JUNIOR CYCLE

History Revision

Dermot Lucey and Stacy Stout

GILL EDUCATION

Gill Education
Hume Avenue
Park West
Dublin 12
www.gilleducation.ie
Gill Education is an imprint of M. H. Gill & Co.

© Dermot Lucey and Stacy Stout 2023

978 0 7171 9067 6
Design by Liz White Designs
Print origination by Ailbhe Hooper

Illustrations: Jeremy Bays, Andrii Yankovskyi, Derry Dillon and Oxford Designers & Illustrators

All rights reserved.
No part of this publication may be copied, reproduced or transmitted in any form or by any means without written permission of the publishers or else under the terms of any licence permitting limited copying issued by the Irish Copyright Licensing Agency.
At the time of going to press, all web addresses were active and contained information relevant to the topics in this book. Gill Education does not, however, accept responsibility for the content or views contained on these websites. Content, views and addresses may change beyond the publisher or author's control. Students should always be supervised when reviewing websites.

For permission to reproduce photographs, the authors and publisher gratefully acknowledge the following: © Adobe Stock: 14, 15, 18, 20, 64, 75, 121L, 121C, 121BR, 134, 184; © akg-images: 28; © Alamy: 4, 33, 48, 67, 79, 80, 85, 97L, 97C, 105, 106, 110, 117, 121TR, 124TL, 124TC, 136, 140TR, 140BL, 140BC, 144, 145, 149, 152, 154, 156, 157, 176, 198; © Eddie Kelly/The Irish Times: 147; © Irish Archives Resource: 211; © National Museum of Ireland: 19B; © Photograph by Robert Shaw, The Discovery Programme, CHERISH Project. This project is funded through the Ireland–Wales Programme 2014–2020, part of the European Regional Development Fund: 212; © Shutterstock: 121CR; © Wikimedia Commons: 19T, 31, 40, 44, 62, 65T, 71, 84, 89, 90, 97R, 102, 124BL, 124BC, 124BR, 124TR, 140TL, 140TC, 140BR, 217.

The authors and publisher have made every effort to trace all copyright holders, but if any has been inadvertently overlooked, we would be pleased to make the necessary arrangement at the first opportunity.

Introduction – Revising for the Junior Cycle History Exam v
1. How Do Historians Find Out About the Past? 1
2. How Do Archaeologists Find Out About the Past? 7
3. Life in Ancient Rome 10
4. Early Christian Ireland 17
5. Life and Death in Medieval Times 23
6. The Renaissance – Changes in the Arts and Science 30
7. Conquest and Colonisation in the Age of Exploration 37
8. Martin Luther and the Reformation – The Historical Importance of Religion 44
9. The Plantation of Ulster, Identity and the Growth of Towns 51
10A. The American Revolution 57
10B. The French Revolution 63
11. Exploring the 1798 Rebellion – The Impact of the Physical Force Tradition 69
12. Causes, Course and Consequences of the Great Famine 73
13. The Parliamentary Tradition in Irish Politics – Daniel O'Connell and C. S. Parnell 79
14. Impact of the GAA 84
15. The Rise and Impact of Nationalism and Unionism in Ireland, 1911–23 88
16. Life in Soviet Russia 101
17. Life in Nazi Germany 107
18. The Causes of World War II 115
19. World War II, 1939–45 – Course and Impact 119
20. The Holocaust 128
21. The Impact of World War II on Ireland, North and South 133
22. The Cold War 138
23. The Changing Experience of Women in 20th-Century Ireland 146
24. The 1960s – An Important Decade in World History 151
25. The 1960s – An Important Decade in Irish History 159

- **26.** The Troubles in Northern Ireland 166
- **27.** The European Union and Ireland's Links with Europe 177
- **28.** Technology and Historical Change 184
- **29A.** Patterns of Change – Health and Medicine 192
- **29B.** Patterns of Change – Crime and Punishment 196
- **Assessment Overview** **203**
- **Guidelines for Answering Exam Questions** **210**
- **Glossary** **219**

Introduction – Revising for the Junior Cycle History Exam

Organise for Less Exam Stress – Revising for the Junior Cycle History Exam

You should take **plenty of time** to revise for your exams.
1. The key to good revision is **good organisation**.
2. Good organisation helps to **relieve the stress of exams**. It puts you in **control**.

Revision Planning

First, you must lay out a **Revision Plan**.
This is how to lay out a **six-week Revision Plan**.

> **How many topics to be studied?**
> **29 topics/chapters** to be revised in *Less Stress More Success*
> This is an average of **5 topics/chapters per week**

Plan your week from **Monday to the following Sunday**.

Week	Chapters to study	
1	1.	How Do Historians Find Out About the Past?
	2.	How Do Archaeologists Find Out About the Past?
	3.	Life in Ancient Rome*
	4.	Early Christian Ireland
	5.	Life and Death in Medieval Times*
		*You can **choose** to study **either** an ancient civilisation **or** a medieval civilisation.
2	6.	The Renaissance – Changes in the Arts and Science
	7.	Conquest and Colonisation in the Age of Exploration
	8.	Martin Luther and the Refo...

Six-week Revision Plan

The **six-week Revision Plan** can be used:
1. before pre- or mock exams
2. before the final JC History exam in June.

This is a plan for 2024. It can be adapted for other years, depending on the dates of Easter and the final JC History exam in June (see www.schooldays.ie).

Week	Chapters to study	
1	1.	How Do Historians Find Out About the Past?
	2.	How Do Archaeologists Find Out About the Past?
	3.	Life in Ancient Rome*
	4.	Early Christian Ireland
	5.	Life and Death in Medieval Times*
		*You can **choose** to study **either** an ancient civilisation **or** a medieval civilisation.
2	6.	The Renaissance – Changes in the Arts and Science
	7.	Conquest and Colonisation in the Age of Exploration
	8.	Martin Luther and the Reformation – The Historical Importance of Religion
	9.	The Plantation of Ulster, Identity and the Growth of Towns
	10A.	The American Revolution
		OR
	10B.	The French Revolution
	11.	Exploring the 1798 Rebellion – Impact of the Physical Force Tradition
3	12.	Causes, Course and Consequences of the Great Famine
	13.	The Parliamentary Tradition in Irish Politics – O'Connell and Parnell
	14.	Impact of the GAA
	15.	The Rise and Impact of Nationalism and Unionism in Ireland, 1911–23
4	16.	Life in Soviet Russia
	17.	Life in Nazi Germany
	18.	The Causes of World War II
	19.	World War II, 1939–45 – Course and Impact
	20.	The Holocaust
	21.	The Impact of World War II on Ireland, North and South
5	22.	The Cold War
	23.	The Changing Experience of Women in 20th-Century Ireland
	24.	The 1960s – An Important Decade in World History
	25.	The 1960s – An Important Decade in Irish History
	26.	The Troubles in Northern Ireland
6	27.	The European Union and Ireland's Links with Europe
	28.	Technology and Historical Change
	29A.	Patterns of Change: Health and Medicine
		OR
	29B.	Patterns of Change: Crime and Punishment

The **best preparation** for the Junior Cycle History exam is to **revise the course fully over a six-week period after your mock (or pre-) exams**.
If the Easter Break falls within that six-week period, then treat the **two weeks of the Easter Break as one week of the Revision Plan**.
Once you have revised the course fully, then do another **quick revision** of the course over the **remaining weeks before the exam in June**.

What Do You Do When You Are Studying?

1. Keep your study as **active** as possible so you don't get bored.
2. You should **vary your study** between subjects where you have 'learning' to do and those where there is written work.
3. Give a **focus** to your study. Begin with: 'What am I learning for this study period?'
4. Use your **notes** or your **textbook** – follow the *Less Stress More Success* revision books.
5. Underline or highlight key information.
6. The *Less Stress* revision notes are divided into **sub-headings** and **points** so that you can study them in short sections.
7. **Tick off** each topic in your Revision Plan after you have studied it.
8. After studying each short section, you should **test yourself** again to ensure that you have learnt the information.
9. Use the **QR code** for **Revision Questions** at the end of each chapter to test how much you have learnt.
10. **Each topic** should be **revised** at **regular intervals**.
11. **Repeated revision** is important in the weeks and months before the Junior Cycle exam.

> **Study sessions**
> - **Length** of study session: 30–40 minutes
> - **Test** after each session
> - Quizlet, key words
> - **Understand the meaning** of 'a pattern of settlement', 'the parliamentary tradition', 'the physical force tradition', 'international co-operation', etc.
> - Also **understand historical terms** such as 'cause and consequence', 'commemoration', 'decade', 'impact of', 'significance of', and 'pre-20th century'.
> - Revision Questions

> No phones, devices, music or TVs – they are a distraction. Instead, tune in to relax when you are taking a break.

Note the **importance of source analysis** when you are studying.

> Know the **strengths** (advantages) and **weaknesses** (limitations) of each of these types of sources.

> **Types of source**
> - Manuscripts
> - Paintings
> - Cartoons
> - Photographs
> - Newspapers
> - Documents
> - Graphs

Dos and Don'ts of Studying

Do

- Organise with a **written plan**
- Spend **no more than 30–40 minutes** on any one History topic at a time
- **Test yourself** after each revision session
- Take **regular short breaks** when revising a number of subjects
- Keep to a **routine**
- Stay healthy
- Have **regular meals**
- Get **exercise**

Don't

- **No late nights**
- If you must, have all your goals or targets met for the week so that you can take the next morning off
- **No cramming**
- Sometimes you may think that if you revise too soon, you will have it all forgotten. The reality is that **if you don't revise, you will have nothing learnt to forget**.

Your notes

The closer you get to the exam, the more you have to **depend on notes**, rather than the full textbook. Revision notes, such as the *Less Stress More Success* series, **summarise** the key information. They link **content or knowledge with historical skills**, which is the basis for many of the marks in the Junior Cycle exams. You will be able to revise large sections of your History course quite quickly.

Your friends

Your friends are a **great support**. They can help you with difficult parts of the courses. They will support you when everything is not going well.
(For Guidelines on Answering Exam Questions, see page 210)

Stress relief

You will need to feel **some pressure** because this will spur you to work and to give your best. But you must not let that pressure take over. When you are following your plan, you will feel more **confident** about your work. As you get to know more about your course, this will encourage you to work more.

INTRODUCTION – REVISING FOR THE JUNIOR CYCLE HISTORY EXAM

Revision Plan for Junior Cycle History

Topics for Study	Tick (✓) every time you revise a section
1. How Do Historians Find Out About the Past? • History; sources – written, visual, aural, oral, tactile; evidence; fact; opinion; viewpoint; bias; objective; reliable; useful; chronology	☐ ☐ ☐ ☐
2. How Do Archaeologists Find Out About the Past? • Archaeology: finding sites, excavation, testing evidence, new technology	☐ ☐ ☐ ☐
3. Life in Ancient Rome • Sources for life in Ancient Rome: written, visual, aural, oral, tactile • Life in Ancient Rome; achievements of Ancient Rome	☐ ☐ ☐ ☐
4. Early Christian Ireland • Sources for Early Christian Ireland: written, visual, aural, oral, tactile • Coming of Christianity; early Irish monasteries; contribution of Christianity to Early Christian Ireland	☐ ☐ ☐ ☐
5. Life and Death in Medieval Times • Sources for life and death in medieval times: written, visual, aural, oral, tactile • Medieval people, medieval society • Black Death: causes; progress; impact (consequences) • Achievements of Norman civilisation	☐ ☐ ☐ ☐
6. The Renaissance – Changes in the Arts and Science • Sources for the history of the Renaissance; written, visual, aural, oral, tactile; change; historical significance • Causes of the Renaissance • Changes in painting; sculpture; architecture; literature • Changes in Renaissance science • How was the Renaissance historically significant?	☐ ☐ ☐ ☐
7. Impact of Conquest and Colonisation in the Age of Exploration • Sources for conquest and colonisation in the Age of Exploration; written, visual, aural, oral, tactile • Impact of conquest; impact of colonisation	☐ ☐ ☐ ☐
8. Martin Luther and the Reformation – The Historical Importance of Religion • Sources for the Reformation; written, visual, aural, oral, tactile; historical importance/significance • Causes of the Reformation • Martin Luther; course of Reformation; consequences of the Reformation	☐ ☐ ☐ ☐

> When you are asked a question about the lives of people in an **ancient** or **medieval** civilisation, you should use information from **Ancient Rome**.

9. The Plantation of Ulster, Identity and the Growth of Towns
- Sources for the plantations and the growth of towns; written, visual, aural, oral, tactile
- Efforts to conquer Ireland: plantations, Laois–Offaly, Munster plantations
- Plantation of Ulster
- Influence on identity
- Growth of towns

10A. The American Revolution
- Sources for the American Revolution: written, visual, aural, oral, tactile
- Causes, course, consequences

10B. The French Revolution
- Sources for the French Revolution: written, visual, aural, oral, tactile
- Causes, course, consequences

*You can **choose** to study **either** the American Revolution **or** the French Revolution.*

11. Exploring the 1798 Rebellion – Impact of the Physical Force Tradition
- Sources for the 1798 Rebellion: written, visual, aural, oral, tactile
- Physical force tradition
- Causes; course; impact (consequences)

12. Causes, Course and Consequences of the Great Famine
- Sources for the Great Famine: written, visual, aural, oral, tactile
- Causes; course (progress); consequences (results)

13. The Parliamentary Tradition in Irish Politics – O'Connell and Parnell
- Sources for the parliamentary tradition; written, visual, aural, oral, tactile
- Parliamentary tradition, significance
- Daniel O'Connell and C. S. Parnell (if you have not studied Chapter 15)

*You can **choose** to study **two** of the following leaders:*
- *Daniel O'Connell*
- *C.S. Parnell*
- *Edward Carson (p. 90)*
- *John Redmond (p. 89)*

14. Impact of the GAA
- Sources for the GAA: written, visual, aural, oral, tactile
- Foundation of GAA; impact of GAA

INTRODUCTION – REVISING FOR THE JUNIOR CYCLE HISTORY EXAM

15. Rise and Impact of Nationalism and Unionism in Ireland, 1911–23 • Sources for rise and impact of nationalism and unionism: written, visual, aural, oral, tactile • Rise, impact • What was nationalism and unionism? • Home Rule Crisis, 1912–14 • Edward Carson and John Redmond (if you have not studied Chapter 13) • 1916 Rising • The Independence struggle • Anglo-Irish Treaty, 1921 • The Irish Civil War • Foundation of Northern Ireland	☐ ☐ ☐ ☐
16. Life in Soviet Russia • Sources for life in Soviet Russia: written, visual, aural, oral, tactile • Life in a communist dictatorship, e.g. purges, show trials, industrialisation, collectivisation, women, World War II	☐ ☐ ☐ ☐
17. Life in Nazi Germany • Sources for life in Nazi Germany: written, visual, aural, oral, tactile; propaganda • Life in a fascist dictatorship, e.g. dictatorship, propaganda, women, Jewish people, World War II	☐ ☐ ☐ ☐
18. The Causes of World War II • Sources for the drift to World War II: written, visual, aural, oral, tactile • Causes	☐ ☐ ☐ ☐
19. World War II, 1939–45 – Course and Impact • Sources for World War II: written, visual, aural, oral, tactile • German victories; turning points; war in East Asia; Allied victory; consequences of the war	☐ ☐ ☐ ☐
20. The Holocaust • Sources for the Holocaust: written, visual, aural, oral, tactile • Significance of genocide; other genocides • Causes of the Holocaust; course of the Holocaust; consequences of the Holocaust	☐ ☐ ☐ ☐
21. The Impact of World War II on Ireland, North and South • Sources for the impact of World War II: written, visual, aural, oral, tactile • Neutrality in action; Northern Ireland	☐ ☐ ☐ ☐
22. The Cold War • Sources for the Cold War: written, visual, aural, oral, tactile • Causes of Cold War; impact of Cold War – Berlin, Korea, Cuba	☐ ☐ ☐ ☐

23. The Changing Experience of Women in 20th-Century Ireland
- Sources for the changing role of women: written, visual, aural, oral, tactile
- Early decades; 1960s onwards

24. The 1960s – An Important Decade in World History
- Sources for the 1960s in world history: written, visual, aural, oral, tactile
- Issues; events; personalities

25. The 1960s – An Important Decade in Irish History
- Sources for the 1960s in Irish history: written, visual, aural, oral, tactile
- Changes in Republic of Ireland; changes in Northern Ireland

26. The Troubles in Northern Ireland
- Sources for the Troubles: written, visual, aural, oral, tactile
- Causes: long-term, short-term; course; consequences

27. The European Union and Ireland's Links with Europe
- Sources for the EEC/EU: written, visual, aural, oral, tactile
- Origins of the EEC/EU; EU and international co-operation; EU and human rights; EU and justice
- **Ireland's links with Europe:** Early Christian Ireland; the Normans; the Reformation; Nine Years' War; 1798 Rebellion; 1916 Rising; World War II; Ireland and the EEC/EU

28. Technology and Historical Change
- Sources for technology and historical change: written, visual, aural, oral, tactile
- Invention of the printing press; ships and navigation; steam engine; nuclear energy

29A. Patterns of Change: Health and Medicine
- Sources for health and medicine: written, visual, aural, oral, tactile
- Ancient Rome; Renaissance; industrial society; modern times

29B. Patterns of Change: Crime and Punishment
- Sources for crime and punishment: written, visual, aural, oral, tactile
- Ancient Rome; medieval times; industrial society; modern times

> You can **choose either** health and medicine **or** crime and punishment.

1 How Do Historians Find Out About the Past?

 After studying this chapter, you should be able to:
- Understand the job of the historian.

Key Words
history
evidence
prehistory
source
primary
secondary
written
visual
aural
oral
tactile

The Job of the Historian

What is history?

History is the story of the past based on **evidence**.

What is prehistory?
Prehistory is the history of people before writing was invented, based on **archaeological evidence**.

What is evidence?

Evidence is the information which proves or disproves the story of the past. Historians get their evidence from **sources**.

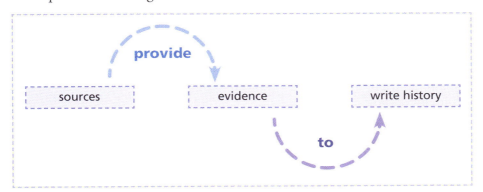

What is a primary source?

A **primary** source comes **directly from the time that is being studied**. It is a **first-hand account** of what happened.
Examples: a diary, a newspaper

What is a secondary source?

A **secondary** source comes **from after the time being studied**. Secondary sources are **based** on primary sources and other secondary sources.
Example: your history textbook

Sources

What are the different types of sources?

1. **Written** sources (things that are written or typed)
   - **Manuscripts** are books written by hand.
   - An **autobiography** is the story of a person's own life.
   - A **biography** is written by a historian about another person's life.
   - A **census** (of population) records information about families, businesses, housing, education.
   - **Newspapers** are another kind of published source.
2. **Visual** sources (things that can be seen)
   - Photographs, paintings, documentaries
   - Cartoons and drawings
   - Maps
3. **Aural** sources (things that can be heard)
   - Interviews
   - Podcasts
4. **Oral** sources (things that are spoken)
   - Interviews
   - Recordings
5. **Tactile** sources (things that can be touched)
   - Artefacts (objects)
   - Buildings

Key Words

archive	biased
museum	objective
library	propaganda
digital	reliable
fact	useful
opinion	limitations
interpretation	chronology
viewpoint	timeline

exam focus

Archives, museums and libraries are all examples of repositories of historical evidence.

Where are sources stored?

1. An **archive** collects mainly **written** (documentary) sources.
   Example: National Archives of Ireland
2. A **museum** collects and stores **objects** (artefacts) for study and display.
   Examples: National Museum of Ireland, local museums
3. A **library** stores books.
   Examples: National Library of Ireland, your local county or city library
4. Some of these sources are stored on **microfilm** (a small film) or **microfiche** (a scaled-down copy), which can be viewed with a magnifying lens.
5. **Websites** are now used by museums, archives and libraries to make available **digital copies** of the sources – documents, newspapers and photographs – that they hold.

Differences and similarities

Archives	Museums	Libraries
Stores mainly written documents	Stores mainly artefacts (objects)	Stores mainly books
Primary sources	Primary sources	Mostly secondary sources
		Autobiographies are primary sources
Must be preserved or conserved	Must be preserved or conserved	Most books can be replaced
Handled carefully with gloves	Handled carefully with gloves	Gloves are not needed for handling the books
Must be studied/researched in the archive	Must be studied/researched in the museum	Books can be borrowed

How do historians use sources?

Historians must distinguish between **fact** (something that happened; true) and **opinion** (a view or belief about something).

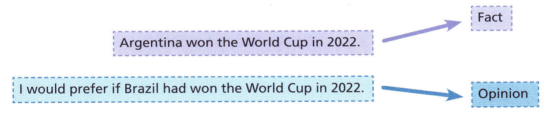

Historians need to **cross-check** between different sources to ensure their facts are **accurate**.

Historians can provide different **interpretations** (versions) of the same events because their **sources** or their **viewpoint** may be different. A historian's viewpoint or **point of view** (also called **perspective**) can be influenced by gender, beliefs, values and interests.

What is bias?

Historians are **biased** if they deliberately **favour one side** over the other.

The job of the historian is to be as **objective** as possible. Being **objective** means that historians must not be influenced by **personal opinions** when researching and writing history.

key point

A historian's description and analysis of the past (an account) is called an **interpretation**.

What is propaganda?

Propaganda is using information to influence people's opinions or to convince people that a particular belief is true.

How reliable is a source?

A source is **reliable** when you can **trust** that the information in it is **accurate** and **true**.

How useful is a source?

A source is **useful** when it **provides information** about the topic you are **researching**.

A Nazi propaganda poster showing Hitler as a great leader: 'One people, one empire, one leader!'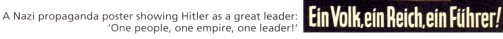

What are the **usefulness** and **limitations** (weaknesses) of some sources?

Source	Usefulness (strengths) of source for historians	Limitations (weaknesses) of source for historians
Newspapers	• Provide eyewitness accounts • Provide information on political, social and economic aspects of the time • Provide photographs • Different newspapers provide different viewpoints	• Can report incorrect information • Can be biased • Could be used for propaganda
Diaries and letters	• Provide personal opinions of writers • Can explain motives or reasons for actions	• Can be biased • Can have incorrect information
Photographs	• Can provide first-hand view of events or scenes • Provide information on political, social and economic aspects of the time	• Can be altered for propaganda purposes • Only record a moment in time

HOW DO HISTORIANS FIND OUT ABOUT THE PAST?

Videos and documentaries	• Can show live action of events	• Can be selective • Can be used for propaganda
Cartoons	• Show political and social views of the time	• Biased • Used for propaganda • Used to get across a point of view
Artefact (object)	• Show objects made by people at the time	• Can be fake
Interview	• Can provide views of eyewitnesses	• Memory can be faulty • Can deliberately mislead • Can exaggerate role in events

What is chronology?

Chronology is putting events in **order of time** (when they happened), starting with the earliest.

- Decade = 10 years
- Century = 100 years
- An age = a number of decades or centuries
- BC = the years before the birth of Christ
- AD = the years after the birth of Christ

Some historians use BCE (Before Common Era) instead of BC, and CE (Common Era) instead of AD.

Examples – Which century?
3rd century BC = 299 BC to 200 BC
5th century AD = 400 AD to 499 AD
545 AD = in the 6th century
1589 AD = in the 16th century

> **key point**
> A **timeline** is a line or graph that shows the dates when events happened; puts events in chronological order.

> **exam focus**
> It is important to **put events in the correct chronological order when answering questions**.

Sample Question

The timeline below relates to exploration and conquest in the New World. Examine the timeline and answer the questions which follow.

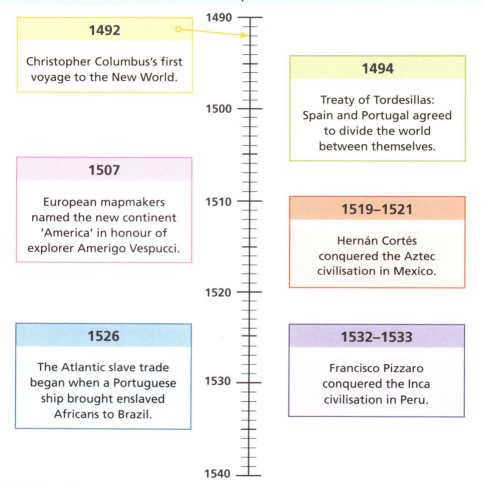

(a) How many decades are represented on the timeline?
   5 decades
(b) Draw arrows to link each event to the correct date on the timeline. The first arrow has been done for you.

Junior Cycle History Examination 2022, Q3

Revision Questions
Scan the QR code for more revision questions.

2 How Do Archaeologists Find Out About the Past?

After studying this chapter, you should be able to:
- Appreciate the work of the archaeologist.

Archaeology

Archaeology is the story of the past from **material remains**. Material remains are **artefacts** and **buildings**.

What are artefacts?

Artefacts are **objects** made by people.
Examples: spears, pots, coins and rings

Key Words
archaeology
artefacts
geophysical survey
rescue or salvage archaeology
crop marks

What is the difference between history and archaeology?
History depends mostly on **written sources** for evidence, while **archaeology** depends mostly on **objects** (artefacts, ruins). However, historians often use archaeological evidence, and archaeologists often use written sources.

Key words can be used in the wording of questions. Define and explain these words or terms when you are answering questions.

How do archaeologists find sites?

1. **Above ground**
   Some sites are above ground.
   Examples: castles, pyramids
2. **Below ground**
   Some are found **by chance** (or by accident) when people are ploughing or building. Others are found by using a **geophysical survey** with scientific instruments to find features under the ground.
   Examples: the Ardagh Chalice was found when two boys were digging for potatoes, and the Terracotta Army was found when people were digging a well in China.

What is rescue or salvage archaeology? This is archaeology undertaken before new roads or buildings are developed.

3. **Stories from history**
   These are legends or biblical stories.
   Example: the story of Troy
4. **Aerial photography**
   This shows **crop marks** (patterns in the way crops grow) which indicate that a feature lies under the soil.
5. **Underwater archaeology**
   This is using sonar, submarines and diving gear to explore sunken wrecks.

Excavation

How do archaeologists excavate sites?

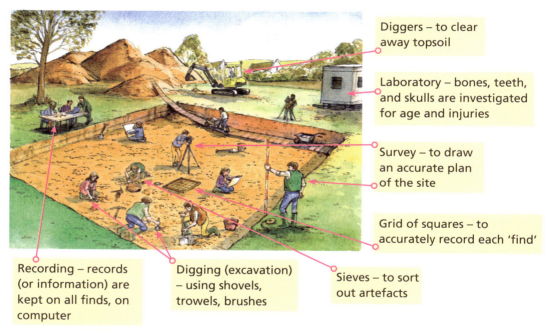

- Diggers – to clear away topsoil
- Laboratory – bones, teeth, and skulls are investigated for age and injuries
- Survey – to draw an accurate plan of the site
- Grid of squares – to accurately record each 'find'
- Sieves – to sort out artefacts
- Digging (excavation) – using shovels, trowels, brushes
- Recording – records (or information) are kept on all finds, on computer

What instruments (or tools) do archaeologists use when excavating a site?

Archaeologists use lots of tools, including trowels, sieves, brushes, picks, measuring tapes and storage bags.

How do archaeologists date objects?

1. **Stratigraphy**: When layers are laid down in the earth, the oldest layers and finds are at the bottom and the youngest layers and finds are at the top.

Key Words
stratigraphy
tree-ring dating
dendrochronology
carbon-14 dating
post-holes
conservation

HOW DO ARCHAEOLOGISTS FIND OUT ABOUT THE PAST?

2. **Tree-ring dating** (also called **dendrochronology**): Archaeologists can tell when a tree was growing by studying the **pattern of rings**. The pattern of rings on a piece of wood is compared with the record of tree-ring growth in Ireland, which is held in Queen's University, Belfast.
3. **Carbon-14 dating**: All humans, plants and animals contain **carbon-14**. When they die, the amount of carbon-14 in them declines. When a plant, person or animal was alive can be worked out by measuring the amount of carbon-14 remaining in the sample of wood, or in the human or animal bone which was found.
4. **Coins and pottery**: Objects found alongside these objects may be from the same time period.

What is conservation?

Conservation is the **protection** and **preservation** of ancient objects so that they do not decay. This is usually done in a **museum**.

> **key point**
> **What are post-holes?**
> These are darkened patches of soil where posts rotted away. They **show the shape and size of buildings.**

> **History, archaeology and tourism**
> Many of the most popular tourist sites in Ireland are based on history and archaeology. *Examples: Bunratty Castle, Co. Clare; Newgrange, Co. Meath*

Exam Question

(e) Explain why drone technology is a useful tool for archaeologists.

Photographs taken by drones show up crop marks (patterns in the way crops grow) which indicate that a feature lies under the soil.
Other possible answers include:
- *Drones can access areas which are difficult to investigate for likely archaeological sites.*
- *Drones are cheaper to operate than helicopters or airplanes for aerial photography of historic areas.*
- *During excavation, drones provide an aerial view of the entire site, which is very important if it is a large site.*

Junior Cycle History Examination 2022, Q1

Revision Questions
Scan the QR code for more revision questions.

3 Life in Ancient Rome

By the end of this chapter, you should be able to:
- Investigate the lives of people who lived in Ancient Rome
- Explain how the achievements of Ancient Rome contributed (added) to European and world history.

Key Words
excavated
Forum
amphitheatre
public baths
patricians
domus
villas
cena
plebeians
insulae
dole
aqueducts
Colosseum
Circus Maximus
strigil
legions
centuries
murals
mosaics
frescoes
catacombs

Ancient Rome
When you are asked a question about the lives of people in **an ancient or medieval civilisation**, you have a **choice** between **Ancient Rome** and the **Norman civilisation** in medieval times.

What happened in Pompeii and Herculaneum?
Mount Vesuvius erupted and covered the towns of **Pompeii and Herculaneum**. The ruins of Pompeii have been **excavated** (dug up) by **archaeologists** to show what life was like in a Roman town.

The Roman Empire

1. In Roman legend, Rome was founded by **Romulus**.
2. Rome actually grew from villages on the hills around the River Tiber.
3. Rome conquered all the land around the Mediterranean Sea. Its empire stretched north to **Hadrian's Wall** between Scotland and England.

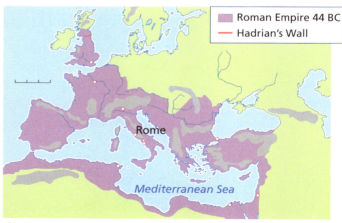

The Roman Empire

LIFE IN ANCIENT ROME

Roman towns

Romans built new towns on a **grid pattern**, surrounded by walls.
The main buildings were:
- The *Forum* or marketplace
- The **amphitheatre**
- The *public baths*.

key point
The *amphitheatre* was a circular or oval building with a central space for **gladiatorial contests**.

Ancient Roman Lives – How Did Rich and Poor Romans Live?

Who were the patricians?

1. Well-off Romans were called **patricians**. This small number of rich families controlled power in Ancient Rome. The men became politicians or generals.
2. Patricians lived in private houses (called a *domus*), which were surrounded by walls. They also had **country** *villas*, which were worked by slaves.
3. **Marriage** was arranged to increase the family's wealth.
4. Richer Romans had three meals a day, including the *cena* – the main meal – in the evening, after the baths. **Slaves** cooked and served the food.

key point
Patricians were the rich or well-off Romans.

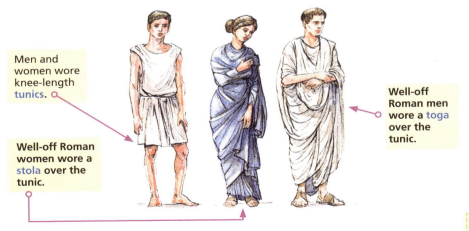

Men and women wore knee-length **tunics**.

Well-off Roman women wore a *stola* over the tunic.

Well-off Roman men wore a *toga* over the tunic.

Who were the plebeians?

1. The poorer Romans were called **plebeians**. Plebeians included shopkeepers, tradesmen, craftworkers and the very poor.

key point
Plebeians were the poorer Romans.

2. The poorer classes ('**plebs**') lived in *insulae* (apartment blocks), which were four to six storeys tall. There were shops on the ground floor.
3. The residents depended on **public toilets** and on the **public fountains** because there was no water supply in the *insulae*.
4. Poorer families depended on bread or a kind of porridge made from wheat and barley. The government also gave out free grain to poorer people because there was so much poverty. This was called the *dole*.

Roman women

- In Rome, **a woman's place** was in the home, obedient to her husband.
- Roman women were expected to have children and run the **household**. In rich homes, the slaves did the work; in poorer homes, women also worked in markets and the baths.
- Daughters were allowed to **marry** at 12 years of age. They had to have a **dowry** for their husbands.

key point

What was the source of water in Roman towns? Water was supplied to Romans towns via the **aqueducts** – channels or bridges for carrying water.

Education

- **Poorer children** did not learn to read and write.
- **Richer children** went to a primary school called a *ludus* at age seven, where they learnt to write on wax tablets.
- **Boys** went to secondary school, where they studied history, philosophy, geometry and the writings of the Greek and Latin authors. Some received training in public speaking for use in politics.
- Richer **girls** ended their education at **primary school** because they were often married off at an early age – around 14.

Religion

- Religion was important to the Ancient Romans, who celebrated many religious festivals. They worshipped many gods and goddesses; **Jupiter** was the father of the gods and **Venus** was the goddess of love.
- The Romans used bronze and marble to make **statues** of gods and goddesses. In their houses and apartments, there were statues to their **household gods**.

Funerals and burial customs

- Some Romans believed that their spirit was carried across the **River Styx** to the underworld by **Charon**, the ferryman. They placed a **coin** in the mouth of the dead person to pay the ferryman.

- When **rich Romans** died, they were dressed in a toga for their funeral. They were carried in a procession of relatives, musicians and mourners before they were **cremated**. Their ashes were placed in **urns** (pottery jars) and buried in cemeteries outside the town or city walls.
- **Poorer Romans** also had processions. They were then cremated and their ashes were buried in simple graves.

What language did the Ancient Romans speak?
Latin was the language of Ancient Romans.

How Were Ancient Romans Entertained?

Leisure and entertainment

- **Gladiators** were slaves who had to fight each other or wild animals in an **amphitheatre**, such as the **Colosseum** in Rome. They used swords, nets, tridents (three-pronged pikes), shields and daggers.

What was the Colosseum?
The **Colosseum** was an **amphitheatre** built in the centre of Rome. It was the largest ever built in the Roman Empire and could hold 50,000 spectators.

- **Chariot racing** was held in the **Circus Maximus**, which could hold 250,000 people. Four teams (called Red, Green, Blue and White) raced seven times around a central spine.
- Plays were held in **open-air theatres** in daylight. Actors wore masks.
- Romans went to the **baths** each day in the early afternoon.
  - The baths had a **warm room** (*tepidarium*), a **hot room** (*caldarium*) and a **cold room** (*frigidarium*). Romans rubbed oil onto their bodies to clean themselves. This was scraped off with a *strigil* (a curved instrument to scrape oil and dirt off the body).
  - **Women** had their own baths.

What Jobs Did Ancient Romans Have?

- **Farming** was the most important occupation in Ancient Rome. Slaves did most of the work on the farms, and everywhere else.
- **Richer Romans** (patricians) became generals or senators (politicians).
- **Poorer Romans** (plebeians) worked as craftsmen such as bakers, glassworkers or carpenters in their own workshops.
- Many people worked for the government as tax collectors or in the **Roman army**.

The Roman army

- The army was divided into **legions** (groups of about 5,000 soldiers) and **centuries** (groups of 100 soldiers).
- Some soldiers lived in permanent forts along the border of the empire.
- Soldiers went on long, fast marches and built temporary camps at night.
- They used swords, shields, helmets and javelins.

Julius Caesar was a great Roman general and leader who conquered Gaul (France) and invaded Britain. He was also a gifted **orator** (speaker). He became consul and dictator of Rome. He was **assassinated** on 15 March 44 BC – a date known as 'the Ides of March'.

Slavery

- Most of the work on farms and in towns was done by **slaves** who were owned by Roman citizens or by the government. They were bought and sold at markets.
- The treatment of slaves depended on their owner. Some were very cruel; others were not as harsh.
- Slaves sometimes **rebelled** against harsh treatment. The most serious rebellion was led by **Spartacus**. It took the Roman authorities two years to crush his rebel army of about 90,000 slaves.

What Were the Achievements of Ancient Rome?

Roman art and architecture

- The Romans used **pillars**, **rounded arches** and **domes** in their buildings.

A Roman pillar

A rounded arch

A dome

exam focus

Note how the **achievements of an ancient civilisation – Ancient Rome** – influenced the history of Europe and the wider world.

LIFE IN ANCIENT ROME

- Inside some buildings were **murals** (wall paintings) and **mosaics** (scenes made from small pieces of glass or pottery) on the floors.

key point

These murals were **frescoes** – frescoes were paintings done on wet or damp plaster.

- Many **modern government buildings** and **churches** followed the Roman style – for example, the White House in Washington DC.

key point

The style of Roman (and Greek) art and architecture is described as '**classical**'. The **classical style** of Greek and Roman art, architecture and literature (writing) was later copied during the **Renaissance in Italy** in the 15th and 16th centuries (see Ch. 6).

St Peter's Basilica in Rome

Concrete

- The Romans used an early form of **concrete** by mixing lime with volcanic ash. This made their buildings **stronger**, e.g. the aqueducts.

Towns and cities

- Many cities owe their **origins to Roman builders and planners** – for example, London, Paris and Lyon. The Romans planned their new towns in a **grid pattern**.

The spread of Christianity

- Christianity spread from Palestine to Rome. Christians refused to follow the state gods of Rome, so they were persecuted. Christianity became the state religion after **Emperor Constantine** converted to the religion.
- The bishop of Rome became the **Pope**, or leader, of the Roman Catholic Church.
- Christians buried their dead in the **catacombs** (underground tunnels and passages). They were not cremated.

Language

- Many **modern languages** such as French, Italian, Portuguese and Spanish are based on Latin, the language of the Romans.
- The **English language** contains many words derived from Latin. For example, the word *aquarium* comes from the Latin word *aqua* (meaning *water*).

Calendar

- Julius Caesar created a **calendar** of **365 days** on which the modern calendar is based. He also called one month **July**, after himself.

Sample Question

Which of the achievements of an ancient or medieval civilisation of your choice was the most important? Explain you answer.

Name of civilisation: *Ancient Rome*

Most important achievement: *The spread of Christianity was the most important achievement of Ancient Rome. This was a new religion which spread all over the Roman Empire. It was spread to the New World and Africa during the Age of Exploration (see Ch. 7). During the Reformation (see Ch. 8), a split occurred in Christianity, which divided into the Roman Catholic religion and Protestant religions.*

Revision Questions

Scan the QR code for more revision questions.

4   Early Christian Ireland

After studying this chapter, you should be able to:
- Summarise the arrival of Christianity to Ireland
- Explain how we know so much about Early Christian Ireland
- Discuss how Christianity had an impact on culture and society in Early Christian Ireland
- Consider the historical importance of Christianity on the island of Ireland.

Key Words
historical significance
contribution
geophysical survey
aerial photography
excavations
annals

Historical significance – important events, people and developments that resulted in great change.

Contribution – the part played by a person or thing in bringing about a result or impact or outcome.

The Arrival of Christianity to Ireland

Timeline

c. 500 BC–400 AD	• Before the arrival of Christianity, Ireland was dominated by Celtic culture. • The **druids** (priests) controlled Celtic religion. • The Celts believed in **many gods**, e.g. Dagda.
431 AD	• Pope Celestine sent **Palladius** to Ireland as a **missionary**.
432 AD	• St Patrick came to Ireland as a missionary.
Sometime before the death of St Patrick, which historians think was in 461 AD	• Details about St Patrick's life and the arrival of Christianity in Ireland can be found in **St Patrick's Confession**. His *Confession* contains no dates. • St Patrick on the Irish people: 'never before did they know of God except to serve idols and unclean things. But now, they have become the people of the Lord, and are called children of God'.
480 AD	• **St Brigid** founded a church in **Kildare**.
484 AD	• **St Enda** established a monastery on the **Aran Islands**.

500–599 AD	• From the 6th century onwards, many more monasteries were built in Ireland, for example:
	  • 520 AD St Finnian established a monastery at **Clonard, Co. Meath**.
	  • 549 AD St Ciarán founded **Clonmacnoise, Co. Offaly**.
	  • 560 AD St Colmcille founded a monastery at **Drumcliffe, Co. Sligo**.
	• Irish missionaries also began setting up monasteries abroad, for example:
	  • 563 AD St Colmcille founded **Iona in Scotland**.
	  • 590 AD St Columbanus began founding monasteries in Europe.

500–699 AD	• **Monastic art** flourished, e.g. the **Book of Durrow**.
600–1000 AD	• Monastic **metalwork** boomed, e.g. the **Tara Brooch** and the **Ardagh Chalice**. • Many **high crosses** were carved, e.g. **Muiredach's Cross, Co. Louth**.
Late 700 AD–950 AD	• **Viking and local raids** on monasteries begin, e.g. 823 AD the monastery on **Skellig Michael** was attacked.

How Do We Know About Early Christian Ireland?

1. What have we learned from tactile sources?

Example: monastic buildings

Skellig Michael

- This is a small monastery in a remote location, which tells us that some monks preferred a more **isolated lifestyle** to focus on praying.
- **Beehive huts** found here show us where monks lived.

Skellig Michael

Armagh

- Large monasteries like Armagh, Glendalough and Clonfert were built along important routes and were important **centres of economic activity**.

Glendalough

- Many early Christian monasteries like Glendalough had a **round tower**.
- These were used as **belfries** when a bell was rung to call monks to services.
- They were also used to **store valuable goods**. A door was built high into the wall to protect the tower and make attacks more difficult.

2. What have we learned from written sources?

Examples: Manuscripts, monastery rules

Manuscript: The Book of Durrow
- This tells us that early Christian monks could **write in Latin** and that they **wrote on vellum** (calfskin).

Manuscript: The Book of the Dun Cow
- This tells us that the monks began **writing in Irish** as it is the oldest Irish manuscript.

The Book of Kells

Monastery rules of St Columbanus
Some rules of St Columbanus:
- *'The service of justice shall be quietness and peace.'* This tells us that **silence** was an important part of life in a monastery.
- *'The food of the monks shall be coarse, consisting of cabbage, vegetables, flour mixed with water, and a biscuit, and taken toward evening.'* This tells us that the monks had a very **basic diet**.

3. What have we learned from visual sources?

Examples: Metalwork, high stone crosses, illuminated manuscripts

Clonmacnoise Crozier
The **Clonmacnoise Crozier** (bishop's staff) tells us that monks were influenced by Celtic designs (**La Tène style**). They also used gold, amber, silver and enamel to make such items, which helps to explain why the Vikings raided monasteries.

The Clonmacnoise Crozier

High crosses and illuminated manuscripts
High crosses like the **Cross of the Scriptures** and illuminated manuscripts like the **Book of Kells** tell us that early Christian monks were trying to help the **illiterate** understand the stories of Christianity.

The Monastery at Clonmacnoise

How archaeologists researched the monastery at Clonmacnoise
- A **geophysical survey** showed Clonmacnoise was a large site.
- **Underwater archaeology** showed the remains of a bridge that crossed the River Shannon.

- **Aerial photography** showed that Clonmacnoise had a third protective ring that surrounded the monastery.
- **Archaeological excavations** show that there is evidence of craftwork, metalwork, stone-cutting and farming at Clonmacnoise.

How historians researched the monastery at Clonmacnoise

- The **annals** (historical records) and **other manuscripts** provided evidence for the history of Clonmacnoise.
- Historians say the annals tell us about the rules and work of monasteries. They say Clonmacnoise was a major centre of Christian art and learning.
- The annals record the building of the cathedral at Clonmacnoise in 909 AD.
- Eighth-century manuscripts said there were two or three rings around large monasteries.
- Accounts tell us that St Ciarán (the founder of Clonmacnoise) looked for a site for his monastery – *'Here will I live'* – and began building in 549 AD.

The high cross and monastery at Clonmacnoise

The Historical Significance of Christianity on the Island of Ireland

1. Changed culture and society in Early Christian Ireland	A. Celtic religion was replaced with Christianity. • The **importance of the druids declined**. B. **Christian culture replaced pagan culture**. Christian festivals like All Saint's Day were introduced to replace pagan festivals like Samhain. C. Christianity brought **reading and writing** to Ireland. • The first reading and writing was in **Latin**, the language of the Catholic Church, but soon manuscripts were being written in Irish, e.g. the **Book of the Dun Cow**. • **Written history began** during the Early Christian period.

2. Contributed to art	A.	Monasteries produced **manuscripts** (handwritten books).
		• The **Cathach** is a copy of the psalms in Latin and is one of the **oldest existing manuscripts** in Ireland.
		• **The Book of Kells** is a highly decorated **illuminated (illustrated) manuscript** and is kept in Trinity College.
	B.	Monks also carved Bible stories onto high crosses to **teach illiterate people** (people who can't read or write) about Christianity.
		• e.g. the **Cross of the Scriptures, Clonmacnoise**.
	C.	Monks also excelled in the field of **metalwork**. They produced **chalices**, **croziers and brooches** decorated with gold, amber and enamel.
		• Intricate gold wiring on such objects was called **filigree** (gold wiring on metalwork).
		• Examples include the **Derrynaflan Chalice** and the **Cross of Cong**.
3. Created greater links with Europe (see pages 181–3)		• Irish missionaries **created links between Ireland and Europe**, e.g. Columbanus went to Gaul (France).
4. Became part of the Irish identity		• St Patrick's Day (17 March) is our **national holiday**. It is celebrated in Ireland and abroad in cities like New York, where it **unites the Irish Diaspora**.
5. Influenced laws and society		• Christianity **influenced many laws** in Ireland, e.g. divorce was allowed in Celtic Ireland but then it was illegal until 1996.
		• Many schools and hospitals have a **religious ethos**.
6. Provided opportunities for tourism		• Many historical sites from Early Christian Ireland are now **popular tourist attractions**, e.g. **Glendalough** and **Skellig Michael**.
7. Has led to discrimination on the island of Ireland		• The **Penal Laws** discriminated against non-members of the Church of Ireland, e.g. Catholics and Presbyterians.
8. Caused conflict		• There have been many **conflicts** in Ireland because of religion, e.g. **the Troubles** (see Ch. 26).

Connections

The significance of Christianity on the island of Ireland can also be seen in later chapters:

The Plantations, Chapter 9
1798 Rebellion, Chapter 11
Daniel O'Connell, Chapter 13
The Troubles, Chapter 26

Sample Question

Pick a topic from your Junior Cycle History course that you can link to archaeology, for example:
- a named ancient or medieval civilisation
- early Christian Ireland
- a pattern of settlement in Ireland
- another named topic of your choice.

How did archaeological evidence help you to learn about three different aspects of that topic?
(See Sample Answer, p. 214)

Revision Questions

Scan the QR code for more revision questions.

5 Life and Death in Medieval Times

aims
After studying this chapter, you should be able to:
- Describe the feudal system
- Explore the lives of different medieval people
- Outline some of the ways people died during medieval times
- Explain the impact of the Black Death.

exam focus

Medieval times
When you are asked about the lives of people in **an ancient or medieval civilisation**, you have a **choice** between **Ancient Rome** and the **Norman civilisation** in medieval times.

Key Words

medieval times	peasant	Cistercian
feudal system	motte and bailey	Augustinian
fief	moat	novice
vassal	wattle and daub	Rule of St Benedict
knight	commons	friar
manor	crop rotation	anti-Semitism
demesne	Benedictine	flogging

How was Medieval Society Structured?

1. Life during **medieval times** (or Middle Ages) was structured around the **feudal system** (social hierarchy).
2. **Land** was very important during medieval times. The king owned all the land but gave some to local subjects like **barons/lords and bishops**. During the **fief** (the ceremony for handing over the land), the lord had to swear an **oath** to become a **vassal** of the king.
3. The barons and bishops gave land to **knights** (soldiers on horseback) who promised to fight for and obey their lords. Knights were given **manors**, villages with land around them. Knights kept some land (the **demesne**) and divided the rest amongst the **peasants**.

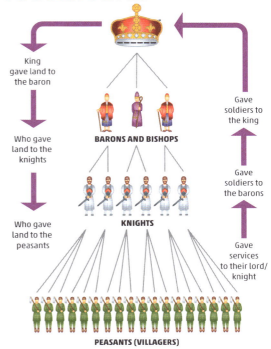

The feudal system

Life in a Medieval Castle

The king divided his land up amongst lords and bishops. Each lord had to build a castle on his land.

Motte and bailey castles

The first castles were **motte and bailey** castles.
1. The **motte** was a mound of earth with a timber tower or **keep**. It was surrounded by a wooden fence or wall.
2. The **bailey** was the courtyard below the motte. Workshops, kitchens, stables, lodging for soldiers and a hall where the lord did business were built here. The bailey was surrounded by timber fence or **moat** (dry or water-filled ditch built around a castle).

Stone castles

Later, **stone castles** were built as they were much stronger, e.g. Edinburgh Castle, Scotland. The **Normans** built stone castles in Ireland, e.g. Carrickfergus Castle in Co. Antrim, Trim Castle in Co. Meath and Kilkenny Castle.
1. Like motte and bailey castles, stone castles had a **keep** and a **bailey**.
2. They also had many defensive features:
    - A **moat** surrounded the castle.
    - A **curtain wall** was built around the castle.
    - **Turrets** (towers) were built. Soldiers shot arrows from these.
    - A **drawbridge** was used to cross the moat. This was lifted to stop people from entering the castle.
    - A **portcullis** was an iron grill that was raised to allow people to enter and leave.
    - A **gatehouse** protected the gate of the castle.

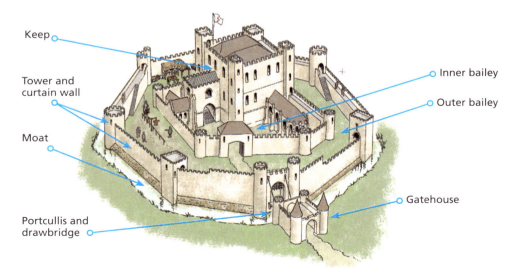

LIFE AND DEATH IN MEDIEVAL TIMES

Attacking a stone castle was difficult. Different methods were used, including a battering ram, siege, fire arrows and mining.

Life inside the castle

The life of the lord
- Organised business of the castle
- Kept his territory under control
- Carried out the wishes of the king
- **Held court** and settled disputes
- Went to the king's court when called
- Hobbies included hunting, **hawking** and **jousting** (medieval sport)

(Shared)
- Marriage was not a love match; instead, it forged links between families
- Took in children of other lords (**fosterage**). Pages did chores for the lord and lady of the castle
- Held **banquets** in the great hall where **minstrels** entertained people
- Spent time in the **solar**, the private rooms of the lord's family

The life of the lady
- Came with a **dowry** (gifts that the lady brought with her when she got married)
- Ensured the daily running of the castle went smoothly
- In charge of the food stores, baking and brewing
- Gave directions to the servants
- Responsible for her daughter's education
- Hobbies included embroidery, spinning flax and wool

Explore the Life of a Medieval Knight

There were **three stages** of training to become a **knight**.

1. At the age of seven, they became **pages** and were **fostered** by another lord and went to live in his castle. They learned good manners, horse riding and dancing, and helped the lady of the castle.
2. At 14, they became **squires**. They helped the lord dress for jousts and battles. They practised with weapons like lances, swords and shields.
3. At 21, they were **dubbed** knights by their lord. The knight would spend the night before the ceremony in prayer. During the ceremony, the knight had to kneel before their lord. The lord then struck them on the shoulder with the flat of the sword and said, 'Arise, Sir …'

key point

Knights were specially trained **soldiers on horseback** during the Middle Ages. They were usually the sons of lords or other knights.

The knight followed a strict code of conduct called **chivalry**. He promised to protect women and children, be truthful, generous and loyal.

Knights took part in **jousts**.

Knights were given **manors**, a village and surrounding land. The knight kept some land called the **demesne** and the rest was rented to **peasants**.

Explore the Life of a Medieval Peasant

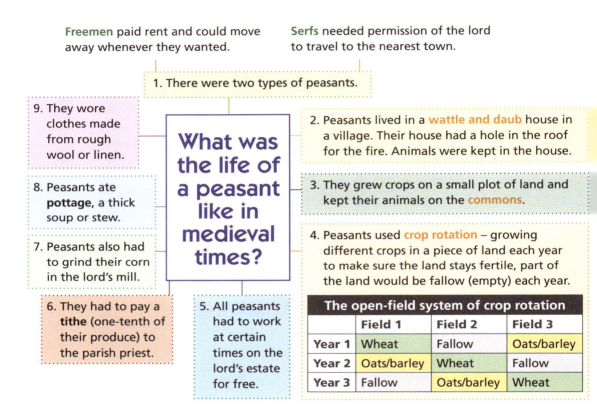

Life in a Medieval Town

During medieval times, towns were given **royal charters** by the king, which gave them permission to have a town government, fairs and markets and their own courts.

They also collected tolls (taxes) to repair the town walls.

Merchants and **craftsmen** were the main two groups in a medieval town.

Merchants

1. **Merchants bought and sold goods**.
2. Some brought goods back from places like China and India.
3. They attended **fairs and markets**. Markets were held once a week. People from outside the town sold produce like eggs, vegetables and milk. Merchants and traders sold clothes, knives, pots and pans. Fairs were much bigger and held once or twice a year. They were usually held outside the town walls in a fair green. Merchants and traders came from far and near to buy and sell goods.

Craftsmen

1. Craftsmen made and sold goods in their **workshop**. A sign over the door with a symbol showed what the workshop sold.
2. A workshop was run by a **master craftsman**. He also trained apprentices.
3. Training to become a craftsman started at 14. An **apprentice** lived with the master craftsman's family and slept in the workshop.
4. After seven years, the apprentice made a **masterpiece** to prove his skill.
5. He then became a **journeyman** who travelled around working wherever he could to gain experience.
6. **Guilds** controlled the standard of craftsmanship. They also set prices and decided who could be a craftsman.
7. The guild took care of members when they got sick.
8. Each guild had its own **coat of arms**.
9. In larger towns and cities, craftsmen of the same trade worked in the same street, e.g. Baker Street, Cook Street or Miller Street.
10. Some family names also come from medieval trades, e.g. Smith, Potter and Taylor (Tailor).

Achievements of a medieval civilisation – the Normans
Norman conquests: The Normans **conquered** England, Wales and Ireland. Ireland and England were linked for the next 800 years. **Feudalism:** The Normans brought a **new style of government** and **land ownership**. **Castles:** The Normans introduced **motte and bailey** and **stone castles**. **Warfare:** The Normans introduced a new style of **warfare**, using **knights** on horseback. **Architecture:** The Normans built **Romanesque-style** churches.

Religious Life in Medieval Times

- The Catholic Church played a very **important role** in the Middle Ages.
- Many medieval people became **monks** and **nuns**.
- Monks lived in **monasteries** and nuns lived in **convents**.

Be careful – don't confuse the medieval monk with the early Christian monk!

- There were many different **religious orders**, e.g. the **Benedictines**, the **Cistercians** and the **Augustinians**.
- To become a monk or a nun, the person had to join a religious order as a **novice**.
- They learned the **Rule of St Benedict** and helped with the work in the monastery or convent.
- If the **abbot** or **abbess** was satisfied with the novice's progress, the novice then became a monk or nun.
- Monks and nuns took three **vows**:
    1. **Poverty** – they would give up all possessions
    2. **Chastity** – they would not marry or have children
    3. **Obedience** – they would obey the order of their abbot or abbess.
- Life in a religious order was **highly structured** and revolved around work and prayer, e.g. **matin prayers** were said in the morning and **vespers** in the evening.
- Some monasteries, abbeys and convents became very **rich**. They were **criticised** for not following the vow of poverty.
- As a result, new orders like the **Dominicans** were founded. These **friars** wandered from place to place, preaching and looking after the sick and poor.

Connections
This later became an important cause of the Reformation (see Ch. 8).

Death in Medieval Times
The Black Death
- The Black Death was a plague that spread across Europe from 1348 to 1351. It was a significant cause of death in medieval times.
- The plague began in Asia. Most historians believe it was spread by **fleas on rats**.
- Dead bodies had a grey/black appearance from boils on the skin.
- People believed many different things caused the plague:
    1. **Poisonous air**
    2. **Vapours** coming from lakes and bogs
    3. **Jewish people**.
- There was a rise in **anti-Semitism** (hatred of Jewish people). There were even massacres of Jews across Europe, e.g. the **Basel Massacre**.

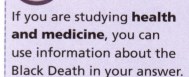

If you are studying **health and medicine**, you can use information about the Black Death in your answer.

The Dance of Death

LIFE AND DEATH IN MEDIEVAL TIMES

- Plague doctors wore masks stuffed with **herbs** to overcome the smells.
- **Flagellants** believed that by flogging (beating) themselves they would make up for their sins and save themselves from the plague.
- Bodies were buried in **mass graves** in large pits.
- Somewhere between **30–60%** of the people in Europe were killed.
- It took almost 150 years for the population of Europe to recover.
- The plague had a significant impact on the **economy**. Because so many peasants were killed, survivors demanded higher wages and tenants got lower rents.

Other causes of death in medieval times

1. Many people died in **battle**, e.g. Richard III.
2. The **Crusades** were a series of religious wars with the aim of reclaiming the Holy Land from Islamic rule. Historians have estimated between 1 million and 9 million died because of the Crusades.
3. **Jousting** was a dangerous sport, e.g. the Duke of Brittany was killed in 1186 during a joust.
4. Other diseases such as **cholera** and **typhus** were common killers during the Middle Ages.
5. Historians have suggested that between 30–50% of children died before reaching adulthood.
6. It is estimated that 1 in 3 women died in childbirth.

Exam Question

(a) From your knowledge of medieval times, write an account of life and/or death in a medieval setting of your choice.
Choose a setting such as one of the following:
- a medieval manor
- a medieval town
- a medieval castle
- another medieval setting of your choice.

Write about at least two of the following:
- living conditions
- working life
- leisure
- defending the settlement
- religion
- illness and death
- any other theme(s) relevant to life and death in medieval times.

SEC Sample Paper, Q3

Revision Questions
Scan the QR code for more revision questions.

6 The Renaissance – Changes in the Arts and Science

After studying this chapter, you should be able to:
- Appreciate change in the arts and sciences during the Renaissance
- Understand differences between medieval and Renaissance art
- Appreciate the contribution of key artists to changes in the arts
- Appreciate the contribution of key scientists to changes in the sciences
- Explain how the Renaissance is historically significant.

What was the Renaissance?

The **Renaissance** was the **revival** or **rebirth** of interest in the learning of Ancient Greece and Rome. It began in Italy in the **14th century**, mainly in the city of Florence, and spread to other European countries.

Key Words
Renaissance
perspective
fresco
gothic
sfumato
anatomy
astronomy
vernacular
historically significant

When you are asked a question about **appreciating change** in the **arts** and **sciences**, you can use **examples** from the **Renaissance**.

Perspective is a painting technique developed during the Renaissance in which three-dimensional objects are made to look real on a two-dimensional surface; the way that objects appear smaller when they are further away.

What changes occurred in art and architecture?

Painting

There were **significant changes** made between medieval and Renaissance paintings.

THE RENAISSANCE – CHANGES IN THE ARTS AND SCIENCE

	Medieval painting	Renaissance painting
	The Annunciation by Simone Martini, c. 1333. Uffizi Gallery, Florence. **No depth** (no perspective) Painted wood panels Lifeless people No variety in colour	*The Annunciation* by Piermatteo d'Amelia, c. 1487. Isabella Stewart Gardner Museum, Boston. **Perspective** (depth; 3D) Renaissance-style clothes Realistic people Variety of colours
Themes	**Religious message only** – scenes from the Bible and the lives of saints	Renaissance artists painted **many different themes** – religious themes, portraits of leaders and their wives, nature and landscape
Materials	**Egg yolk** with powered colours, which dried quickly so changes could not be made	**Oil** with colours so that the paint dried more slowly and artists could vary colours and shading; increased use of **canvas**
Perspective was one of the most important changes	Two-dimensional – the paintings lacked depth	Three-dimensional – the paintings had depth

> **key point**
>
> A **fresco** was a painting done on **damp plaster** so that the painting became part of the plaster.
> *Example: Michelangelo's ceiling in the Sistine Chapel*

Sculpture

Sculptures became more realistic.

Medieval sculpture	Renaissance sculpture
Religious themes Lacking in feeling Often part of a church or cathedral	People were **more realistic** and lifelike Stand-alone sculptures

Architecture

Architecture followed the style of Ancient Rome.

Medieval architecture	Renaissance architecture
Gothic-style architecture	Roman-style architecture (also called **classical** architecture)

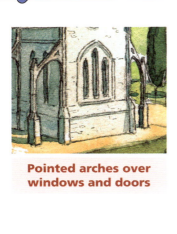
Pointed arches over windows and doors

Gothic or medieval
A **Buttresses**
B **Flying buttress**

Spire

Renaissance

Dome

Columns

Rounded arches over doors and windows

Artists

What contribution did **Leonardo da Vinci** make to changes in the arts and sciences?

1. Leonardo da Vinci was born near Florence. He was **apprenticed** to Master Verrocchio.
2. He went to work for the ruler of Milan, designing fortifications.
3. Leonardo **experimented** with **different styles and techniques** in his paintings.
4. Leonardo created some paintings which are regarded as some of the best works of art.
   - He also developed a new technique of painting, **sfumato**.
   - He used **perspective** to paint **backgrounds** with landscape, plants and rocks.
5. He painted *The Virgin of the Rocks* on canvas. He used a **sfumato** style in this painting.
6. Da Vinci painted *The Last Supper* on a dining room wall of a monastery in Milan. It was not a true fresco, because da Vinci used oil paints.
7. He kept **notebooks** containing his ideas and studies.
8. He studied **astronomy**, geology and **engineering**. He also studied **human anatomy** by dissecting dead bodies.
9. His notebooks have designs of **machines** such as a helicopter and a tank.

10. Even though Leonardo came up with very interesting ideas, his notebooks were not published in his lifetime, so **he did not contribute** to new scientific ideas.
11. He painted the *Mona Lisa* in Florence. This also used the **sfumato** style.
12. He died in France.

What contribution did Michelangelo make to changes in the arts?

1. Michelangelo was born near Florence. He was **apprenticed** to Master Ghirlandaio.
2. Michelangelo **mastered** many different art forms.
    - He was a **painter**, a **sculptor** and an **architect**.
3. Two of Michelangelo's most famous sculptures are the *Pieta* and *David*.
    - The *Pieta* features Mary holding the dead Jesus.
    - *David* portrays the boy who killed the giant, Goliath.
4. He carved **very lifelike figures** out of marble.
5. Michelangelo painted two large **frescoes** in the **Sistine Chapel** in Rome.
    - He painted **four scenes** from the Old Testament about the creation of the world on the ceiling.
    - He painted the *Last Judgement* behind the altar.
6. Michelangelo **designed the dome** of St Peter's Basilica in Rome.
7. He also **designed the Campidoglio**, a square with buildings in a **classical design**.
8. Michelangelo's painting and sculpture **influenced many artists** at the time and since, especially his **realistic portrayal** of the human body.

Sfumato was a painting technique which Leonardo used to **blur** the outlines of figures and **blend** them into their surroundings.
Example: La Giaconda (the 'Mona Lisa') by Leonardo da Vinci

What contribution did Sofonisba Anguissola make to changes in the arts?

1. Sofonisba Anguissola was an Italian artist.
    - She set an **example** for other women when she became an **apprentice** to local painters. She was also guided by **Michelangelo**.
    - She excelled at painting **portraits**, including self-portraits and portraits of her sisters, such as *The Chess Game*. She also painted religious themes. As a woman, Sofonisba was not allowed to study anatomy (the human body). Instead, she developed informal settings for her portraits.

2. She was **court painter** to the **King of Spain**. Here she painted portraits of the king and the queen, and others in the Spanish court.
3. Sofonisba was the **first woman painter** who achieved **international fame**.
   - Younger artists sought her advice.
   - Famous male artists, such as Caravaggio, also learned from her.
   - She became an **example** for later female artists.

How Significant were Developments in Renaissance Science?

Changes in understanding of the universe

1. Astronomy is the study of the universe.
2. In the Middle Ages, people believed that the **earth was the centre** of the universe.
3. During the Renaissance, **Copernicus**, a Polish-born monk and astronomer, said the **sun** was the **centre** of the universe and that the earth and the other planets revolved in **circles** around it.
4. He published his views in *On the Revolutions of the Heavenly Sphere*.
5. **Kepler**, a German astronomer, agreed with Copernicus that the sun was the centre of the universe.
6. But Kepler said the earth and the planets revolved around it in **elliptical** (oval) orbits.
7. Later, **Isaac Newton**, an English scientist, developed his **law of gravity** from Galileo's and Kepler's work.

What contribution did **Galileo** make to changes in the sciences?

1. Galileo was a **Renaissance scientist** who was born in **Pisa**, Italy. Galileo became a **professor of mathematics** in Padua University. He believed he could apply mathematics to the study of the world.
2. He proposed the **pendulum clock** after observing the chandeliers swinging in Pisa Cathedral. He concluded that the swing took the same time whether it was long or short.
3. One of his discoveries was the **theory of the speed of falling bodies**. He said that solid objects all fall at the same speed. Before this idea, people believed that heavier objects fell faster than lighter objects.
4. Galileo invented his own **telescope** to study the universe.
5. His important astronomical discoveries include observing four of the moons of **Jupiter**, the mountains and craters on the moon, and sunspots.

6. Galileo used his observations to support the ideas of Copernicus that the **sun**, not the earth, was the centre of the universe.
7. When Galileo supported this new idea, he got into trouble with the **Catholic Church**. He was summoned to Rome to appear before the **Court of Inquisition**, a church court.
8. Galileo was forced to deny the idea of a sun-centred universe. He was placed under **house arrest** in his house in Florence, until his death.
9. Galileo is called the **Father of Modern Science** because his ideas were based on **scientific methods** of close observation and experimentation.
10. His ideas were added to by other scientists: **Kepler** showed that the earth went around the sun in an **elliptical** path, not a circular path, as Galileo believed; **Newton** discovered the laws of gravity based on Galileo's ideas about the speed of falling objects.

How Significant were Developments in Renaissance Literature?

How did Shakespeare contribute to the development of literature?

1. Shakespeare was a **Renaissance writer** of plays and poetry. He was born in Stratford-upon-Avon and later went to live in London.
2. He became an **actor** and **writer of plays** with the **King's Men**, a theatre company. They performed in the **Globe Theatre**, which was an **open-air theatre** on the banks of the River Thames.
3. Shakespeare wrote **38 plays**, which were performed before Queen Elizabeth and King James as well as at the Globe.
4. Shakespeare took his ideas from **classical** (Greek and Roman) literature as well as the history of England.
   - His plays included **tragedies** such as *Hamlet*, *Romeo and Juliet* and *Macbeth*; his **comedies** included *The Merchant of Venice* and his **histories** included *Henry V* and *Julius Caesar*. Shakespeare also wrote poems and sonnets (14-line poems).
   - His plays were **published widely** on the **printing press**.
5. His plays contributed to the use of the vernacular language (the language of the people) rather than Latin, which was the language of learning during the Middle Ages.
   - He influenced the development of the English language; he contributed to the **standardisation of the language**.
   - He made theatre appeal to the **wider public**.

What is the meaning of historically significant or important? It is a person, issue or event in history that is considered important in effecting (causing) historical change.

Summary: Why is the Renaissance historically significant?
Use examples from what happened **during** the Renaissance to write more on the **results or influence** of the Renaissance to show how **historically significant** it was.
1. The Renaissance fostered a **questioning spirit** in which old ideas were no longer accepted without question.
2. There were **new developments** in **painting, sculpture and architecture**. These included **perspective, sfumato** and **classical architecture**.
3. The questioning spirit of the Renaissance led to **new knowledge** in geography, science, medicine and astronomy.
4. This questioning spirit also led to the **Age of Exploration**, the **Reformation** and to further **scientific discoveries**.
5. **The printing press** led to increased education and literacy. It also spread new ideas.

Sample Question
Apart from art, select **two** areas of learning in which change took place during the Renaissance era, e.g. literature, architecture, medicine, science.
Outline **one** key change that occurred in each area.

First area of learning: *Literature*
Change: *Latin was the language used for writing in medieval times. During the Renaissance, Shakespeare, the greatest playwright in the English language, spread the use of the vernacular – the language of the people. He invented new words, e.g. lonely, and his plays helped to standardise the rules and grammar of the English language.*

Second area of learning: *Science*
Change: *In medieval times, people thought that the earth was the centre of the universe. During the Renaissance, Copernicus, a Polish astronomer, showed that the sun was the centre of the universe. He thought the earth went on a circular orbit around the sun. But Kepler showed that the orbit was elliptical.*

It is important to note the word **'change'**, and to be able to show changes in your answer by pointing out **what went before** and **what the change was**.

Revision Questions
Scan the QR code for more revision questions.

7 Conquest and Colonisation in the Age of Exploration

After studying this chapter, you should be able to:
- Explain what the age of exploration was
- Outline key developments in shipbuilding and navigation
- Identify important Portuguese and Spanish explorers
- Define 'conquest' and 'colonisation'
- Evaluate the impact of conquest on people
- Evaluate the impact of colonisation on people.

Key Words
caravel	quadrants	conquest	Cuzco
lateen	cross-shafts	Aztecs	colonisation
rudder	Portolan chart	Montezuma	Middle Passage
carrack, nao	Treaty of	Tenochtitlan	*hacienda*
compass	Tordesillas	Inca Empire	encomienda
astrolabe	conquistador	Atahualpa	system

What was the Age of Exploration?

In the 15th and 16th centuries, Europeans – especially the Portuguese and Spanish – began to explore the world.

Technology and historical change in the Age of Exploration

Without **technological developments** in shipbuilding and navigation, the Age of Exploration would not have been possible.

What were the main developments in shipbuilding?

1. New ships called **caravels** were built.
2. These ships were **carvel-built**. That means boards on the side of the ship were fitted **edge to edge**.
3. Caravel used **square** and **lateen** (triangular) sails.
   - **Lateen sails** were used to sail against the wind
   - **Square sails** were used to sail faster with the wind following behind
4. Caravels were steered by **rudders**.
5. Caravels had **castles** (raised structures) on the decks at the front and back. Sailors could spot enemy ships more easily from castles.
6. Later, a larger ship called a **carrack** or **nao** was built for longer voyages.

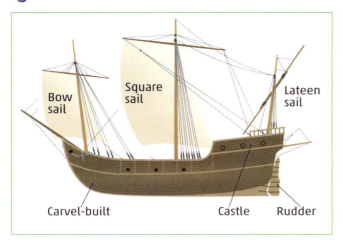

A caravel

What were the main developments in navigation?

| Compass | • This was used to tell sailors which direction they were sailing in.
• They were often unreliable because iron objects on the ship affected them. |
|---|---|
| Latitude and longitude | • **Latitude** means how many **degrees north or south** of the equator it was.
• Sailors used **astrolabes**, **quadrants** and **cross-shafts** to work out the latitude.
• **Longitude** – degrees east and west – could not be worked out until the 18th century, when an accurate clock called a **chronometer** was developed. |
| Maps | • **Portolan charts** were the earliest maps used by sailors.
• They showed places along the coast joined by straight lines.
• These lines gave the course or direction, which the sailors followed by compass.
• Soon mapmakers developed new ways of drawing maps that included the whole world. |
| Speed | • Speed was measured using a **log and line** and a **sand-glass**.
• The line, with a log tied to the end of it, was thrown out of the ship.
• The line was marked by **knots**.
• The speed of the ship was calculated by measuring the time it took the knots on the line to pass through a sailor's hand. |

These developments made the transportation of people and goods across the Atlantic possible, e.g. the slave trade.

They also led to larger sea battles and the development of powerful naval fleets, e.g. the Spanish Armada.

CONQUEST AND COLONISATION IN THE AGE OF EXPLORATION

The Portuguese Explorations

The Portuguese explored along the African coast, hoping to find a route to Asia and the Spice Islands.

Prince Henry the Navigator led the Portuguese explorations.

c. 1420	**Prince Henry the Navigator** organised voyages down the coast of Africa
1444	**African slaves** were brought to **Lisbon**
1488	**Bartholomew Diaz** rounded the **Cape of Good Hope** in the southern tip of Africa
1497–99	**Vasco da Gama** sailed to **India**
1500–01	**Pedro Cabral** reached the coast of **Brazil**
c. 1530	African slaves were brought to Brazil

The Spanish Explorations

Sponsored by **Kind Ferdinand** and **Queen Isabella**, Columbus's aim was to sail west to reach the East.

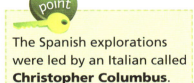

The Spanish explorations were led by an Italian called **Christopher Columbus**.

1492	Columbus's first voyage. He explored islands off the coast of America.
1494	• The **Treaty of Tordesillas** was agreed after Columbus's first voyage. • The Pope wanted to **prevent war** between Spain and Portugal. • They drew a line on the globe from north to south. All lands discovered to the west of this line were Spanish and all land to the east of the line was Portuguese. • Brazil became Portuguese, while the rest of South America belonged to Spain.
1502	The Spanish took African slaves to Cuba.
1519	• **Magellan's** voyage around the world began. • **Cortés** begins the conquest of the **Aztec Empire** in **Mexico**.
1532	**Pizzaro** conquered the **Inca Empire** in **Peru**.
c. 1550	The **yearly shipment** of silver to Spain from the New World began.

Columbus is a **contentious** (controversial) historical figure. Some people view him as a hero; he had an idea that he could reach India by sailing west, and was determined to see the trip through even when supplies were running low. Places have been named after him and monuments have been put up in his honour. But Columbus was extremely cruel to the natives that he encountered, and many people think he should be viewed as a murderer and villain. Some statues of Columbus have been removed and some places have replaced Columbus Day with Indigenous Peoples' Day.

The Conquest of the Aztecs and the Incas

1. According to the **Treaty of Tordesillas**, all of the land on the new continent, apart from Brazil, belonged to Spain.
2. Spanish **conquistadors** (conquerors) began the **conquest** (forced takeover) of these lands.
3. They were looking for gold and silver.

Cortés and the Aztecs

Hernán Cortés

1. **Cortés** was responsible for the defeat of the **Aztec Empire** in **Mexico**.
2. 1519 – Cortés sailed to **Mexico** with **11 ships** and **500 men**.
3. As Cortés marched inland towards the **Aztecs**, he encountered native tribes who did not like the **heavy taxes** and **slavery** imposed on them by the Aztecs. Many of these natives had also been used as **human sacrifices** to the Aztec gods.
4. **Montezuma**, the Aztec emperor, came to greet Cortés as he approached the Aztec capital, **Tenochtitlan**.
5. The Spaniards were initially allowed into the city but were forced out after the murder of Aztec priests and the death of Montezuma.
6. 1521 – Cortés got help from neighbouring tribes and led 100,000 men against the Aztecs.
7. Tenochtitlan was destroyed and the Aztecs were forced to work as **slaves** in mines or in the fields.
8. Cortés rebuilt Tenochtitlan as **Mexico City**.
9. The Spaniards brought cattle, plants, ploughs and hundreds of priests to establish a colony in the Aztec lands, and renamed them **New Spain**.
10. Cortés returned to exploring and discovered **California**. Many places in the southwest of North America have Spanish names, e.g. **Los Angeles** and **San Francisco**.

Pizarro and the Incas

1. **Pizarro** set out to conquer the **Inca Empire** in **Peru**.
2. He captured and killed the Inca emperor, **Atahualpa**.
3. Pizarro and his men then captured the Inca capital, **Cuzco**.
4. They seized the Inca treasures and melted them down for gold.
5. The Spaniards fought amongst themselves, and Pizarro was killed by his own soldiers.
6. The Spaniards later discovered gold and silver mines.
7. For the next 100 years, gold and silver was mined by the Incas, who died in their thousands.

8. Peru and Bolivia supplied about **65%** of the gold and silver sent to Spain in the 16th century.
9. Spain became very wealthy.
10. Spanish ships travelling across the Atlantic were often attacked by English ships, leading to war between the two countries.

What was the Impact of Conquest on the New World?

What was the impact of conquest on the New World?

1. Destroyed empires like the Aztecs and the Incas. The native population of New Spain went from 25 million in 1492 to 1.25 million c. 1600.

2. Brought European diseases to the New World.

3. Gold and silver was sent to Europe and made Spain incredibly wealthy.

4. The Americas were opened up to other European countries, e.g. in 1497–98 **John Cabot** explored the coast of North America on behalf of England.

5. Native peoples were brutally treated.

6. Many natives were **enslaved**.

7. New animals and plants were introduced to the New World, e.g. **horses** and **grapes**, and many new animals and plants were sent from the New World back to Europe, e.g. potatoes and **peanuts**. This was called the **Columbian Exchange**.

8. New **farming methods** were introduced in the Americas.

9. European languages, culture and religion replaced native languages, culture and religion.

What was the impact of colonisation?

Colonisation means settling among and establishing control over native people.

1. The slave trade	• Shortages of native people to work on the estates of Europeans in the Americas led to slaves being brought from Africa. This was called the **trans-Atlantic slave trade**. • Portugal controlled the slave trade. • It is estimated that **12.5 million slaves** were shipped from Africa to North and South America between the 16th and 19th centuries. • About 1.8 million slaves died in the **Middle Passage** (on the way to the Americas). • Conditions onboard slave ships were awful. • Even though the trans-Atlantic slave trade stopped in 1807, slavery was not abolished in the United States until 1865.
2. Plantations	• Large farms called **plantations** developed across North America and the Caribbean. • They grew crops like tobacco, cotton and sugar. • They were worked by slaves in brutal conditions. 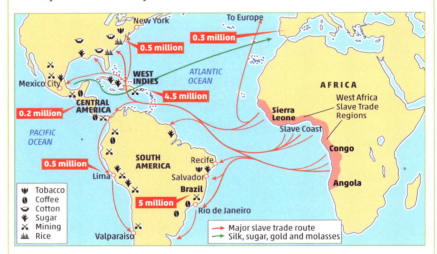
3. Spanish system	• The Spanish developed their land using *haciendas* (large estates bought from or granted by the Spanish king). • Landowners used the **encomienda system** to work their land. This gave landowners the right to use free native labour on their *haciendas*. In return, landowners gave the native people protection and a Christian education. • This system created a small, rich ruling class who were in control of the majority of the poorer population.
4. Religion	• Catholicism replaced many native religions.
5. Language	• **Spanish** and **Portuguese** often replaced native languages.
6. Architecture	• Spanish-style architecture spread to the Americas. • **Cathedral Metropolitana** in Mexico City was built in the **European Baroque style**.

CONQUEST AND COLONISATION IN THE AGE OF EXPLORATION

7. Impact on Spain	• Spain became the **richest** country in Europe. • Every year from the middle of the 16th century to the end of the 18th century, a Spanish treasure fleet sailed from the Americas to Spain. • Spain controlled a huge new empire that was available for **settlement**, **investment** and **exploitation**. • The flow of silver into Spain caused **inflation** (rising prices). • Spanish landowners benefited as the value of their land increased, but the standard of living of other Spaniards got worse.
8. Impact on Portugal	• Portugal also **prospered** from its empire. • Much of this wealth was in the hands of a small ruling class. • From 1881 to 1991, over 1.5 million **Portuguese people immigrated to Brazil**.

Sample Question
What impact did the conquest of the Aztecs have on people?

The conquest of the Aztecs had a negative impact on the Aztecs and a positive impact for Spain.

The Aztec capital, Tenochtitlan, was destroyed. The Aztec leader, Montezuma, was killed. The Aztecs were forced to work as slaves in mines or in the fields. New farming methods, religion (Christianity), language (Spanish) and culture were introduced and replaced Aztec ones.

Spain became incredibly wealthy following the destruction of the Aztec Empire. Gold and silver were sent to Spain. The Spanish language and Catholic religion spread to the New World. The Aztec Empire was replaced by a colony called New Spain. Tenochtitlan was rebuilt as Mexico City.

Revision Questions
Scan the QR code for more revision questions.

8 Martin Luther and the Reformation – The Historical Importance of Religion

aims After studying this chapter, you should be able to:
- Consider the historical significance of the Reformation
- Evaluate the role played by Martin Luther in the Reformation
- Consider the historical significance of the Catholic Counter-Reformation
- Reflect on the impact of the Reformation
- Consider the significance of Luther today.

The Reformation

What is the meaning of historically significant or important?
It is a person, issue or event in history that is considered important in **effecting historical change**.

Key Words
historically significant
Reformation
reformer
justification by faith alone
indulgences
excommunicated
Protestants
Catholic Counter-Reformation or Catholic Reformation
vernacular
Inquisition
heresy
intolerant

What was the Reformation?

1. The **Reformation** was a religious movement in the 16th century that led to the formation of the Protestant churches. It began in **Germany** as a **protest** against abuses in the Catholic Church.

Martin Luther

MARTIN LUTHER AND THE REFORMATION – THE HISTORICAL IMPORTANCE OF RELIGION

What were the causes of the Reformation?

Causes of the Reformation

1. The influence of the Renaissance: The Renaissance encouraged a questioning spirit, so some people criticised the Catholic Church and said it was not following the Bible.

2. Abuses: People were critical of abuses in the Catholic Church, such as **1. nepotism** – appointing relatives to church positions; **2. simony** – buying and selling church positions; **3. pluralism** – having more than one parish or diocese; **4. absenteeism** – being absent from your parish or diocese; **5. bad organisation** – many priests were uneducated, so they could not read the Bible or preach.

3. The printing press: Criticism of the Catholic Church was **spread quickly** through books and pamphlets.

4. The power of princes and kings: Rulers wanted to **control** their countries, including the power of the Catholic Church.

5. The wealth of the Catholic Church: Princes and kings wanted the **wealth** of the Catholic Church to build up their countries.

The Actions of One Reformer: Martin Luther

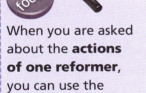

exam focus

When you are asked about the **actions of one reformer**, you can use the information from the life of **Martin Luther**.

1505	Luther ordained as a priest
1511	Luther began lecturing in Wittenberg University
1517	*95 Theses* published
1521	Luther excommunicated by Pope
1521	Luther at Diet of Worms
1530	Confession of Augsburg
1546	Death of Luther

1. **The Reformation began in Germany in the early 16th century, when Martin Luther criticised the Catholic Church**.
2. Luther was an **Augustinian** monk who was **Professor of Theology** at Wittenberg University.
   - He was worried about **salvation** (going to heaven), but he read in the Bible that 'the just man shall live by faith alone' (**justification by faith alone**). Luther said that **only faith in God** would allow a person to get to heaven. *Renaissance questioning*
3. He criticised John **Tetzel** for preaching **indulgences** (acts or prayers to reduce the amount of punishment for sins).

4. In 1517, Luther wrote his **95 Theses** in Latin and sent them to the Archbishop of Mainz. Some said he also pinned them on the church door at **Wittenberg**. The **95 Theses** criticised the Catholic Church and demanded its reform.

    Printing press

5. Very soon, Luther's theses were translated into **German**, printed and distributed all over Germany.

6. Many Germans agreed with Luther, because they **did not want to pay money to the Pope in Rome** and because the **priests** were **ignorant of the Bible**.

    Abuses in Catholic Church

7. The **Pope** acted against Luther.
    - He ordered Luther to meet **Cardinal Cajetan**, but he couldn't persuade Luther to change his ideas.
    - Luther then debated with a theologian, **John Eck**, but again Luther did not change his mind.
    - The Pope then sent Luther a **papal bull** (letter) ordering him to withdraw his teachings or else be **excommunicated** (banned from the sacraments).
    - Luther publicly burned the papal letter; the Pope **excommunicated** him.

8. Luther and his followers engaged in a **propaganda war** with the Catholic Church. They produced pamphlets and cartoons criticising the Catholic Church.

    Printing press

9. The emperor, **Charles V**, brought together the **Diet of Worms** – a meeting of the princes of the empire. Luther was invited there, but he refused to change his views in front of the emperor.

    Power of princes

10. Charles V then issued the **Edict of Worms** to arrest Luther.

11. **Frederick the Wise**, the ruler of Saxony, took Luther and hid him in **Wartburg Castle** so that he would be safe. Here, he spent the next year translating the **New Testament** into German so that ordinary Germans could read the Bible.

    Printing press

12. Luther's ideas got support from other **princes**. They protested to the emperor that they wanted to practise their own religion, so they became known as **Protestants**.

    Power of princes

13. Some of Luther's followers (with Luther's approval) wrote out the **Confession of Augsburg**, which was a statement of **Lutheran beliefs**, but it was rejected by the emperor.

MARTIN LUTHER AND THE REFORMATION – THE HISTORICAL IMPORTANCE OF RELIGION

14. Luther died in 1546, before the divisions between Catholic and Protestant princes broke into war.
15. The war lasted for nine years. It was ended by the **Peace of Augsburg** (1555). This stated that rulers were **free to decide the religion of their own states**. This led to states becoming either Catholic or Protestant.

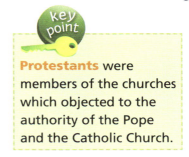

key point

Protestants were members of the churches which objected to the authority of the Pope and the Catholic Church.

Some differences between the Catholic Church and Luther's religion

	Sacraments	Clergy	Head of the church	Church services
Catholic beliefs	Seven sacraments	Clergy were specially educated; clergy cannot marry	The Pope	Mass in Latin
Luther's beliefs	Two sacraments – baptism and eucharist	Any Christian can be a clergyman; clergy can marry	Princes and kings	Mass in the **vernacular** (the language of the people)

Why was the Reformation Historically Significant or Important?

exam focus

What were the results of the Reformation?
'Results' = 'effects' = 'impact' = 'consequences' = **showing historical change**

1. Other reformers

Luther's actions led others to begin their own Reformation.
- **John Calvin** founded the **Calvinist** or **Presbyterian** religion in Switzerland. This spread to many other countries, including Scotland, Ireland and America.
- **Henry VIII** began the Reformation in **England** when he broke away from the Catholic Church. This led to the development of the **Church of England**. The changes in religion in England were also introduced into **Ireland**.

2. The Catholic Counter-Reformation

Luther's actions resulted in the **Catholic Counter-Reformation**. This refers to the efforts of the Catholic Church **to reform itself** and **to stop the spread of Protestantism**.

(i) The Council of Trent

The Council of Trent was a council of the cardinals and bishops to reform the Catholic Church. It resulted in statements of **Catholic faith** (beliefs) and **discipline** (rules), including:
- A list of seven sacraments
- Priests were special people, so they could not marry
- Simony, nepotism, pluralism (abuses) were **banned**
- Catholics must be taught from a **catechism** (a book with questions and answers about the Church's teachings).

Ignatius Loyola

Results of the Council of Trent
- The Catholic religion became the **most important Christian religion** in Europe.
- There were **greater divisions** between Catholics and Protestants in Europe.

(ii) Religious orders: Ignatius Loyola and the Jesuits

The **Jesuits** (Society of Jesus) was a religious order founded by **Ignatius Loyola**.
- He wrote the *Spiritual Exercises* as a guide to train his followers.
- He was an ex-soldier, so the Jesuits were organised like an **army**, with a governor-general at their head. They followed strict discipline.

The work of the Jesuits

The Jesuits spread the Catholic religion through preaching and deeds of charity.
- They founded **schools and colleges** to teach the sons of nobles and merchants – the future leaders.
- They became **missionaries** to Ireland, India, Japan and other countries.

(iii) The Court of Inquisition

The **Inquisition** was a **court of the Catholic Church** which tried people accused of **heresy** (beliefs contrary to the Catholic Church).
- It was **mainly active** in Spain and Italy.
- It **used torture** to get people to confess.

MARTIN LUTHER AND THE REFORMATION – THE HISTORICAL IMPORTANCE OF RELIGION

- **Punishments** included wearing a Sanbenito (a special garment to mark out people being punished), whipping and burning at the stake.

The **result** of the work of the Inquisition was that **Protestantism was crushed in Spain and Italy**.

3. Religious divisions in Europe

As a result of the Reformation and Catholic Counter-Reformation, Europe was **divided** between Catholic and Protestant countries.
- **Catholic** = Spain, Italy, Ireland
- **Protestant** = England, Scotland, Holland, Norway

4. Wars of religion

These divisions between Catholics and Protestants resulted in **civil wars** and in **wars between countries**.
- There were **civil wars** in England, France and Germany.
- There was a war between **Spain and England**, in which Spain attacked England with its Armada (fleet of ships), and was defeated.
- There was the **Thirty Years' War (1618–48)**, which involved Sweden, Denmark, states of Germany, Austria and other countries.

5. Intolerance and persecution

- Catholics and Protestants were intolerant of each other's religion (they refused to tolerate or respect the views of the opposing religion).
- Catholics and Protestants **persecuted each other**. In different countries, Catholics and Protestants brought in **laws** which persecuted members of the other religion.
- In France, Catholics massacred French Calvinists known as **Huguenots** in the **St Bartholomew's Day Massacre** in 1572.
- There were many persecutions and massacres during the **Thirty Years' War**.

When you are writing about the **historical importance (significance)** of the Reformation, **you do not have to confine yourself** to the immediate changes brought about by the Reformation. You can **mention changes/effects up to the present day**.

6. Art and architecture
- Protestant churches followed a **plain style** in their altars and windows.
- Catholic churches were richly decorated – the **Baroque style** of art and architecture was used in Catholic paintings and churches.

7. Education
Protestant churches wanted everybody to be able to read the Bible. This led to the **expansion** of education and literacy.

8. Christianity today
- Christianity remains divided today.
- In 2017, the 500th anniversary of Luther publishing his **95 Theses** was celebrated, especially in Germany.

Sample Question
The Reformation was a very important episode in the history of Christianity in Europe.
Name a reformer that you studied: *Martin Luther*
What was the long term result of the reformer's actions in the history of the Reformation?
Christians were now divided between the Catholic Church and the Protestant churches. This division led to religious wars in Germany, France, the Thirty Years' War in Europe and the English Civil War. Christians are still divided today though there are efforts made to reach better understanding between the different churches.

Revision Questions
Scan the QR code for more revision questions.

9 The Plantation of Ulster, Identity and the Growth of Towns

After studying this chapter, you should be able to:
- Explain what the word 'identity' means
- Summarise the main events of the Ulster Plantation
- Recognise how the Ulster Plantation changed identity on the island of Ireland
- Explain how the growth of towns influenced identity on the island of Ireland.

The Plantation of Ulster

Background

1. **Gaelic chiefs** and clans like the O'Neills of Tyrone and the O'Donnells of Donegal were the main rulers of Ulster.
2. In 1594, the **Nine Years' War** began when the Ulster chiefs rebelled against efforts by the English government to impose English law and the Protestant religion.
3. The Ulster chiefs, led by **Hugh O'Neill**, won a number of battles, e.g. the **Battle of Yellow Ford**.
4. **Philip II** of Spain sent ships with 4,000 soldiers to help the rebellion.
5. They landed at **Kinsale**, Co. Cork, but were surrounded by an English fleet and army.
6. When O'Neill and O'Donnell came to help, they were defeated at the **Battle of Kinsale** in **1601**.
7. In 1607, O'Neill and the other Ulster chiefs **fled Ireland** for the continent. This was called the **Flight of the Earls**.
8. King James I **confiscated** their land.

Reasons for the Ulster Plantation

There were a number of reasons why King James I wanted to carry out the **Ulster Plantation**.
A. He wanted to create a **loyal and Protestant population**.
B. King James I wanted to **protect England** by making sure that other countries, like Spain and France, couldn't use Ireland as a base to attack England.

Key Words
Nine Years' War
Battle of Kinsale
Flight of the Earls
plantation
contentious
undertakers
servitors
bawn
tories
controversial
arable farming
unionists
paramilitary
nationalists
partition

If you are asked about a **plantation**, you should write about the **Ulster Plantation**.

C. He wanted to **spread the Protestant religion** because he thought Catholics would be disloyal to the crown.
D. King James I thought that **English culture was superior** to Irish Gaelic culture.
E. He wanted to **gain money** for the crown from rents. King James I also wanted to pay soldiers and officials who fought in the Nine Years' War by granting them land in Ulster.

The Ulster Plantation is an example of a **contentious** (controversial) topic.

The plantation in practice

1. Land was confiscated in six counties: **Fermanagh**, **Armagh**, **Tyrone**, **Derry**, **Donegal** and **Cavan**.
2. Land was split into **crown land** and **church land**.
3. Church land was given to the **Church of Ireland** and **Trinity College**, **Dublin**.
4. Crown land was used for towns, schools and plantation.

5. Land for plantation was divided into **1,000, 1,500 and 2,000 acre estates**. The Articles of Plantation gave land to **undertakers** (English and Scottish settlers), **servitors** (English soldiers and officials who were owed money after the Nine Years' War) and **loyal Irish**.
6. All three groups had to protect their land with a **bawn** (stone wall), and sometimes a stone house or tower.
7. Derry was renamed **Londonderry**, as the guilds of London merchants brought settlers to the county.
8. From the point of view of the English government, the Ulster Plantation was more successful than previous plantations in Munster and Laois-Offaly, because:
   - It increased the **influence of English law**, the English **language** and English **farming methods**.
   - It ensured a **loyal** population.
   - They spread the **Protestant religion**.
9. The Ulster Plantation led to a later migration of more Scottish settlers in the late 17th century.

How Did the Ulster Plantation Influence Identity on the Island of Ireland?

The Ulster Plantation had a significant influence (impact) on identity on the island of Ireland.

1. **New population arrived**
    - Settlers came from Scotland and England.
    - By 1641, there were about 40,000 Scottish and English settlers in Ulster.
    - Between 1690 and 1698, 80,000 Scottish people came to Ulster due to famine in Scotland.
2. **Changes in land ownership and religion**
    - Planters were either **Presbyterian** or **Church of England**.
    - This differed from the religion of the Gaelic Irish, who were **Catholic**.
    - Planters brought their own clergy and took over Catholic churches.
    - **Land ownership changed** from Gaelic chiefs to English and Scottish settlers.
    - Some Gaelic Irish remained as **tenants** with new landlords, but others lived as outlaws or 'tories' in the mountains and woods. They attacked the planters.
    - Changes in land ownership created a level of **resentment** between settlers and the Gaelic Irish.
3. **New towns were built**
    - Planters introduced **town life** to Ireland.
    - More than 20 new towns were planned and built, e.g. **Derry/Londonderry**, **Letterkenny** and **Dungannon**.
    - They had **straight**, **wide streets** with a **central square** or **diamond**.
    - Towns were surrounded by **stone walls** for protection.

The name Derry/Londonderry remains a controversial topic today. Road signs in the Republic of Ireland use 'Derry', while many in Northern Ireland read 'Londonderry'. In some areas, the 'London' part of these signs is painted over. Sometimes you will see both names used, e.g. 'Derry/Londonderry' is often used by www.visitderry.com.

4. **The economy changed**
    - The planters introduced new farming methods.
    - They used arable farming (growing crops) rather than pastoral farming (keeping animals).
    - New crops like **flax** were grown.
    - Woods were **cut down** and the timber was **exported**.
    - **Trade prospered** and roads, inns and mills were developed.

5. **Gaelic Irish culture declined**
   - The culture and language of the Gaelic Irish **declined** because the Gaelic chiefs lost their power.
   - The English language became more **widespread** during the 17th century.
6. **The law changed**
   - **English Common Law** replaced Brehon Law.
7. **Different identities emerged**

   Unionists
   - **Unionists** are mostly Protestant and want to keep a **connection** with Britain.
   - Unionist organisations include the **DUP** (political party) and the **UVF** (paramilitary group).
   - Many unionists view themselves as British.

   Nationalists
   - Most **nationalists** are Catholic and want a **unified** Ireland under Irish rule.
   - Nationalist groups include **Sinn Féin**, the **SDLP** (political parties) and the **IRA** (**paramilitary** group).
   - Many nationalists view themselves as Irish.
   - Some people in Northern Ireland view themselves as British *and* Irish.
8. **Different identities caused conflict**
   - Divisions between the Catholic Irish and Protestant Scottish and English settlers has caused **conflict**.
   - The 1689 victory of **Protestant William of Orange** over **Catholic King James II** is commemorated each year on the **12 July** with parades. These parades often end up in violence.
   - Conflicts between nationalists and unionists in the early 20th century led to the partition (division) **of Ireland** and the creation of Northern Ireland in 1920. Northern Ireland is part of Britain.
   - When Northern Ireland was established, the nationalist community was **discriminated** against by the majority unionist government. This discrimination led to the **Troubles**, a 30-year period of violence in Northern Ireland.

Summary of the impact of the Ulster Plantation on identity

	Before the Ulster Plantation	**After the Ulster Plantation**
Population	Most people were Gaelic Irish. Controlled by Gaelic Irish chiefs like the O'Neills	Many new settlers from Scotland and England, e.g. 40,000 by 1641
Religion	Most were Catholic	Settlers were Presbyterian or Church of England (Anglican)
Economy	Used pastoral farming (animals)	Used more arable farming (crops)

THE PLANTATION OF ULSTER, IDENTITY AND THE GROWTH OF TOWNS

Towns	Most people lived in the countryside	Introduced town life
		Built many new towns, e.g. Coleraine
Culture	Irish language and culture dominant	English language and culture became widespread
		Scots language came to Ulster with the Scottish settlers
Law	Brehon Law used	English Common Law introduced
Conflict	Conflict between Gaelic chiefs and English government	Conflict between Catholics/Protestants nationalists/unionists became a more common feature

How did the Growth of Towns Influence Identity on the Island of Ireland?

exam focus

If you are asked about a **pattern of settlement** in an exam, you could write about the **growth of towns**.

Era	Examples	Features	Impact on identity
Early Christian Ireland saw the development of monastic towns	Kells and Cashel	Some monastic towns became important centres of **economic activity**, e.g. Clonmacnoise (see Ch. 4)	Promoted **Christianity**
The **Vikings** raided monastic settlements. They built and developed towns along the coastline.	Waterford, Wexford, Dublin, Cork and Limerick	Built **embankments** with timber walls around the settlement for defence. These towns **traded** with other Viking towns around Europe	**Spoke Norse**, some words like 'market' (*margadh*) originate from Norse
The **Normans** developed Viking towns and built over 50 new towns	Kilkenny, Athenry, Trim and Fethard	Built on monastic sites or near water	Originally spoke French and then English. Used **different language, laws and customs** to Gaelic Irish in the countryside

Towns were a central feature of the **Plantations**. They were administrative hubs.	Bandon, Killarney, Omagh and Donegal	Wide streets Central square or diamond for markets	Gaelic Irish lived outside the town walls These suburbs were sometimes called 'Irishtown' Towns became a **hub for English and Scottish culture**
In the **18th century**, some landlords developed estate towns	Kenmare, Abbeyleix, Birr and Westport	Wide streets crossed in an 'X'. Town connected to Big House at one end and a Church of Ireland at the other	Towns centred around the 'Big House' and the English **landlord system**

Sample Question
Consider a controversial issue from more than one perspective.

The Plantation of Ulster can be seen as a controversial issue.
The majority of **unionists** might view the Ulster Plantation as a positive thing.
Many unionists are the **descendants of settlers** who came to Ireland during the Ulster Plantation.
Most unionists are Protestant because most of the Scottish and English settlers were Protestant.
Unionists want to keep the link or connection with Britain.
The majority of **nationalists** might view the Ulster Plantation as a negative thing.
Because of the Ulster Plantation, the Gaelic Irish language and culture declined.
Most nationalists are Catholic. Protestant settlers took over Catholic churches and some of the land confiscated after the Flight of the Earls was given to the Church of Ireland.
When Northern Ireland was established in 1920, nationalists were discriminated against by the unionist government.

Revision Questions
Scan the QR code for more revision questions.

10A The American Revolution

When you are asked to examine the **causes, course and consequences of one revolution** in pre-20th-century Europe and/or the wider world, you can use information from **either** the **American Revolution OR** the **French Revolution**.

After studying this chapter, you should be able to:
- Name and explain the main causes of the American Revolution
- Outline the main events of the American Revolution
- Assess the consequences of the American Revolution.

America in 1850

Key Words
colony
revolution
Navigation Acts
Seven Years' War
Stamp Act
Sons of Liberty
'No taxation without representation'
Boston Massacre
Boston Tea Party
Intolerable Acts
Common Sense
Battles of Lexington and Concord
Continental Army
Declaration of Independence
Battle of Yorktown
Treaty of Paris
federal government

The 13 colonies in America before the American Revolution

1. By the middle of the 18th century, English settlers had established **13 colonies** along the eastern coast of North America, e.g. **Georgia**, **New York** and **Virginia**.
2. The population grew rapidly because of a high birth rate, low death rate, European immigration and the trans-Atlantic slave trade.
3. Relations between the American colonies and Britain grew worse during the 18th century and eventually resulted in the **American Revolution**.
4. A revolution is when a government is overthrown by force.

> **key point**
>
> A **colony** is an area of land controlled by a foreign power.
>
> A **revolution** is when a government is overthrown by force.

What Were the Main Causes of the American Revolution?

1. The Navigation Acts
- The **Navigation Acts** were an English attempt to control America.
- These laws stated that some American products like sugar, tobacco and tea could only be sold through England.
- England made a lot of money acting as the middleman (dealer/agent).

2. The Seven Years' War and British debt
- During the **Seven Years' War** (1756–63), Britain and America joined forces to defeat the French, who had colonies in Canada and America.
- The war **increased British debt**.
- To pay for this debt, Britain insisted that the Americans be taxed to pay for the cost of the war.
- Americans were also taxed to cover the cost of keeping British soldiers in America.

3. The Stamp Act and the Sons of Liberty
- To help pay for the war, the British also passed the **Stamp Act** (1764).
- This meant Americans had to pay to have **newspapers and legal documents stamped** by government officials.
- The **Sons of Liberty** protested against the Stamp Act by **burning stamps** and **attacking stamp officials**.

4. Increased taxation and 'no taxation without representation'
- The British parliament introduced another series of taxes.
- The **Quartering Act** meant that local towns and villages had to provide housing and food for any British soldiers based there.

- The **Sugar Act** imposed a tax on sugar imports.
- The **Townshend Acts** of 1767 taxed items such as paint, paper, glass and tea.
- Many Americans believed that the British parliament had no right to impose taxes, as America was not represented in the London parliament.
- This became known as 'no taxation without representation'.

5. The Boston Massacre

- On 5 March 1770, British troops killed five colonists (Americans) who were throwing stones and snowballs at the British soldiers.
- This became known as the Boston Massacre.
- It was a huge **propaganda opportunity** for colonists like the **Sons of Liberty**.
- 'Paul Revere engrave[d] a picture of the scene ... [it] showed British soldiers firing at peaceful Boston Citizens. That wasn't the way it actually happened ... but the drawing made good propaganda. It made people furious at the British.' (Joy Hakim, *From Colonies to Country*)

6. The Boston Tea Party

- In December 1773, the **Sons of Liberty** organised the Boston Tea Party.
- Colonists, dressed as Mohawk people, dumped 342 crates of tea from British ships into Boston Harbour.
- They were **protesting a British tax on tea** and the perceived **monopoly** (they had no competition) that the East India Company had on the tea trade.
- As a result, Britain introduced the Intolerable Acts.
- These acts **closed Boston Port** until the East India Company had been repaid for the spilt tea.

7. Tom Paine and Common Sense

- Americans were also inspired by the writings of Tom Paine.
- In 1776, Paine wrote *Common Sense*.
- Paine said that America should **fight for complete independence** from Britain.

What Was the Course of the American Revolution?

This timeline lists the main events of the war in **chronological order**. Chronological order means the order in which they happened, starting with the earliest and going forwards towards the present.

1775	1. The **Battles of Lexington and Concord** signified the start of the American Revolution.
	• British commander, **General Gage**, sent 800 British troops to destroy weapons that the Americans were storing at Concord.
	• British soldiers shot 8 and wounded 10 Americans on **Lexington Green**.
	• There were further clashes at Concord and on the British return to Boston.
	• 273 British soldiers were killed or wounded.
	2. The Second Continental Congress in Philadelphia voted to form a **Continental Army** and appointed **George Washington as the Commander-in-Chief**.
	3. At the **Battle of Bunker Hill**, British troops successfully forced Americans off Breed's Hill in Boston.
	• Despite losing, Americans were boosted by how well they fought against the professional British army.
1776	4. Washington and the Continental Army successfully **forced the British out of Boston**.
	5. The American **invasion of Canada failed**.
	6. On 4 July, the Continental Congress voted to adopt the **Declaration of Independence**.
	• 'We hold these truths to be self-evident, that all men are created equal', Declaration of Independence.
	7. Washington and the Continental Army were **defeated in the Battle of Long Island** and had to evacuate New York.
	8. On 24 December, Washington **crossed the Delaware River** and attacked German soldiers who were helping the British at **Trenton**.
1777	9. The year 1777 was an important **turning point** in the war. The **Americans won at Princeton**.
	• Washington hoped such victories would boost morale.
	10. The **British captured Philadelphia**.
	11. American general Horatio Gates forced a large British army to surrender at the **Battle of Saratoga**.
	• This prompted France, and later Spain and Holland, to join the war on the American side.
	• The American cause also encouraged volunteers, e.g. French general **Marquis de Lafayette**.
	12. Washington and the Continental Army spent the winter of 1777–78 at **Valley Forge**, 20 miles from Philadelphia.
	• Half the Continental Army deserted and thousands died of disease. Soldiers endured great hardship and hunger in the freezing cold.
	• The remaining troops were trained by German officer **Von Steuben**. They were now as good as any European army. The remaining men had a new undying loyalty to Washington, who had refused to abandon them and shared in their hardships.
1778	13. Between 1778 and 1781, the war continued with each side winning and losing some battles, e.g. an American and French attack on the British in Rhode Island failed.

THE AMERICAN REVOLUTION

1781	14. The war suddenly ended at the **Battle of Yorktown**. • British commander **Cornwallis (with a force of 7,000 troops)** was surrounded by Washington's forces by land (9,000) and 5,000 French troops and a French fleet at sea. • Cornwallis was forced to surrender to Washington. • This effectively ended the war.
1783	15. In the **Treaty of Paris**, the British government recognised the independence of her former colonies. • This treaty gave America the land **between the Atlantic Ocean and the Mississippi River**.

Consequences of the American Revolution

key point

Consequences means results. These were changes that the American Revolution brought to America and/or the wider world.

1. The United States of America was founded.

The new state continued to extend westwards, which led to clashes with Native Americans, e.g. the Trail of Tears was the forced relocation of 60,000 Native Americans.

The USA started as 13 colonies but now has **50 states**. For example, in 1803, the USA bought territory from France in the Louisiana Purchase.

6. In Ireland, Wolfe Tone and the United Irishmen were inspired to fight for full independence from Britain.

They organised the **1798 Rebellion** (see Ch. 11).

Consequences of the American Revolution

2. The American Constitution (1787) was drawn up.

This created a **federal government** structure. A federal government involves splitting up power between a central national government in Washington and local state governments.

George Washington was the **first president of the United States**.

3. The Declaration of Independence said **'all men are created equal'**.

However, slaves, Native Americans and women **did not have equal rights**.

The Declaration inspired these groups to continue to fight for equality.

5. American victory inspired French people to challenge their king, Louis XVI.

The war cost France a lot of money, which meant increased taxes for lower-class French citizens (*sans-culottes*).

This contributed to the start of the **French Revolution** in 1789.

4. The Declaration of Independence inspired a new type of government.

A republican government, based on the **consent of the people**, and without a king or queen, was set up in America.

Sample Question

The image to the right shows an interpretation of the Boston Massacre. British troops (on the right) are shooting at unarmed American protesters (on the left).

1. a. Which side does this drawing favour – the British or Americans? *This drawing favours the Americans because it shows British soldiers (Redcoats) shooting at unarmed civilians.*

   > The question has been clearly answered.
   > An explanation with specific reference to the source has been given.

   b. How is this drawing an example of propaganda? *This drawing is an example of propaganda because it shows Redcoats shooting at American civilians, but it doesn't show that the Americans were throwing stones and snowballs at the British soldiers first. This drawing tries to make the viewer feel angry at the British soldiers at this seemingly unprovoked attack.*

   > A point has been made.
   > The point has been developed.

2. a. From your study of history, name **one** historical event or issue that has been commemorated. *The USA celebrates Independence Day on 4 July because the Declaration of Independence was adopted by the Continental Congress on 4 July 1776.*

   key point
   Commemoration means remembering an event or person.

   b. Name **two** ways in which a historically significant person has been commemorated. *Washington DC, the capital of the United States, and Washington State are both named after George Washington.*

Revision Questions

Scan the QR code for more revision questions.

10B The French Revolution

After studying this chapter, you should be able to:
- Examine the main causes of the French Revolution
- Outline the main events or course of the French Revolution
- Assess the consequences of the French Revolution.

Key Words	
causes	guillotine
French Revolution	*sans-culotte*
course	republic
'Liberty, Equality, Fraternity'	Reign of Terror
	consequences

When you are asked to **examine the causes, course and consequences of one revolution** in pre-20th-century Europe and/or the wider world, you can use information from **either** the **American Revolution OR** the **French Revolution**.

The Major Events of the French Revolution

1789	Meeting of Estates-General
	Storming of the Bastille
	Declaration of the Rights of Man
	Women's March to Versailles
1791	Flight to Varennes
1792	France declares war on Austria
	France becomes a republic

1793	Trial and execution of Louis XVI
	Reign of Terror begins
1794	Robespierre arrested and guillotined
	Reign of Terror ends

What Were the Main Causes of the French Revolution?

Causes of the French Revolution:
1. Absolute monarchy
2. Age of Enlightenment
3. Privileges of nobility and clergy
4. The American Revolution
5. The meeting of the Estates-General
6. The Fall of the Bastille

key point: The **causes** explain **why** events happened.

1. **Absolute monarchy:** The king, **Louis XVI**, had **full power** over everyone. He believed he got his power from God. This was called the **divine right of kings**. The French people thought King Louis XVI was too powerful. People also did not like his wife, **Marie Antoinette**, because she was Austrian and was too well-off.

2. **Age of Enlightenment:** The 18th century was an era when scientists, artists and other thinkers believed that the use of reason could solve all problems. Some French thinkers (such as Rousseau) believed that the king should **share power** with parliament.

3. **Privileges of the nobility and clergy:** The clergy were known as the **First Estate** and the nobility were known as the **Second Estate**. The nobility and clergy did not pay taxes. The nobles had complete power over their peasants (farmers). The **peasants and middle classes** were the **Third Estate**. They paid taxes to run the country. The peasants also paid taxes to the clergy and nobility. They **did not like** having to pay any more taxes.

4. **The American Revolution:** Some French leaders wanted to follow **the example of America**, which got rid of its all-powerful rulers. France helped America during the revolution and now France was nearly **bankrupt**. The king needed to raise **taxes**.

5. **The meeting of the Estates-General:** The king called the **Estates-General** (or parliament) together to pass more taxes. The **Third Estate** wanted all three estates to meet as one, but the **First and Second Estates** wanted to vote separately. Eventually, the Third Estate got its way, and they formed the **Constituent Assembly** (later called the **National Assembly**).

6. **The Fall of the Bastille:** People in Paris suffered from **bread shortages** and **high prices**. They attacked the Bastille – a large prison fortress – because they thought it stored arms. The Bastille was captured on **14 July**. This **sparked off the French Revolution** – the violent overthrow of the government.

What Was the Course of the French Revolution?

> **key point**
> The **course** outlines the **main events**.

The fall of the Bastille encouraged the middle classes and the peasants to take **further action**.

1. The **National Assembly** abolished the privileges of the nobility and the clergy.
2. They issued ***The Declaration of the Rights of Man and of the Citizen***, which said all men are born free, that all were equal before the law and that people had freedom of speech.
3. '**Liberty, Equality, Fraternity**' became the **slogan** of the French Revolution. The **tricolour** became the flag of the revolution.

THE FRENCH REVOLUTION

What was the meaning of 'Liberty, Equality, Fraternity'?
Liberty – All people should be free
Equality – All people are equal
Fraternity – All people share common interests

Maximilien Robespierre

4. The **market women and fishwives of Paris** marched to the **Palace of Versailles** and forced the king and queen to live in Paris.
5. **King Louis XVI** was plotting with his brother-in-law, the emperor of Austria. He attempted to leave France secretly, but he was recognised at Varennes and brought back to Paris.
6. **War** broke out between France and Austria and later Prussia.
7. The *sans-culotte* (working-class people in Paris) were still suspicious that the king was plotting against the revolution, so they put him and his family in prison.
8. France was declared a **republic** (government without a king) in 1792. Evidence of the king's plotting was found, and he was executed by **guillotine** (which chopped off the heads of victims). His wife, Marie Antoinette, was executed later.
9. **Reign of Terror**: The **Committee of Public Safety** was set up to overcome the dangers facing the revolution. Its **president** was **Robespierre**.
10. Robespierre was a member of the **Jacobins**, a political group in revolutionary France. As France was faced with more and more trouble, Robespierre believed that **strong government** and a **reign of terror** were needed to save the revolution.
    - France was in **danger** from war as Britain, Holland and Spain joined Austria and Prussia against the revolution.
    - Apart from the war, Robespierre and the Committee faced dangers from **opposition** to the revolution from nobles and **rebellion** in different parts of France.

A guillotine

The *sans-culottes* were members of the lower class who supported a republic. A **republic** is a government without a monarch (king/queen) and ruled by representatives elected by the people.

11. Robespierre decided that **violence and terror** were the only ways to save the revolution.

    - He brought in the **Law of Suspects**, which punished anyone thought to be against the revolution. About 2,500 people were killed in Paris and over 16,000 in the rest of France, many by the **guillotine**, the new symbol of the **Reign of Terror**.

    The **Reign of Terror** was a time during the French Revolution when many massacres and public executions were carried out to crush opposition and maintain the power of the Committee of Public Safety.

    - Robespierre put down the **rebellions** in different parts of France with great cruelty, including 30,000 killed in Lyon.
    - To fight the war, Robespierre organised **mass enlistment** in the French army. There were over 1 million soldiers in the French army, much larger than the other armies. The French army saved the revolution from defeat.
    - Then Robespierre brought in the **Law of Maximum**, which controlled rising prices by putting a maximum price on many goods.
12. Robespierre and the Committee **succeeded in overcoming the problems** they faced, but they did this by using methods which were very harsh.
13. Once the revolution was no longer in danger, many people, including the **sans-culotte**, turned against Robespierre. They thought he had too much power.
14. He was arrested and tried. He was **guillotined** and over a hundred of his supporters were also executed.

What Were the Consequences of the French Revolution?

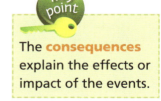

The **consequences** explain the effects or impact of the events.

1. **Rise of Napoleon: Napoleon** took control of France after the Reign of Terror. He established the **Napoleonic Code**, which influenced the laws of continental Europe.
   He led France in a war to **take over Europe**, but he was defeated in the invasion of Russia and eventually at the **Battle of Waterloo**.
2. The **ideas** of the French Revolution – 'Liberty, Equality and Fraternity' – spread to other countries. These ideas influenced the development of the modern world as people wanted greater **freedom** and equality: the **power of monarchy** was reduced and people demanded a **greater say** in running their governments (**democracy**).

3. **Ireland** was influenced by the ideas of the French Revolution. The **United Irishmen** was founded to spread the ideas of revolutionary France. **Wolfe Tone** got the French government to help the United Irishmen rebel against the British government in Ireland. This became part of the **physical force tradition** in Irish history (see Ch. 11).
4. On the other hand, **Daniel O'Connell** disliked the violence of the French Revolution, and he believed that **parliamentary and peaceful means** was the way to achieve Catholic Emancipation and Repeal for Ireland, and to abolish slavery (see Ch. 13).
5. **Abolition of slavery**: Slavery was abolished in France by the revolutionary leaders.
6. **Middle-class power**: The middle classes got more power in France as the clergy and nobility lost much of their power.
7. **Metric system**: The French introduced the metric system, which spread to the rest of Europe.

Sample Question
Many important changes in the history of Ireland, Europe and the wider world have been caused by revolutions. Often revolutions involved overthrowing the rule of monarchs (kings or queens). **Source A** shows Louis XVI, King of France, as he is about to be executed in Paris in 1793, during the French Revolution.

1. Which person in the image do you think is the king? Explain your choice. *The king is the person with his hands tied behind his back, facing the crowd. His shirt is pulled back from his neck so that the guillotine can cut off his head more easily. The person on the left is a revolutionary because he is wearing the cap with an emblem of the revolution. The person in the brown robe is a priest.*
2. How reliable are images such as this as sources of evidence about the past? Explain your answer. *A source is reliable if you can trust that the information is accurate and true. We are not told if the artist was present at the execution or when the drawing was done. If the artist was not present, then we cannot trust sources like this.*
3. What were conditions in the country like before the revolution began?
   See *What Were the Causes of the French Revolution?* on page 63
4. What were some of the main events that happened during the revolution?
   See *What Was the Course of the French Revolution?* on page 64
5. How did the country change as a result of the revolution?
   See *What Were the Consequences of the French Revolution?* on page 66

   Sample 7, NCCA Junior Cycle History Assessment Items

Revision Questions

Scan the QR code for more revision questions.

11 Exploring the 1798 Rebellion – The Impact of the Physical Force Tradition

exam focus

If you are asked about a **pre-20th-century rebellion** in Irish history, you should write about the **1798 Rebellion**.

After studying this chapter, you should be able to:
- Explain the term 'physical force tradition'
- Explore the 1798 Rebellion
- Outline the impact of the physical force tradition on Irish politics.

Key Words
nationalism
unionism
parliamentary means
physical force tradition
passive resistance
Protestant Ascendancy
Penal Laws
subdivided
United Irishmen
sectarian violence
Act of Union
republic

The Physical Force Tradition

1. There were two main political traditions in Ireland – **nationalism** and **unionism**.
2. Unionists wanted to **maintain British rule** in Ireland.
3. Nationalists wanted to **gain independence** from Britain.
4. Nationalists **disagreed** on how they would achieve independence.
5. Some wanted to use **parliamentary means** (see Ch. 13). That means using **peaceful methods** and politics to get greater independence for Ireland.
6. Others supported the **physical force tradition**. That means using an **armed rebellion** or **uprising** to get an independent Ireland.
7. The **1798 Rebellion** is a pre-20th-century example of a rebellion and is an example of the physical force tradition.

Political traditions in modern Ireland

Nationalism → Independence
- Parliamentary tradition
  - Peaceful persuasion
  - Passive resistance
  - Pass laws
  - Mainly Catholic
- Physical force tradition
  - Armed uprising/rebellion
  - Mainly Catholic

Unionism
- Maintain union with Britain (after 1800)
- Mainly Protestant

What Were the Causes of the 1798 Rebellion?

1. The power of the Protestant Ascendancy

The **Protestant Ascendancy** controlled the land and power in Ireland, even though they were only 15% of the population.

2. Catholic and Presbyterian discontent

The **Penal Laws** were used by the Protestant Ascendancy to control the Catholics and Presbyterians.

Even though some of the laws were **repealed** (abolished), Catholics and Presbyterians were still banned from parliament. They also paid **one-tenth** of their crops to support the Anglican clergy.

6. The foundation of the United Irishmen

The **United Irishmen** was a group founded in Belfast to unite all religions and to reduce English power in Ireland. Later, they planned a rebellion in Ireland.

Causes of the 1798 Rebellion

5. The influence of the French Revolution

The principles of the French Revolution (**liberty, equality and fraternity**) were popular in Ireland, especially among Presbyterians in Belfast.

3. Poverty in the countryside

The population rose rapidly in the 18th century, so farms were **subdivided** (split up). This made families worse off.

4. The influence of the American Revolution

The Americans won their independence from Britain in 1783. This was an **example** for many in Ireland.

Who was Theobald Wolfe Tone?

1. **Theobald Wolfe Tone** was present at the founding meeting of the **United Irishmen**.
2. He came to prominence when he wrote *An Argument on behalf of the Catholics of Ireland* (1791); *'Ireland requires a strength in the people to counteract (cancel out) the influence of the [British] Government.'*
3. When the United Irishmen was banned, Tone went to America and France looking for support for an Irish rebellion.
4. France was at war with Britain (see Ch. 10B on the French Revolution).
5. France gave a fleet of **43 ships, 15,000 soldiers** and commander **General Hoche**.
6. **Bad weather** meant they failed to land in **Bantry Bay** in 1796.

What Were the Key Events in the 1798 Rebellion?

1. The British government took action to stop the upcoming rebellion. British commander, **General Lake**, used his troops to burn houses, flog and torture suspects and confiscate arms in Ulster and Leinster.

EXPLORING THE 1798 REBELLION – THE IMPACT OF THE PHYSICAL FORCE TRADITION

2. Information from spies led to the arrest of United Irishmen leaders, including **Lord Edward Fitzgerald**.
3. The Rising still went ahead in Dublin, Kildare and Meath where the **mail coaches** were attacked. But the attacks were easily put down.
4. In **Wexford**, Father John Murphy and Bagenal Harvey defeated **yeomanry** (part-time soldiers) and militia (full-time soldiers) at **Oulart Hill**; they captured **Enniscorthy** and **Wexford** town.
5. Over 100 Protestants were burned in a barn in **Scullabogue** and 100 were killed in Wexford town.
6. The rebels (**Croppies**) were defeated at New Ross and Arklow as they tried to move out of Wexford. Then they were defeated in a major battle at **Vinegar Hill**.
7. A rising in **Ulster** was also defeated, and the leaders, **Henry Joy McCracken** and **Henry Munro**, were executed.
8. French troops led by General **Humbert** landed in Killala, Co. Mayo. They defeated the British at the **Races of Castlebar**. But they were beaten in Ballinamuck, Co. Longford.
9. When Tone arrived in Donegal with a French fleet, he was captured. He was tried for treason, found guilty and sentenced to death. He died by suicide before he could be executed.
10. **Reasons for failure:** The **Rising of 1798** was defeated because of poor organisation, stronger government forces, spies and insufficient French help.

Defeat at Vinegar Hill by George Cruikshank

The Impact of the 1798 Rebellion

1. Death and destruction	• Between **10,000 and 30,000** people were killed. • Towns like **New Ross** were destroyed.
2. Memory	• Many local communities failed to commemorate the 1798 Rebellion. • The first known 1798 memorial was erected in **Bunclody** in 1875.
3. Catholics and Protestants in conflict	• The United Irishmen aimed to 'unite the whole people of Ireland', but sectarian violence created mistrust between Catholics and Protestants. • Due to events like the **Scullabogue Massacre**, 'both sides believed the worst of each other'.
4. Act of Union	• The Act of Union was passed, which abolished the Irish parliament. • For the next 120 years, Irish Members of Parliament (MPs) and Irish lords sat in the Houses of Parliament in London.

Sample Question
Explore how the physical force tradition impacted on Irish politics, with particular reference to a pre-20th century example of a rebellion.

The physical force tradition means using an armed rebellion or uprising to get an independent Ireland. The 1798 Rebellion is an example of the physical force tradition and had a significant impact on Irish politics.

In response to the 1798 Rebellion, the Act of Union (1800) closed the Irish parliament. Irish MPs and Irish lords now had to travel to Westminster. Ireland was now ruled directly from London. Politicians like Daniel O'Connell and Charles Stewart Parnell spent the next 100 years trying to restore this parliament in Dublin.

The United Irishmen put forward the idea of a republic. This is a form of government where the state is ruled by representatives of the country. The United Irishmen influenced later generations to fight and die for a republic, e.g. the 1916 Rising. Following the 1798 Rebellion, many believed that a republic would only be gained through the use of physical force. There were three significant uprisings during the 19th century: the Rising of 1803, the Young Irelanders Rising of 1848 and the Fenian Rising of 1867.

The Rising of 1803 began when a riot broke out on Thomas Street. Robert Emmet was hung for leading this failed rebellion in Dublin. Over 100 years later, Countess Markievicz studied this rising while plans were being made for the 1916 Rising.

In 1848, Young Irelanders, including William Smith O'Brien, attacked the Royal Irish Constabulary (police) in Ballingarry, Co. Tipperary. Two were killed and the leaders were sent into exile in Tasmania (Van Diemen's Land).

On 5 March 1867, risings took place in Dublin, Cork City and Limerick. The largest of these engagements took place at Tallaght where the Fenians were eventually driven off by the RIC. Even though this rising failed, the Irish Republican Brotherhood continued to exist and later organised the 1916 Rising.

Revision Questions
Scan the QR code for more revision questions.

12 Causes, Course and Consequences of the Great Famine

aims

After studying this chapter, you should be able to:
- Investigate the causes, course and consequences of the Great Famine
- Examine the significance of the Irish Diaspora.

Key Words

absentee landlords	causes	coffin ships
cottiers	blight	consequences
workhouse	public works	Irish Diaspora
evicted	*laissez-faire*	historically significant

Rural Ireland in the 1840s

1. Ireland was a mainly **agricultural** country in the 1840s.
2. **Landlords**:
   - There were 20,000 landlords. Some landlords were **absentee landlords** (not living on their estates, but instead in Dublin or England).
   - The landlords rented land to **tenants** who paid rent twice a year to the landlord's agent.
3. **Tenants**:
   - **Large farmers** rented over 30 acres. They hired labourers to work on the farm. They lived in two-storey houses.
   - **Small farmers** – rented between 5 and 15 acres. They lived in thatched cottages and depended on the **potato** as their main food.
4. **Cottiers** were labourers who rented a small plot of land – up to an acre – from a farmer. In return, they worked for the farmer to pay off the rent. They lived in one-room cabins.
5. **Landless labourers** were very badly off. They lived in mud cabins on the edge of towns and depended on the **potato** for their food.
   - **Spailpeens** were wandering labourers who travelled around looking for work.
6. **Poverty and the workhouse**: Poor people went to the **workhouse** for help. These were sometimes tenants who were **evicted** (expelled, thrown out) from their farms.

Before the Great Famine, the British government set up **Poor Law Unions** (areas), each of which had a **workhouse**. Poorer people had to go to the local workhouse if they needed help. Families were split up and conditions were bad in the workhouses.

The **causes** explain **why** events happened.

What Were the Causes of the Great Famine 1845–50?

1. **Rise in population:** The population grew from 6.8 million in 1821 to 8.2 million in 1841. As the population grew, people got poorer, especially labourers, cottiers and small farmers.
2. **Subdivision of the land:** Farmers divided their farms in order to give land to their sons and a dowry to their daughters. Subdividing the farms made families poorer.
3. **Dependence on the potato:** Poorer families depended on the potato to live. The potato was almost the only food for about half the population.
4. **The Blight:** Blight is a disease which attacks and rots potatoes. Those who depended on the potato, especially small farmers, cottiers and landless labourers, had no other food when the blight struck. They starved.

What Did the British Government Do?

1. **Indian corn:** In 1845, the British prime minister, **Sir Robert Peel**, imported £100,000 worth of **Indian corn** (maize), enough to feed 1 million people. The corn was sold through government depots. Some people called it **Peel's Brimstone** because people were not used to cooking it and they found it was hard to eat. However, it did reduce the impact of the famine in 1845.
2. **Public works:** Peel also set up **public works** – government organised work schemes to build roads and piers. However, pay was low and people often had to walk long distances to get to the work.

3. *Laissez-faire*: In 1846, a new government led by **Lord John Russell** believed in *laissez-faire* – the view that if governments interfered in the economy, it would make matters worse. The government **stopped** buying corn, but **expanded** the public works schemes so that 750,000 people were employed on them.
4. **Soup kitchens:** These were first set up by the **Quakers** (or Society of Friends). Soup was cooked in **large boilers** and given to the poor.
   - The government then passed the **Soup Kitchen Act** in 1847 to set up their own soup kitchens. **Three million people** were fed in the soup kitchens, but then the government **closed them down** and said people had to get help through the **workhouses**.
5. **Workhouses:** In 1848, there were over 200,000 people in the workhouses, so they were very overcrowded and disease spread quickly. About 800,000 were helped with 'outdoor relief'.
6. **Disease:** People died from **typhus** and **relapsing fever**. More died from diseases, which were spread in crowded workhouses and towns, than from starvation. Disease affected rich and poor alike.

Where Did People Emigrate to?

1. People left for **Britain**, **America and Canada**. Around 250,000 left in 1847. Some were helped by landlords; others sent one family member to work and to send money home to pay for other family members. By 1851, 1 million people emigrated.
2. Many people sailed in '**coffin ships**' – ships in very poor condition where disease spread. Some sank on the way.

A replica of a famine ship, the *Jeanie Johnston*, in Dublin

exam focus

What were the **consequences** of the Great Famine?
'Consequences' = 'Effects' = 'Results' = 'Impact' = **showing historical change**

What Were the Consequences of the Great Famine?

1. **Fall in population**: The population fell by 2 million – 1 million emigrated and 1 million died from starvation and disease.
   - The **cottiers** and **labourers** were worst hit; so also was the west of Ireland.

- The population **continued to fall after the famine** due to **late marriages** and **emigration**.
- Emigration during and after the famine created the Irish Diaspora – the spread of Irish emigrants and their descendants around the world.

2. **Subdivision ended:** Dividing up the farms between members of the family ended; instead, the farms were given to the eldest son and others emigrated. As a result, farms got larger.
3. **Decline of the Irish language:** The Irish-speaking areas in the west and south-west of Ireland were worst hit by death and emigration. After the famine, families learnt English for emigration, so Irish-speaking areas continued to decline.
4. **Politics:** Bitterness against England grew because people **blamed** the British government for the famine. Emigrants helped later groups such as the Fenians and the leaders of the 1916 Rising.

What is the meaning of historically significant or important? It is a person, issue or event in history that is considered important in **effecting historical change**.

What Was the **Significance** of the Irish Diaspora?

Emigration

People emigrated from Ireland well before the Great Famine. But there was a huge increase in emigrants during the famine, and emigration continued for long after the famine.

Emigration to the USA

1. Between 1845 and 1855, 1.5 million people emigrated from Ireland to the USA. Irish emigration to the USA continued for the rest of the 19th century.
2. The Irish lived mostly in the **cities**, such as New York, Boston and Philadelphia.
3. Irish emigrants were mainly **Catholics** and worked largely in **unskilled jobs**, and lived in slum conditions.
4. They were often **resented** by the local population, who were Protestant and better-off. Some advertisements read, **'No Irish Need Apply'**.
5. Irish emigrants **blamed** the British government for the famine deaths and for emigration. They supported opposition to British rule in Ireland.

CAUSES, COURSE AND CONSEQUENCES OF THE GREAT FAMINE

6. Over the decades, **Irish-Americans** got **more prosperous**. They contributed to popular entertainment (Bing Crosby, Maureen O'Hara), sport (Muhammad Ali, Tom Brady), industry (Henry Ford), literature (Georgia O'Keeffe, Anne Rice) and politics (Presidents Kennedy, Nixon, Reagan, Clinton and Obama).

Emigration to Britain

1. Irish people emigrated to Britain during and after the famine, as that country was **industrialised** during the 19th century.
2. Irish emigrants lived in the **larger cities** such as Liverpool, Manchester, Glasgow and London, often in **slum conditions** with overcrowding and poor sanitary conditions.
3. They worked in mostly **unskilled jobs**, especially in factories and construction, where they constructed canals, railways and later roads.
4. The Irish emigrants experienced **discrimination** and **anti-Irish racism**.
   - Cartoons depicted the Irish with **monkey-like features**.
5. Over the decades, the Irish emigrant population **rose up the social and political ladder** in Britain. They contributed to theatre, television and radio, sport, and to the medical, teaching and other professions.

Exam Question

Over one million people emigrated from Ireland in the 1840s/1850s. The following sources relate to a ship containing Irish emigrants which arrived in New York on 30 November 1853. Examine the sources and answer the questions which follow.

Source 1: extract from a newspaper report describing the ship and its passengers.

The ship, Marathon, left Liverpool on the 22nd of September, with 522 passengers, mostly Irish. She arrived at New York after a voyage of 59 days, during which she lost 64 persons to an outbreak of cholera.
The passengers were in a state of the most wretched poverty and filth. They were lodged on two decks, one above the other. The decks were covered with reeking filth.
The passengers' provisions [food supplies] were exhausted three weeks before the ship came into port. Had the ship been delayed for a few days longer, the people would have starved.

Source 2: extract from seven columns in the ship's passenger list.

1	2	3	4	5	6	7
Rose Moore	25	Female	Servant	Ireland	U.S.A.	
John Fitzpatrick	24	Male	Labourer	Ireland	U.S.A.	
Mary Fitzpatrick	15	Female	Servant	Ireland	U.S.A.	
Johannah Fitzpatrick	40	Female	Servant	Ireland	U.S.A.	
John Fitzpatrick	50	Male	Labourer	Ireland	U.S.A.	Died
John Fitzpatrick	5	Male	Child	Ireland	U.S.A.	
Mary Reilly	29	Female	Servant	Ireland	U.S.A.	Died
Patrick Reilly	9	Male	Child	Ireland	U.S.A.	Died
Margaret Reilly	7	Female	Child	Ireland	U.S.A.	
Bridget Reilly	5	Female	Child	Ireland	U.S.A.	Died

(a) From where did the Marathon set sail and how long did the journey take?
Starting point: Liverpool
Length of journey: 59 days

(b) How many of the passengers survived, and how many died, on the voyage to New York?
Survived: 458
Died: 64

(c) Margaret Reilly is one of the passengers named in Source 2.
What **facts** could a historian write about her, using information from both sources?
Margaret Reilly sailed on the Marathon from Liverpool to New York.
She was 7 years of age.
She came from Ireland.
She survived the voyage.

Junior Cycle History Exam 2022, Q5

Revision Questions
Scan the QR code for more revision questions.

13 The Parliamentary Tradition in Irish Politics – Daniel O'Connell and C. S. Parnell

If you are asked about two leaders involved in the **parliamentary tradition**, you could write about **O'Connell** and **Parnell OR Redmond** and **Carson** (Ch. 15).

After studying this chapter, you should be able to:
- Explain the term 'parliamentary tradition'
- Investigate the role and significance of Daniel O'Connell
- Investigate the role and significance of C.S. Parnell.

Key Words
parliamentary tradition	Home Rule
Catholic Emancipation	Land War
abolished	Land Act
repeal	Kilmainham Treaty
Act of Union	Phoenix Park murders
monster rallies	Irish National League

What is the Parliamentary Tradition?

1. **Parliamentary tradition** refers to using peaceful methods like mass demonstrations and politics to get greater independence for Ireland.
2. **Daniel O'Connell** and **Charles Stewart Parnell** were two 19th-century leaders involved in the parliamentary tradition.

Daniel O'Connell: The Liberator

1775	• Daniel O'Connell was born in **Co. Kerry**.
1793	• O'Connell witnessed scenes from the **French Revolution** and was in France when the French king, Louis XVI, was executed.
1798	• His time in France, combined with **violence** he saw during the **1798 Rebellion**, solidified his anti-violence approach to achieving change.
1798	• O'Connell began practice as a **barrister**. • He was called **'The Counsellor'**.
1823	• O'Connell founded the **Catholic Association** to lead his campaign for **Catholic Emancipation** (Catholic freedom from discrimination).
1824	• The **Catholic Rent** (a penny a month) was organised to finance the campaign for Catholic Emancipation.

1828	• He won the **Clare by-election**.
1829	• The **Catholic Relief Act** was passed, which allowed Catholics to take their seats in parliament. • O'Connell's peaceful methods of achieving his goals spread far and wide. • He became known as **'The Liberator'**.
1830	• O'Connell was re-elected to Clare. • He was the first Catholic in modern times elected to the **House of Commons**.
1833	• O'Connell helped to pass the **Slavery Abolition Act**, which abolished slavery in the British Empire.
1840	• He set up the Repeal **Association** to campaign for an end to the **Act of Union**, which closed the Dublin parliament.
1841	• O'Connell was elected the Lord Mayor of Dublin.
1843	• 1843 was meant to be the **Year of Repeal**. • Monster rallies were held all over the country. • Monster meeting at **Clontarf** was cancelled because O'Connell feared it would result in violence. • The repeal campaign failed because the British government feared it would lead to the break-up of the union of England, Scotland and Wales.
1847	• O'Connell warned the British government about the **severity of the Great Famine** in Ireland. • At the age of 71, O'Connell **died** in Genoa, Italy, while on his way to meet the Pope.
1864	• The foundation stone for the O'Connell Monument on O'Connell Street, Dublin, was laid.

Charles Stewart Parnell: the 'Uncrowned King of Ireland'

1846	• Charles Stewart Parnell was born in **Co. Wicklow**.
1875	• He was elected as a Home Rule MP (Member of Parliament) for Meath.
1876	• Parnell came to prominence for defending the **Manchester Martyrs** (Fenians/IRB who shot a policeman while trying to free their colleagues from a prison van).
1879	• The Land League was formed. • Parnell was **president** of the Land League. • The Land War began. This consisted of increased agrarian outrages (incidents, crimes) in the countryside between landlords and tenants.
1880	• Parnell was elected MP for Cork City. • Parnell became **leader** of the Home Rule Party. • Parnell's affair with a married woman called **Katherine O'Shea** began.
1881	• Gladstone introduced the Land Act, which provided fair rents for the tenants and a land court would decide the rents. • Parnell was interned (imprisoned) in **Kilmainham Gaol**.

THE PARLIAMENTARY TRADITION IN IRISH POLITICS – DANIEL O'CONNELL AND C. S. PARNELL

1882	• **Kilmainham Treaty** was agreed. Gladstone improved the Land Act, Parnell agreed to use his influence to stop the violence in the countryside. • **Phoenix Park murders** took place. Two high-ranking officials in the British government were murdered by a Fenian group in 1882. • **Irish National League**, an organisation which wanted to help poor tenant farmers, was formed.
1885	• Parnell and the Home Rule Party did so well in the 1885 general election that they held the **balance of power** in Westminster.
1886	• The **first Home Rule Bill** was introduced.
1887	• The *London Times* published letters in articles called **Parnellism and Crime** which seemed to show that Parnell supported the Phoenix Park murders. • A **Special Commission** showed that the letters had been **forged** by a journalist called **Richard Piggott**. • Parnell's name was cleared and his **popularity soared**.
1889	• The O'Shea Divorce case began. • Captain O'Shea **filed for divorce** from his wife Katherine. He named Parnell in the proceedings, which caused a **scandal**.
1890	• Home Rule Party **split** when Gladstone said his Liberal Party could no longer bring forward a Home Rule Bill if Parnell continued as leader of the party.
1891	• Parnell died and was buried in Glasnevin Cemetery.
1911	• The Parnell Monument on O'Connell Street in Dublin was erected.

Sample Question
Outline the role and significance of **two** leaders involved in the parliamentary tradition that you have studied.

Daniel O'Connell was the most significant Irish politician in the first half of the 19th century.

*Events during the French Revolution and 1798 Rebellion encouraged O'Connell to believe in a **non-violent approach** to achieve change. He provided an alternative to the physical force tradition.*

*One of the last Penal Laws **prevented** Catholics from taking their seats in parliament, even if they were elected. In 1823, O'Connell founded the **Catholic Association**, which led to his campaign for **Catholic Emancipation**. He organised a **Catholic Rent** (a penny a month) to pay for the campaign. O'Connell held **peaceful meetings** in Ireland and Britain to put pressure on the British government. He was elected to Clare in 1828, which forced the government to pass the **Catholic Relief Act** (1829). This allowed Catholics to take their seats in parliament. O'Connell was known as 'The Liberator'.*

O'Connell was an **abolitionist** (he wanted to get rid of slavery). He helped to pass the **Slavery Abolition Act 1833**, which abolished slavery in the British Empire. O'Connell also favoured **Jewish emancipation**.

O'Connell led a campaign to **repeal the Act of Union** so that a parliament would be established in Dublin. He set up the **Repeal Association** with **Repeal Rent**. O'Connell said 1843 would be the **Year of Repeal**. '**Monster meetings**' (huge peaceful rallies) were held all over the country, but the campaign **failed** as the British government feared that giving repeal to Ireland would break up the union of England, Scotland and Wales.

Parnell was the most significant Irish politician at the end of the 19th century. Parnell was an influential member of the **Home Rule Party**. Home Rulers wanted a parliament in Dublin to deal with **internal affairs**, like education, in Ireland, while Westminster would still deal with external matters, like trade. He founded the **Irish National League**, which was organised in each constituency. Members now sat together in parliament and worked together as a **united** group. The party paid Home Rule MPs and they had to take an **oath** to vote with the party. Parnell was also involved in the **land campaign**. Parnell and **Michael Davitt** formed the Land League, which aimed to get **fairer rents** for tenants and **tenant ownership** over the land they were renting and working. When **crime** in the countryside between tenants and landlords broke out (the **Land** War), the Land League forced PM Gladstone to bring in land reform for tenants in the **1881 Land Act**. The act said a land court would decide fair rents for tenants. Parnell favoured the act but asked tenants to **test** it in the courts. Parnell and other leaders were sent to **Kilmainham Gaol** in 1881. While Parnell was in jail, crime in the countryside increased and Gladstone realised Parnell needed to be released. In 1882 they agreed to the **Kilmainham Treaty**, which improved the Land Act, while Parnell promised to use his influence to stop the violence in the countryside.

One of the most significant areas that Parnell was involved in was the introduction of **the first Home Rule Bill** for Ireland. After the 1885 election, Parnell and the Home Rule Party held the **balance of power** in Westminster. This meant Gladstone and the Liberal Party needed the support of the Home Rule

Party to get into power. Parnell supported Gladstone and the Liberals because they promised to introduce a Home Rule Bill. Gladstone's Home Rule Bill (1886) provided for a parliament in Dublin to deal with internal Irish affairs. However, it was defeated in the House of Commons.

Revision Questions
Scan the QR code for more revision questions.

14 Impact of the GAA

exam focus

If you are asked about a **sporting**, **cultural** or **social movement**, you should write about the **GAA**.

aims

By the end of this chapter, you should be able to:
- Outline the foundation of the GAA
- List key people involved in the GAA
- Examine the impact of the GAA on Irish life.

Key Words
impact
anglicisation
cultural revival
infiltrated
separatist tradition
historical revisionism

The Foundation of the GAA

1. The Gaelic Athletic Association (GAA) was founded in **Hayes Hotel**, **Co. Tipperary**, on 1 November 1884 by **Michael Cusack**.
2. Unlike existing organisations for 'gentlemen', Cusack welcomed labourers, policemen, etc. and included nationalists in the governing body.
3. **Maurice Davin** was elected president of the GAA.
4. **Archbishop Croke of Cashel**, **Parnell** and **Davitt** (land campaign) became patrons. **Cusack** was the secretary before being sacked in 1886.
5. In 1887, the **first All-Irelands** were held. **Limerick** won the football final and **Tipperary** won the hurling.
6. The **'American Invasion'** tour of 1888 was **disastrous** and the GAA lost money.
7. The **Camogie Association** was established in 1904.
8. In 1913, the GAA purchased playing fields on **Jones Road**, Dublin. This was named **Croke Park** and became the headquarters of the GAA.
9. **Three hundred and two** players took part in the **1916 Rising**, but the Central Council distanced themselves from the involvement.
10. In 1918, **Gaelic Sunday** took place. British authorities attempted a crackdown on GAA activities by insisting no matches could take place without prior written permission. The GAA objected and they decided to defy the order and hold a match in every parish in Ireland at precisely the same time – 3 p.m. on Sunday 4 August.

Michael Cusack

11. In response to Michael Collins's **Squad** killing 12 British Intelligence Officers and two policemen, British forces entered **Croke Park** and killed 14 civilians. Later, two IRA officers were killed. This became known as **Bloody Sunday** 1920 (see Ch. 15).
12. The year 1961 saw the highest attendance at a GAA match with **90,556** people attending.
13. In 1971, **Rule 27** was lifted (you could now play **GAA and 'foreign' sports**).
14. The **LGFA** (Ladies' Gaelic Football Association) was established in 1974. Both the LGFA and Camogie Association are run **independently** of the GAA but with its active support.
15. In 2001, **Rule 21** was lifted (**British security forces** were now allowed to play).
16. In 2007, **Rule 42** (ban on foreign sports being played in GAA stadiums) was amended to allow the Ireland VS England rugby match to take place. The match was symbolic as the **British national anthem** would be played at the site where British forces killed 14 civilians on **Bloody Sunday 1920**.

A Gaelic football match at Croke Park in the early 1920s

What **Impact** Did the GAA Have on Irish Life?

1. The GAA **boosted the cultural revival** and prevented further **anglicisation** (making things more English)	• The GAA was part of the cultural revival at the end of the 19th century. • This promoted all things Irish and wanted to **reduce English influence** in all aspects of Irish life, e.g. people should play Irish sports instead of English sports.
2. Increased **pride** in Irish culture	• **Coiste na Gaeilge** promotes the use of the Irish language. • In 1969, **Scór** was set up. It's a cultural contest in céilí, singing and storytelling.
3. Contributed to the **political revolution**	• In the late 19th century, the GAA was infiltrated (taken over) by the **Irish Republican Brotherhood (IRB)/Fenians** who used the GAA as a cover for training young men for a future rising. • The GAA was part of the separatist tradition. Some believed that the full revival of Gaelic culture could not be achieved without a fully independent country. • The GAA took part in the **centenary of the 1798 Rebellion** and the **funerals** of prominent Fenians, e.g. **James Stephens**. • Over **300** players took part in the **1916 Rising**.

4. Saved native games	• **Rule 27** forbade members of the GAA from playing and watching **'foreign' sports**. • This ban was not lifted until **1971**. • The GAA also created **written rules** for Gaelic games for the first time.
5. Promoted Irish games **abroad**	• The Department of Foreign Affairs says there are over **400** GAA clubs abroad. • The GAA has maintained **links** between the **Irish Diaspora** (see page 76) and the Irish in Ireland. For example, Gaelic Park in New York became a centre for Irish emigrants who went to watch football and hurling matches on Sundays.
6. Developed local and community spirit	• Clubs were established in most counties and contributed to a **rise in local pride**. • The GAA created inter-parish and inter-county **rivalries**. • By 1901, there were 411 GAA clubs in Ireland. • GAA clubs also became the focus of **social activity**. The club house often became the community centre for meetings, dances and concerts.
7. Women and Gaelic games	• The **Camogie Association** (est. 1904) and the **Ladies' Gaelic Football Association** (est. 1974) are both run **independently** of the GAA, but with its active support.
8. Importance of Croke Park	• **Croke Park** has become the most important sporting venue in Ireland. • The stadium is one of the largest in Europe and can fit **82,300** people. • It hosts all the major football and hurling matches each year. • These events make an important contribution to Dublin's **economy**.

Sample Question

In the decades after 1916, the history of the Easter Rising was rewritten by men and women who wished to claim for themselves – or for the organisations they loved – a central part in the Rising.

In sporting terms, the great example of this is provided by the GAA.

The Association – and its historians – claimed that, unique among Irish sporting organisations, the GAA had provided the great bulk of the men who fought in 1916.

As William Murphy has written, GAA players were indeed more likely to have participated in the Easter Rising in Dublin than most other sectors of society … it is also the truth that … the response of the GAA was to flat-out deny any involvement in 1916.

More than that, there were also many more GAA men fighting in British army uniforms in France than there were in the GPO.

Any rounded account of the GAA's involvement in 1916 must acknowledge this basic truth – and accommodate it in any meaningful history of the Easter Rising.

Adapted from: 'The GAA and the Rising', by Paul Rouse, independent.ie

How is this source an example of historical revisionism?

Historical revisionism is reviewing, changing or revising a point of view by looking at new information or going back over old information.

Historical revisionism means reviewing or changing a point of view by looking at new information or going back over old information. This source is an example of historical revisionism because it highlights the fact that 'the history of the Easter Rising was rewritten by men and women who wished to claim for themselves' a central part in the Rising.

This source tells us that the GAA, and its historians, claimed that 'the GAA had provided the great bulk of men fought in 1916'. This is supported by William Murphy, who has written that 'GAA players were indeed more likely to have participated in the Easter Rising in Dublin than most other sectors of society', but the rewritten history ignored or glazed over the fact that the immediate response of the GAA was to 'flat-out deny any involvement in 1916'. The source also says that a fully rounded account must acknowledge that 'there were also many more GAA men fighting in British army uniforms in France, than there were in the GPO'.

Revision Questions

Scan the QR code for more revision questions.

15 The Rise and Impact of Nationalism and Unionism in Ireland, 1911–23

 By the end of this chapter, you should be able to:
- Explain nationalism and unionism
- Explain cultural nationalism
- Examine the key events in the rise and impact of nationalism and unionism, 1911–23.

Key Words
nationalists
unionists
Home Rule
passive resistance
abstentionism
cultural nationalism
Castle Document
blood sacrifice
rising
conscription
republic

What Are Nationalism and Unionism?

1. In the early 20th century, Ireland was ruled directly from London. Irish Members of Parliament (MPs) sat in parliament in Westminster. The Lord Lieutenant represented the King of England in Ireland.
2. There were two main political groups:
    - **Nationalists** wanted some form of **self-government** with a parliament in Dublin.
    - **Unionists** wanted to maintain **the union** with Britain.

Who were the nationalists?

There were three main groups of nationalists.
1. The **Home Rule Party** (also called the **Irish Parliamentary Party**) was the largest nationalist group. It was led by **John Redmond**.
    - **Home Rulers** wanted a **parliament in Dublin** to deal with **internal Irish affairs**.
    - The **parliament in London** would deal with **external or foreign affairs**.

The Home Rulers supported the use of **peaceful or parliamentary means** for achieving **Home Rule**.

THE RISE AND IMPACT OF NATIONALISM AND UNIONISM IN IRELAND, 1911–23

John Redmond, leader of the Home Rule Party

- John Redmond served as a Home Rule MP for New Ross, North Wexford and later Waterford City between 1881 and his death in 1918.
- He **opposed** the use of force and **supported** the **use of peaceful means** to achieve Home Rule for Ireland.
- After general elections in 1910, Redmond and the Home Rule Party held the **balance of power** in Westminster. They supported the **Liberal Party** in return for the Third Home Rule Bill (see *The Home Rule Crisis, 1912–14* below).
- Redmond achieved the passage of the Third Home Rule Bill, but it was suspended until after World War I.
- He encouraged the **Irish Volunteers** to join the British army. This led to a split, with the great majority following him.
- After the 1916 Rising, the popularity of his party declined. Redmond **died** before the defeat of the Home Rule Party in the 1918 general election.

2. The **Irish Republican Brotherhood (IRB)** was a secret revolutionary organisation.
   - The IRB wanted **complete independence** from Britain.
   - They wanted to establish a **republic**.
   - They wanted to use **physical force** to achieve their aims.
3. **Sinn Féin** was founded by **Arthur Griffith**.
   - Sinn Féin wanted a **dual monarchy** for Britain and Ireland.
   - They wanted to develop **Irish industry** by using tariffs (customs duties) to protect new industry.
   - Sinn Féin wanted to use **passive resistance** and **abstention from parliament in London** to achieve their aims.

Passive resistance was **non-violent opposition** or refusal to co-operate with the British government.

Abstentionism was the policy of Sinn Féin TDs not to take their seats in parliament in Westminster, but to set up their own parliament in Dublin.

Who were the unionists?

The **Unionist Party** was led by **Edward Carson** and **James Craig**. The majority of unionists lived in the **north-east of Ireland**, around Belfast.
- Unionists were **opposed** to Home Rule. They wanted laws for Ireland to continue to be passed in parliament in Westminster.
- They said '**Home Rule is Rome Rule**' – they believed that Catholics would discriminate against Protestants.
- They believed that **Belfast's industries** would be ruined if Ireland won Home Rule.

Edward Carson, leader of the Unionist Party
- Edward Carson was elected MP for Trinity College, Dublin.
- He became **leader of the Unionist Party** in 1910.
- He was devoted to Ireland and to **the union** between Ireland and Britain: *'It's only for Ireland that I'm in politics.'* He wanted to use Ulster unionist opposition to stop Home Rule for Ireland.
- He led the campaign against the Third Home Rule Bill.
- He continued to lead the Unionist Party until 1921. He did not want Home Rule for any part of Ireland.
He was **disappointed** when a Home Rule parliament was set up in Belfast in 1921.

What is Cultural Nationalism?

At the end of the 19th century and the beginning of the 20th century, there was a **revival of interest** in the language, culture and games of Gaelic Ireland. This was called **cultural nationalism**. The Gaelic revival was promoted by the following:
- The **Gaelic Athletic Association (GAA)**, which promoted Gaelic football and hurling
- The **Gaelic League**, which promoted the use of the Irish language
- The **Anglo-Irish Literary Movement**, which promoted the use of Gaelic folktales and history in the English language.

These ideas influenced **many political leaders** at that time.

I. The Home Rule Crisis, 1912–14

1. In Britain, the **Liberal Party** favoured Home Rule for Ireland, but the **Conservative Party** was opposed to it.
2. After elections in 1910, the Liberal Party was in government in Britain, but it needed the support of the Irish **Home Rule Party**. In return for that support, the Liberal Party brought in the **Third Home Rule Bill** for Ireland in 1912. This would mean:
   - a **parliament in Dublin** to deal with **internal affairs**
   - a **parliament in London** (Westminster) to deal with **external affairs**.
3. The Liberal Party also passed the **Parliament Act**, which said that the **House of Lords** could only delay laws for two years.
   - This meant that the House of Lords would only be able to delay the passing of the **Third Home Rule Bill** for two years so that **by 1914**, Ireland would have a **Home Rule parliament**.

THE RISE AND IMPACT OF NATIONALISM AND UNIONISM IN IRELAND, 1911–23

Timeline of the Home Rule Crisis, 1912–14

1911	Parliament Act passed
1912	Third Home Rule Bill introduced
	Ulster Solemn League and Covenant
1913	Ulster Volunteer Force (UVF) founded
	Larne gun-running
	Irish Citizen Army and Irish Volunteers formed
1914	Curragh Mutiny
	Howth gun-running
	Outbreak of World War I
	IRB decided on a rising
	Home Rule Act passed but suspended until after the war

How did unionists organise opposition to Home Rule?

1. Carson and Craig held **huge demonstrations** against Home Rule.
2. The **Ulster Solemn League and Covenant** was signed by over 200,000 unionist men in September 1912. They swore to defend the union with Britain **by all means**. A similar declaration was signed by **unionist women**.
3. Unionists founded the **Ulster Volunteer Force (UVF)**. They imported arms and ammunition from Germany through the port of **Larne** – 35,000 guns and 5 million rounds of ammunition were smuggled in the **Larne gun-running** (April 1913).
4. The **Conservative Party** supported the efforts of the unionists.
5. **Curragh Mutiny**: Officers of the British army in the Curragh said they would resign rather than enforce Home Rule in Ulster.

The nationalist response

1. Nationalists organised the **Irish Volunteer Force**, led by Eoin MacNeill in November 1913. He wrote an article called **'The North Began'**, where he said nationalists should follow the example of northern unionists.
2. The Irish Volunteers brought in 900 rifles and 25,000 rounds of ammunition on the *Asgard* ship through **Howth**, Co. Dublin, in July 1914.

World War I – the end of the crisis

1. Attempts at getting a **compromise** between both sides **failed**, so it looked likely that Ireland was **heading for civil war**. However, when World War I broke out in August 1914, both nationalists and unionists agreed to help the war effort.
2. The Third Home Rule Bill **became law**, but it was **postponed** until after the war was over.

Ireland in World War I

1. **Unionists** supported the war effort and joined the British army through the **Ulster Division**.
2. **Nationalists:** The Irish Volunteers split. Most members followed Redmond, who wanted Irishmen to fight in the war.

Nationalists split over the war

National Volunteers
- 100,000 followed **John Redmond**
- Supported Irishmen fighting abroad

Irish Volunteers
- 10,000 followed **Eoin MacNeill**
- Opposed to Irishmen fighting abroad

3. A quarter of a million Irishmen joined the British army in **World War I**. They joined the **Irish Guards**, the **Royal Munster Fusiliers** and other regiments. They fought in the **Western Front** in France and in **Gallipoli** in Turkey.

II. The 1916 Rising

1. The **IRB** planned the 1916 Rising. They set up a **Military Council** to organise the Rising.
    - The Council included Patrick **Pearse**, Thomas **Clarke** and Seán **McDermott**.
    - They set **Easter Sunday 1916** as the day for the Rising.
    - They persuaded James **Connolly** and the **Irish Citizen Army** to join them.
2. **Roger Casement** was sent to Germany to get arms. They were loaded on board the *Aud* ship to be taken to Ireland, but the *Aud* was captured off the Kerry coast. Casement was also captured when he got off a German submarine.
3. The Military Council gave a document to MacNeill – called the **Castle Document** – which said that the British government was planning to arrest the leaders.
    - MacNeill authorised **manoeuvres** for the **Irish Volunteers**, but he **cancelled** them when he found out the document was a **forgery**.
4. Pearse and the others decided to go ahead with a **rising in Dublin** on **Easter Monday, 1916**.
    - Pearse was influenced by the idea of a **blood sacrifice** – that the spirit of the Irish people would be woken up by the sacrifice of the leaders.
    - They took over **key buildings** such as the **General Post Office** (**GPO**). Here Pearse read the **Proclamation of the Irish Republic**.

THE RISE AND IMPACT OF NATIONALISM AND UNIONISM IN IRELAND, 1911–23

- The British government sent a gunboat, the *Helga*, up the Liffey, which bombarded the GPO.
- The Volunteers were easily defeated and they surrendered after a week.

What were the results of the 1916 Rising?

Why was the 1916 Rising a failure?
- The Irish Volunteers were **outnumbered**.
- The capture of the *Aud* meant there was **shortage** of guns and ammunition.
- The Rising was **not supported** by the people.
- The British army was **more powerful**.
- The Rising was confined to Dublin.

1. Sixteen of the leaders were **executed**, including Pearse and Connolly in Kilmainham Gaol, and Casement in London.
2. Around **500 people** were killed and **2,500** were injured; £3 million in damage was done to property in Dublin.
3. The British imposed **military (martial) law** and **interned** (imprisoned without trial) 2,000 people.
4. Dubliners were **angered** by the destruction caused by the Rising and the resulting food shortages.
   - But **British actions** – interning thousands and executing the leaders of the Rising – **changed the minds** of many. They began to support the actions and aims of the leaders of the 1916 Rising.
5. The British government called it the **Sinn Féin Rising**, even though Sinn Féin had nothing to do with the Rising. Afterwards, Sinn Féin's popularity rose as younger members joined.

Timeline of the Rise of Sinn Féin, 1916–18

1916	Easter Rising and execution of leaders
1917	New leadership in Sinn Féin
1918	Conscription Crisis German Plot End of World War I General election victory for Sinn Féin

If you are asked about the **impact** of the rise of nationalism and unionism, you can refer to the **results** or **effects**.

The rise of Sinn Féin

Éamon de Valera became **president of Sinn Féin** and **president of the Irish Volunteers**.

The rise in popularity of Sinn Féin occurred because:
- The British government tried to impose **conscription** (compulsory military service) in Ireland in 1918 and Sinn Féin organised opposition to it during the **Conscription Crisis**.

- The British government arrested Sinn Féin leaders in the so-called **German Plot**.
- Sinn Féin had a **younger, active membership** whereas the Home Rule Party had an older membership.

1918 general election

In the 1918 general election, Sinn Féin became the **most popular party** in Ireland.
- They now demanded a **republic** and they followed a policy of **abstentionism** (abstaining from parliament in London).

> **key point**
> A **republic** is a government without a king or queen which is ruled by representatives elected by the people.

How did the results of the 1910 and the 1918 general elections differ?

	1910	1918
Sinn Féin	6	73
Home Rule Party	73	6
Unionists	19	23

III. The Independence Struggle or War of Independence, 1919–21

Sinn Féin followed a policy of **passive resistance** – a policy of opposing the British government by refusing to co-operate with British rule in Ireland.

In 1919, Sinn Féin set up **Dáil Éireann** and an **alternative government**. **De Valera** was elected president of the Dáil, Griffith became Minister for Home Affairs and Michael **Collins** became Minister for Finance.

They declared a **republic**, they asked the **Paris Peace Conference** to recognise it and they set up **Sinn Féin courts**.

> **Key Words**
> flying columns
> Black and Tans
> Auxiliaries
> partition
> Bloody Sunday
> British Commonwealth
> treaty ports
> Boundary Commission
> Oath of Allegiance
> Irregulars
> Regulars
> sectarian riots

War

1. The **Irish Volunteers** – later called the **Irish Republican Army (IRA)** – organised a **guerrilla warfare campaign** – 'hit and run', mostly ambushes on British forces in Ireland.
2. Local **IRA** units began the guerrilla campaign against British forces.
   - In **January 1919**, the first attack was against an **RIC (Royal Irish Constabulary)** patrol in **Soloheadbeg**, Co. Tipperary.
   - They attacked **small RIC barracks** in various parts of the country in order to take its arms and ammunition.

3. Michael **Collins** was **Director of Intelligence** – he organised a spy network. He also organised the **Squad**, a group whose job was to kill spies and detectives.
4. The IRA organised flying columns – small groups of armed men who planned ambushes.

How did the British government respond?

1. **David Lloyd George**, the British prime minister, organised the Black and Tans (ex-soldiers) and the Auxiliaries (ex-officers) to fight the IRA.
   - They carried out **reprisals** (revenge attacks) against families and towns.
2. Lloyd George passed the **Government of Ireland Act 1920**, which set up parliaments in Belfast and in Dublin.
   - Sinn Féin **rejected** the Dublin parliament.
   - However, the **unionists** accepted the **northern parliament** so that six northern counties **formed Northern Ireland**.
   - This created partition (a border) between North and South.
3. Some of the **most serious incidents** of the War of Independence included:
   - **Tomás Mac Curtain**, Lord Mayor of Cork, was shot in front of his family by the RIC (March 1920).
   - **Terence MacSwiney**, Lord Mayor of Cork, died on hunger strike in Brixton prison in England after 74 days (October 1920).
   - Bloody Sunday, **21 November 1920**: Collins's **Squad** killed a group of British agents sent to find him. In retaliation, **Black and Tans** shot into the crowd at a football match in Croke Park, killing 14 people.
   - **West Cork Brigade**, led by Tom Barry, ambushed Auxiliaries at Kilmichael, killing 17 of them (November 1920).
   - A week later, **Auxiliaries** burned down the **centre of Cork City.**
   - **Eighty IRA members** were either captured or killed when the Dublin brigade attacked the **Custom House in Dublin** (May 1921).

Peace

1. **Both sides now wanted peace**.
   - The **IRA** was running out of arms and ammunition while the **British government** was criticised at home and abroad for the actions of the Black and Tans and the Auxiliaries.
2. De Valera came back from **America**, where he spent most of the War of Independence. He agreed a **truce** with Lloyd George, which came into effect on 11 July 1921.

IV. The Anglo-Irish Treaty, 1921

1. Sinn Féin sent a **delegation** led by **Griffith** and **Collins** to London to negotiate a treaty with the British government.
   - **De Valera** refused to go because he wanted to control more extreme members of Sinn Féin and the IRA at home.
2. **Sinn Féin's main aim** was:
   - To achieve a **republic** (complete independence from Britain).

   The **main aim of the British government** was:
   - To keep Ireland within the **British Empire** (or Commonwealth).
3. The **British delegation** was more experienced; it was led by **Lloyd George** and **Winston Churchill**.
4. The terms of the **Anglo-Irish Treaty** were agreed on 6 December 1921.

The terms of the Anglo-Irish Treaty

1. Ireland was now known as the **Irish Free State**.
2. It was a **member** of the **British Commonwealth**.
3. **Members of Dáil Éireann (TDs)** in Dublin would have to take an **Oath of Allegiance** to the Irish government and to the British king.
4. **Three ports** – the treaty ports – at Cobh, Castletownbere and Lough Swilly – would be used by the British navy.
5. A Boundary Commission would be set up to decide the border between North and South.

Treaty debates

1. The **Dáil** was divided over the terms of the Anglo-Irish Treaty.

Arguments For and Against the Treaty	
Pro-Treaty: Griffith, Collins	**Anti-Treaty: de Valera, Brugha**
• The IRA was too weak to continue fighting • The Treaty was a **stepping stone** to full independence	• The Treaty did not give Ireland **a full republic** • The **Oath of Allegiance** recognised the king

THE RISE AND IMPACT OF NATIONALISM AND UNIONISM IN IRELAND, 1911–23

Arthur Griffith

Michael Collins

Éamon de Valera

> The **Oath of Allegiance** was agreed in the Anglo-Irish Treaty. **Members of Dáil Éireann (TDs)** had to take an Oath of Allegiance or loyalty to the Irish government and faithfulness to the King of England.

2. The **Dáil** voted **in favour** of the Treaty by **64 votes** to **57**.
   - De Valera **resigned** as president of the Executive Council; he was replaced by Griffith as president, and he and Collins took over the leadership of the government.
   - In the **general election in June 1922**, there was **huge majority** in favour of the **Pro-Treaty parties**. This strengthened the position of the government.
   General election result:

Pro-Treaty vote	78%
Anti-Treaty vote	22%

V. The Civil War, 1922–23

The causes of the Civil War

The **Pro-Treaty** and **Anti-Treaty** sides grew further apart.

Two sides of the Civil War	
• Pro-Treaty	• Anti-Treaty
• Free State Army/government forces	• Republicans
• Regulars	• Irregulars

1. **There was disagreement over the Anglo-Irish Treaty.**
   - The **Pro-Treaty** side believed that the Treaty gave them the freedom to achieve more freedom.
   - The **Anti-Treaty** side said that a republic had not been achieved.

2. The **Anti-Treaty** side took over the **Four Courts** in Dublin and captured a Free State general.
    - The **British government** put pressure on the Free State government to end the takeover of the Four Courts.

The course of the Civil War

1. The **Free State army**, led by **Collins**, bombarded the **Four Courts**.
    - The Civil War had begun.
    - The Free State army **defeated** the Anti-Treaty forces (Irregulars) in Dublin.
2. The Anti-Treaty forces **retreated** behind a line from Limerick to Waterford, in an area known as the **Munster Republic**.
    - Then the Regulars (Pro-Treaty) attacked the Irregulars in the **Munster Republic**. They captured Limerick, Waterford and Cork.
    - **Griffith** died from a brain haemorrhage.
    - **Collins** was killed in an ambush at **Béal na Bláth, Co. Cork** (August 1922).
3. **W. T. Cosgrave** and **Kevin O'Higgins** took over the Free State government.
    - The Civil War got very bitter. Both sides were guilty of **atrocities**.
    - It **ended** when de Valera got the IRA to call a **ceasefire** in May 1923.

The results of the Civil War

1. Over **900 people** were killed. There was **£30 million** worth of damage done to property. Dublin was ruined for the second time in six years.
2. The country lost able leaders, including Collins and Griffith.
3. There was **great bitterness** between both Pro-Treaty and Anti-Treaty sides for many years after the Civil War.
4. **Two of the main political parties** owe their origins to the Pro- and Anti-Treaty sides in the Civil War.

Pro-Treaty	→	Cumann na nGaedheal	→	Fine Gael
Anti-Treaty	→	Sinn Féin	→	Fianna Fáil

5. The **democratic tradition** was upheld as the victory of the Free State government was supported by the majority of the people.
    - The **parliamentary tradition** was supported in opposition to the **physical force tradition**.

VI. The Foundation of Northern Ireland

1. Northern Ireland was founded by the **Government of Ireland Act 1920**.
   - A parliament was set up in Belfast.
   - The parliament had control of the **internal affairs of Northern Ireland** – education, roads, police and health.
2. The northern parliament was controlled by the **Unionist Party**, led by **James Craig**.
3. There was conflict between Protestants and Catholics.
   - Protestants were **opposed to a united Ireland** because they believed they would be **discriminated** against by a Catholic majority.
   - They also thought the **northern economy** would collapse.
4. Law and order was controlled by an armed police force – the **Royal Ulster Constabulary (RUC)** – and the **B-Specials**, a part-time police force.
5. They used the **Special Powers Act** to arrest and imprison people.
6. There were sectarian riots between Protestants and Catholics.
   - **Catholics lost jobs**; for example, Catholics were expelled from Harland and Wolff shipyards.
   - Many **Catholic houses** were burnt.
   - More Catholics were **killed** than Protestants.
   - The **IRA** continued a campaign in the North, attacking RUC barracks and big houses.
   - The violence ended with the **outbreak** of the Civil War in the South.

Key changes – what was the impact of the rise of nationalism and unionism, 1911–23?
- The Home Rule Crisis, 1912–14
- 1916 Rising
- Decline of the Home Rule Party
- Rise of Sinn Féin
- War of Independence
- Anglo-Irish Treaty and the creation of the Irish Free State
- Civil War
- Foundation of Northern Ireland and partition
- Unionist control of Northern Ireland

Sectarian riots occur between two groups which differ strongly on religious and political beliefs.

Exam Question

Archivist Catriona Crowe gave a talk on the destruction of the Public Record Office. Read this extract and answer the questions which follow.

In April 1922, an armed force of anti-Treaty IRA occupied the Four Courts. The government assault on the Four Courts began on 28 June. At 12.30 on 30 June, there was an enormous explosion, and fire spread to the Public Record Office. Among the records lost in the fire were the census records of 1821, 1831, 1841 and 1851. Other records included church records dating back to 1174, court records, military records, and records dealing with the huge land transfers of the 17th century. Church of Ireland parish records and many wills dating back to the 16th century were also lost.
It was one of the greatest cultural disasters ever to befall any country, and we did it to ourselves. What damage was done to writing Irish history based on primary sources we will never know.

On what date was the Public Record Office (PRO) destroyed?
30 June 1922
What were **three** different types of records destroyed in the fire at the PRO?
Census records, court records, Church of Ireland parish records

Select **one** opinion from the extract above and explain whether you agree or disagree with that opinion.
Opinion: It was one of the greatest cultural disasters ever to befall any country.
Agree/disagree: I agree with this opinion. Family history is a very important part of our culture. The loss of the census records means that families lost important information on their ancestors during the early 19th century.

Junior Cycle History Exam 2022, Q6

Revision Questions
Scan the QR code for more revision questions.

16 Life in Soviet Russia

If you are asked about **life in a communist country**, you should use information on **life in Soviet Russia**.

After studying this chapter, you should be able to:
- Examine life in Soviet Russia, a communist country.

Key Words
dictatorship
democracy
censorship
communism
propaganda
police state
gulag
cult of personality
purge
show trial
Five-Year Plans
collectivisation
Stakhanovite Movement
collective farms
kulaks
kindergartens

During the inter-war years (1918–39), many European countries became **dictatorships**, e.g. Mussolini's rule in Italy, Hitler's rule in Germany and **Stalin's rule** in the **Soviet Union**.

Dictatorship	Democracy
• One ruler/party in power	• Ruler is elected by the people
• Censorship	• Freedom of speech and media
• Use of violence to maintain control	• Respect for the law
• Example: Soviet Russia, Nazi Germany	• Example: Ireland, Britain

Stalin's rule in the Soviet Union is an example of a **communist dictatorship**.
Hitler's rule in Germany is an example of a **fascist dictatorship** (see Ch. 17).
In 1917, **Lenin and the Communist Party** took over Russia in a revolution. After Lenin died in 1924, **Stalin** won the power struggle to take over leadership of the Communist Party and the Soviet Union. Stalin took power in 1928 and continued to rule **Soviet Russia** until his death in 1953.

Features of the communist system in Soviet Russia
- One-party dictatorship
- Government (state) ownership of industry and agriculture
- Control of press, radio, TV and cinema
- Cult of personality
- Police state

What was Soviet Russia?
In 1939, **Soviet Russia (Union of the Soviet Socialist Republics – USSR)** included present-day Russia, Ukraine, Belorussia (now Belarus) and many countries further east. It expanded further after World War II.

What is communism?
Communists wanted to abolish private property. Instead, they favoured state (government) ownership of industry and agriculture.

Life in a Communist Dictatorship

1. **Stalin** and the Communist Party established a **one-party dictatorship** in Soviet Russia (USSR).
2. The **Communist Party** controlled all aspects of life in the Soviet Union – government, army, industry and agriculture.
3. They controlled the **means of communication** – press, radio, TV and cinema. They used **propaganda** to control the views of the people.
4. **Censorship** (control of what is printed or said on the media) was imposed so no criticism of the government was allowed.
5. The Communist Party also organised a **police state** where all opposition was put down. **Gulags** (labour camps) were used to punish people.
6. There was a **cult of personality** developed around Stalin. He was treated like a god.

Joseph Stalin

In a **dictatorship**, all power is controlled by one person or one party.

The **cult of personality** is a feature of dictatorships. The leader of the country is treated like a god, and propaganda is used to create the image of the leader or dictator as all-powerful.

Purges and Show Trials

1. Opposition to Stalin in the Communist Party and the army was **purged** (cleaned out).
2. The most serious **purges** occurred during the **Great Terror** (1936–38). Some leaders were tried in special **show trials** (public trials) and most of them were executed.
3. Thousands of ordinary people were also arrested and sent to **gulags** (labour camps).
4. These arrests and trials were conducted by the **secret police**, the **NKVD**.

Stalin's Show Trials (1936–38)		
First Show Trial, 1936	**Second Show Trial, 1937**	**Great Show Trial, 1938**
• 16 leaders tried • All executed	• 17 leaders tried • 13 executed, four sent to gulags	• 21 leaders tried • 18 executed, three sent to gulags

What Was Life Like in the Gulags?

1. The **gulags** were labour camps. They were mostly found in **Siberia**, far away from western Russia where most of the people lived.
2. Prisoners worked at mining, tree-cutting, farming and in factories.
3. About **19 million people** were sent to gulags between 1929 and 1953.
4. Prisoners worked long hours, often in freezing conditions. They were badly fed.
5. At least **1.6 million** prisoners died.

How Did Industrialisation Affect People's Lives in Soviet Russia?

The **Five-Year Plans** were plans to modernise or industrialise the Soviet Union.

1. Stalin introduced **Five-Year Plans** to modernise Russian industry, and catch up with the West.
2. These Five-Year Plans set **targets** for each industry.
3. Managers and workers who failed to reach their targets were punished.
4. A coal miner, Alexei **Stakhanov**, became the model for all workers. The Stakhanovite Movement encouraged all workers to work for their country.
5. **New industrial cities** were created, especially in Siberia, e.g. Magnitogorsk.
6. Huge **dams** were built to generate electricity.
7. The city (urban) population grew by 29 million between 1929 and 1939.
8. There was **no unemployment**, but there were harsh working conditions and low living standards.
9. The Soviet Union became the **second largest industrial country** in the world by the beginning of World War II.

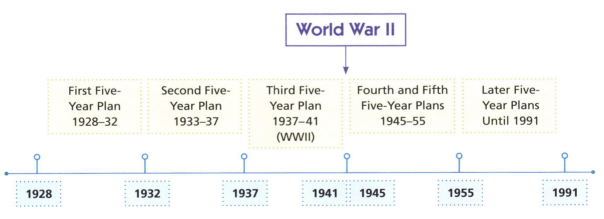

How Did Collectivisation Affect People's Lives in Soviet Russia?

Collectivisation was the plan of the Communist Party to change all privately owned farms into collective farms controlled by the state or government.

1. The government took over all the land. It planned to **modernise farming** with **more machinery** to increase food production.
2. The government created large **collective farms** – private farms were taken over by the government and formed into large farms. Farmers (peasants) were forced to co-operate to work these farms.
3. Many peasants resisted, including **kulaks** (middle-class farmers).
4. Millions were killed or sent to labour camps (**gulags**).
5. Six to eight million died of **starvation** in famines of the early 1930s, including in the **Ukraine** when Stalin took more grain from the collective farms.

What Was Life Like for Women in Soviet Russia?

1. Women's lives changed a great deal.
2. **Creches** (day nursery) and **kindergartens** (schools for children aged four to six years) were developed to allow both husbands and wives to work.
3. Women's place in the workforce was put on a **more equal footing** with the men – they were employed in what were considered men's jobs in the West – construction, engineering and labouring.
4. By 1937, **50% of the workforce** was female – much higher than in the West.
5. There were **child allowances** to encourage larger families, especially after World War II, to replace the huge loss of population.
6. However, many families in the cities lived in **one-roomed apartments**.

Health, Education and Youth

1. **Healthcare** was provided **free** for the people. New hospitals were built and thousands of doctors were trained.
2. **Education** was **free and compulsory** for all young people.
3. A huge **literacy campaign** resulted in most people under the age of 50 being able to read and write.

4. Education was also used for **propaganda**. Stalin was portrayed as the **Great Leader**.
   - His role in the Communist Revolution in 1917 was exaggerated.
5. **Children** also joined communist **youth organisations**, for example the **Little Octobrists**, from seven to nine years of age.
   - They organised sports activities and summer camps, but they were also used for propaganda, teaching the young people communist ideas.

What Was Life Like in Soviet Russia during World War II?

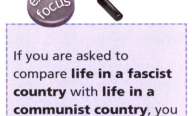

1. In June 1941, the **German army** attacked the Soviet Union (see Ch. 19), advancing towards Leningrad, Moscow and Stalingrad.
2. The Soviet Red Army used a **scorched-earth policy** as it retreated, by burning crops and destroying bridges and factories along the way.
3. The people of Soviet Russia **suffered greatly** in lands conquered by the Germans, and in the three cities of Moscow, Leningrad and Stalingrad.

> If you are asked to compare **life in a fascist country** with **life in a communist country**, you should use information from life in **Nazi Germany** and life in **Soviet Russia**.

   - **Nazi SS** (**Blackshirts,** see Ch. 17) **and police units** following the German army carried out **mass murders**, mainly of Jews and officials of the Communist Party and government.
   - Hundreds of thousands of Soviet troops were taken as **prisoners of war** (POWs). They were treated cruelly – more than 3 million died from starvation or disease.
   - People endured great hardship in the **sieges** of Leningrad and Stalingrad. Over 700,000 people either starved or froze to death in the siege of Leningrad.
4. In areas controlled by the Soviet government, food and clothing were **rationed**. Those working the war industries got more rations, but anybody could be ordered to work for the war industries.
5. About **17 million civilians in Soviet Russia died** in the war, on top of about 10 million soldiers killed.

Stalingrad

Sample Question

'Under the leadership of the great Stalin – onward to communism!'

1. How is this poster an example of the cult of personality? Explain your answer.

In the cult of personality, leaders are treated like gods. In this poster, Stalin is in the centre, above everybody else, pointing his finger towards the sky (heaven) while the people are looking on in admiration.

2. How effective is this poster as an example of propaganda? Explain your answer.

This poster is an effective example of propaganda. Stalin is seen clearly, the colours are bright and the caption has a clear message that following the great Stalin the Soviet Union will be a communist state, with a large, prosperous population and successful industry, as shown on the map in the background.

Revision Questions

Scan the QR code for more revision questions.

17 Life in Nazi Germany

After studying this chapter, you should be able to:
- Differentiate between dictatorship and democracy
- Identify the main characteristics of fascism
- Explain how Hitler and the Nazis came to power
- Examine life in a fascist dictatorship
- Describe life under Nazi propaganda
- Explain how the Nazis controlled the youth
- Discuss life for women in Nazi Germany
- Examine what life was like for Jewish people in Nazi Germany
- Describe what life was like for workers in Nazi Germany.

Key Words
rule by decree
SS
Gestapo
concentration camps
paramilitary
SA
Night of the Long Knives
Propaganda
cult of personality
Nuremberg Rallies
indoctrinated
'Kinder, Küche, Kirche'
Aryan
Herrenvolk
Nuremberg Laws
Kristallnacht
immorality trials
'With Burning Anxiety'
Confessing Church
Lebensraum
rationing
black market
refugees
resistance

How Did Hitler and the Nazi Party Gain Power in Germany?

1. Hitler joined the **German Workers' Party** after World War I.
2. He soon took over as leader and changed the name of the party to the **National Socialist German Workers' Party** (NSDAP), popularly known as the **Nazi Party**.
3. After the **Great Depression** hit Germany in 1929, support for the Nazi Party soared.
4. Soon, they became the largest party in the **Reichstag** (German parliament), and in January 1933, Hitler became **chancellor** (prime minister) of Germany.

From democracy to dictatorship

1. Germany was still a democracy when Hitler became **chancellor** in January 1933.
2. When a Dutch communist set fire to the **Reichstag**, Hitler used this as an excuse to **ban** the Communist Party and give extra powers to the police.
3. After the March 1933 election, Hitler passed the **Enabling Law** in 1933, which allowed him to **rule by decree**. This meant Hitler could pass laws without having to consult anyone.

4. Hitler **banned** all other political parties as well as trade unions.
5. He created a police state:
   - The **SS**, or Blackshirts, and the **Gestapo** (secret police) could arrest anybody, read mail and listen to phone calls.
   - Judges took **oaths of loyalty** to Hitler.
   - **Informers** were encouraged to spy on their families.
   - The media was **controlled**.
   - People who opposed Hitler were rounded up and put into **concentration camps** like **Dachau**.
6. Hitler decided to eliminate a **paramilitary** group called the **SA** because they threatened his power.
   - On the **Night of the Long Knives** (30 June 1934), the SS were used to kill the leadership of the SA.
   - Hitler was now in total control of his organisation and of the state.
7. In August 1934, when **President Hindenburg** died, Hitler combined the position of president and chancellor. He became known as **der Führer** ('the Leader') in the Nazi dictatorship.

What Was Life Like under Nazi Propaganda?

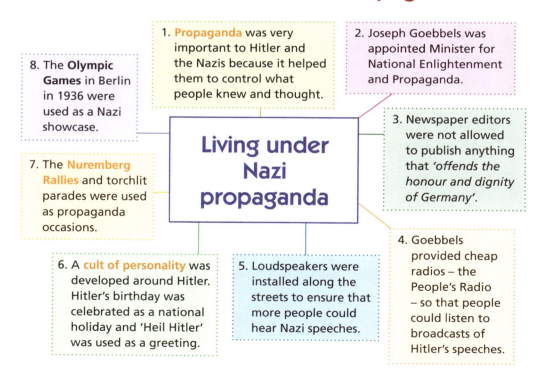

How Did the Nazis Control Young People?

1. Loyalty to the **Führer** was taught from kindergarten to university.
2. History books were **rewritten** to glorify Germany's past.
3. **Physical education** was emphasised.
4. Nazi ideas were also taught in other subjects, such as **maths**. For example, one mathematics textbook included the question *'The Jews are aliens in Germany: in 1933 there were 66,060,000 inhabitants of the German Reich of whom 499,862 were Jews. What is the percentage of aliens in Germany?'*
5. Children joined youth organisations, e.g. the **Hitler Youth** and the **League of German Maidens**.
6. They were indoctrinated (brainwashed) with Nazi ideas.
7. Boys were trained to be loyal future soldiers, while girls prepared to be mothers.
8. Some young people rebelled against Nazi ideas, e.g. the **Edelweiss Pirates** listened to American and British music, and tried to disrupt Hitler Youth patrols.

What Was Life Like for Women in Nazi Germany?

1. Women in Nazi Germany were encouraged to follow a **traditional gender role** as **mothers** with large families.
2. The Nazi ideal for women was *'Kinder, Küche, Kirche'* (children, kitchen, church). Women were encouraged to **give up their jobs** when they got married and women in **state jobs,** such as teachers and civil servants, were **sacked**. Only 11% of university places were given to women. Women were **discouraged** from **smoking** and **wearing make-up**. **Mothers' Schools** were organised to train women in household work. The Nazis also made **Mother's Day** a national holiday.
3. The Nazis wanted to increase the falling German birth rate and increase the Aryan (pure-blooded, white race) population, so they introduced **'marriage loans'** of **1,000 Reichsmarks** to women who had worked for six months and then gave up their job upon marriage.
4. **Maternity benefits**, **family allowances** and medals like the **Motherhood Cross** were also introduced. Contraception was made difficult to obtain and abortion was made illegal in 1933, unless the mother had a 'defect'. Unmarried women were encouraged to have babies with Aryan SS men in a **Lebensborn** home. As a result, the birth rate increased between 1933 and 1939.
5. The Nazis also **sterilised** (made infertile) **320,000** men and women to **preserve the Aryan race** and prevent people with disabilities from having children.

What Was Life Like for Jewish People in Nazi Germany?

1. The Nazis believed that the Germans were the pure-blooded **Aryan race** – the **Master Race** (*Herrenvolk*).
2. Hitler and the Nazis were **anti-Semitic** and the Jewish people were seen as **inferior** and **subhuman** (*Untermenschen*).
3. *'The Jew is responsible for our misery and he lives on it. He has corrupted our race, fouled our morals, undermined our customs and broken our power'*, Goebbels, 1930.
4. As soon as the Nazis came to power in 1933, Jewish people were **persecuted** by the Nazi regime.
5. Things only got worse for the Jews following the outbreak of World War II (see Ch. 20).

Timeline of Jewish persecution in Nazi Germany

1933	• The SA organised a **boycott** of Jewish shops and businesses. • Books by Jewish authors were publicly **burned**. • Jewish civil servants, lawyers and teachers were sacked. Jewish doctors and dentists could not treat Aryans.
1934	• Jewish shops were marked with a **yellow star**. • Jewish people had to sit on separate seats on buses and trains.
1935	• The **Nuremberg Laws** were introduced. • Jewish people were not allowed in the army.
1938	• Jews were forced to change their first names: males would be known as Israel, females as Sarah. • Jewish children were forbidden to go to school and universities. • 9 November – **Kristallnacht** (**The Night of Broken Glass**). The SS organised attacks on Jewish homes, businesses and synagogues in retaliation for the assassination of a German diplomat in France by a Polish Jew.
1939	• By 1939, half of Germany's 600,000 Jewish citizens, including **Albert Einstein**, had emigrated to other countries.

Kristallnacht

What Was Life Like for Christians in Nazi Germany?

Christianity in Nazi Germany

1. Hitler attacked the Christian churches.
2. He did not like the loyalty that the Catholic Church showed to the Pope.
3. Catholic schools were closed. Priests were harassed with **immorality trials**. Catholic youth movements were closed.
4. Pope Pius XI responded by criticising the Nazis in a famous statement called **'With Burning Anxiety'** (1937).
5. Hitler also attacked Protestants who did not agree with him.
6. He set up a Protestant national church.
7. The **Confessing Church** emerged as opponents to the Nazis. One of their leaders, Martin Niemöller, was sent to a concentration camp in 1937.

What Was Life Like for Workers in Nazi Germany?

1. Hitler promised 'work for all', so when he came to power in 1933, he began the **'Battle for Work'** to eliminate unemployment.
2. In 1933, there were **6 million people unemployed**. By 1939, Germany claimed to have **full employment**, but this figure is misleading, because:
   - women were encouraged to give up their jobs
   - many Jewish people were forced to give up their jobs and were not included in this statistic.
3. He began a huge programme of **public works schemes**, which included the construction of 7,000 km of motorways (*Autobahn*) and building hospitals, schools, and public buildings such as the 1936 Olympic Stadium.
4. **Rearmament** began almost as soon as the Nazis came to power but was not publicly announced until 1935. By 1939, **26 billion marks** were being spent on ships, submarines, planes and arms. This created millions of jobs for German workers.
5. The Nazis set up:
   - **Strength through Joy**, an organisation that created leisure activities for workers
   - **Beauty of Labour**, a Nazi programme to improve working conditions, e.g. better canteen food.
6. Hitler encouraged the design and manufacture of the Volkswagen (the 'people's car'). However, cars were not delivered before World War II began.
7. Hitler's plans for *Autarky* (self-sufficiency) were not successful. He planned to conquer lands in Eastern Europe to obtain *Lebensraum* (living space), and the extra food and raw materials that he needed.

8. The living standards of German workers in the non-armaments industries **did not improve** under the Nazis. From 1933 to 1939:
   - wages **fell**
   - the number of hours worked **rose** by 15%
   - serious accidents in factories **increased**.

Life in Nazi Germany during World War II

Rationing	• Food **rationing** began in 1939. • **Vegetable patches** were planted in gardens and parks. • Imitation coffee was made from roasted barley, oats, chicory and acorns. • Clothes were rationed from November 1939. • A shortage of coal meant that people were only allowed warm water twice a week. • Shortages resulted in a thriving **black market**. • From 1944 onwards, there were more severe shortages of food and goods.
Air raids	• In May 1942, the first British air raids deliberately targeting residential areas took place at **Lübeck**. • Over the next three years, **61 German cities** were attacked. • In **Dresden**, 70% of the buildings were destroyed and around 25,000 people were killed. • Raids in November 1943 made **400,000 Berliners homeless**. • Overall, 3.6 million homes were destroyed, **7.5 million people** were made homeless and **300,000–400,000 civilians were killed** in the raids.
Forced labour and refugees	• The Nazis forced people from the occupied countries and prisoners of war to work in Germany. • Many died from bad living conditions, mistreatment and malnutrition. • At the end of the war, **8 million** slave labourers and other displaced persons became **refugees** inside Germany.
Employment	• **13.7 million** German men served in the army during the war. • Women worked in **factories** and as **medics**. • The Nazis often used forced or slave labour, e.g. by 1943, **21%** of the German workforce were foreigners.
Persecution (See Ch. 20 for more on the Holocaust)	• During World War II, the Nazis murdered **6 million Jews** from across Europe, including **3 million Polish Jews in the Holocaust**. • 85% of Germany's **Sinti** and **Roma** people died in concentration camps. • Between 1939 and 1941, over **100,000** Germans with physical and mental **disabilities** were killed in secret. • **Homosexuals, Soviet prisoners of war, Jehovah's Witnesses** and other **'undesirables'** were also killed.

LIFE IN NAZI GERMANY

Resistance (opposition)	<ul><li>The main youth opposition group during the war was the **Edelweiss Pirates**.</li><li>**The White Rose** group was led by brother and sister Hans and Sophie Scholl.</li><li>They published **anti-Nazi leaflets** and **protested** against Nazi policies.</li><li>Some churches and church officials also offered opposition to the Nazis, e.g. **Dietrich Bonhoeffer**.</li><li>During the war, there were also a series of assassination attempts made against Hitler, e.g. the July Plot in 1944.</li></ul>

Comparing Life in Soviet Russia with Life in Nazi Germany

	Soviet Russia – a communist country	Nazi Germany – a fascist country
Dictatorship	<ul><li>One-party dictatorship – Stalin and Communist Party</li><li>Police state</li><li>Purges, show trials</li><li>Gulags</li></ul>	<ul><li>One-party dictatorship – Hitler and Nazi Party</li><li>Police state</li><li>Concentration camps</li></ul>
Propaganda	<ul><li>Control of press, radio, cinema</li><li>Cult of personality</li></ul>	<ul><li>Control of press, radio, cinema</li><li>Cult of personality</li><li>Minister of Propaganda – Goebbels</li></ul>
Industry and agriculture	<ul><li>Government control of industry and agriculture</li><li>Five-Year Plans for industrialisation and collectivisation</li></ul>	<ul><li>Private control of industry</li><li>Programme of public works</li><li>Rearmaments</li></ul>
Women	<ul><li>Women put on a more equal footing with men</li><li>50% of workforce were women</li></ul>	<ul><li>Women encouraged to stay at home and raise families</li></ul>
Health, education and youth	<ul><li>Free healthcare and education</li><li>Education used as propaganda</li><li>Communist youth organisations</li></ul>	<ul><li>Education used as propaganda</li><li>Nazi youth organisations</li></ul>
Treatment of Jews	<ul><li>Anti-Semitism</li></ul>	<ul><li>Anti-Semitism</li><li>Persecution of Jewish people, including the Holocaust during World War II</li></ul>
World War II	<ul><li>Rationing, black market</li><li>Invaded by German army</li><li>Cities bombed; civilians killed</li></ul>	<ul><li>Rationing, black market</li><li>Cities bombed; civilians killed</li><li>Invaded near end of war</li></ul>

Sample Question

How does a dictatorship differ from a democracy? Include **three** points in your answer.

There are many differences between a dictatorship and democracy.

One person or party has complete control in a dictatorship, but a democracy allows lots of different political parties. Hitler and the Nazi Party had complete control in Nazi Germany.

In a dictatorship, violence is used to gain and maintain power, e.g. the SA, SS and Gestapo helped the Nazis come to power and stay in power. This does not happen in a democratic country.

The press is controlled in a dictatorship, but they have freedom of speech in a democracy. In Nazi Germany, the Minister for Propaganda, Goebbels, controlled press, radio and cinema.

Revision Questions

Scan the QR code for more revision questions.

18 The Causes of World War II

If you are asked about World War I or World War II, you should **write about World War II**.

After studying this chapter, you should be able to:
- Identify the main causes of World War II.

Key Words
Treaty of Versailles
reparations
Polish Corridor
Anschluss
Lebensraum
Munich Conference
League of Nations
appeasement
Nazi-Soviet Pact

What Were the Causes of World War II?

There were 10 main causes of World War II.

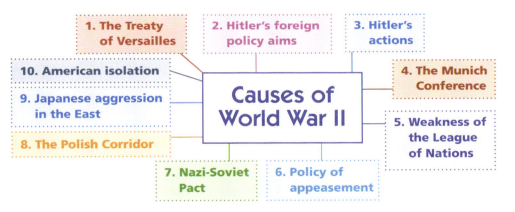

| 1. The Treaty of Versailles | • After World War I, Germany was forced to sign the **Treaty of Versailles**, which severely **punished** Germany. Germans **greatly resented** this.
• Terms included:
  • Germany had to sign a **war guilt clause** accepting full responsibility for World War I.
  • They had to pay **£6.6 billion** in **reparations** (compensation).
  • They could not enter the **Rhineland**.
  • They lost a piece of land called the **Polish Corridor**.
  • The German army was reduced to **100,000**.
  • Union with Austria (*Anschluss*) was **forbidden**. |

2. Hitler's foreign policy aims	• Hitler wanted to make **Germany great** again, but this aim was bound to **disturb peace in Europe** because it meant taking over **non-German territory**.
	• Hitler's foreign policy had three main aims:
	  • Unite all German-speaking people to form a Greater Germany (**Grossdeutschland**)
	  • **Abolish** the Treaty of Versailles
	  • Obtain **Lebensraum** (living space) in Eastern Europe for his Greater Germany.

3. Hitler's actions	• As soon as Hitler came to power, he began to **destroy** the Treaty of Versailles.
	  • 1935 – **rearmament** began.
	  • 1936 – Hitler **remilitarised** the Rhineland.
	  • 1938 – Hitler united Germany and Austria (**Anschluss**).
	• These actions showed Hitler was building up the German military and starting to expand German borders.

4. The Munich Conference	• Next, Hitler laid claim to the **Sudetenland** (the German-speaking part of Czechoslovakia). • Czechoslovakia refused to hand over the Sudetenland. • Britain (Chamberlain), France (Daladier) and Italy (Mussolini) met Hitler at the **Munich Conference** (1938) to sort the issue out. • Czechoslovakia was **not invited**. • The Czechs were forced to **hand over** the Sudetenland. • Chamberlain came home claiming he had achieved **'peace in our time'**, but six months later, Hitler took over the rest of Czechoslovakia. • Hitler could **no longer claim** to be uniting all German-speaking people as he was not welcomed in the rest of Czechoslovakia as he had been in the **Sudetenland**, **Austria** and the **Rhineland**. • Hitler ignored what had been agreed at the Munich Conference and continued to expand the German Reich.

5. Weakness of the League of Nations	• The **League of Nations** was set up after World War I to promote international co-operation and achieve international peace.
	• But **they failed** to stop Hitler, Japan or Mussolini from expanding beyond their borders.
	• The League had a number of **weaknesses**:
	  1. The USA did not join.
	  2. All decisions had to be **unanimous**.
	  3. The League had **no army** to protect weak countries.

6. Policy of appeasement	• Britain and France gave into Hitler's demands because they followed a policy called **appeasement**. • They believed that if they gave into Hitler's demands, then they would **prevent war**. • Hitler saw this as a sign of **weakness** and continued to make more demands.

THE CAUSES OF WORLD WAR II

7. Nazi-Soviet Pact	• Fascists (Nazis) and communists hated each other, but in 1939 Hitler and Stalin surprised the world when they signed the **Nazi-Soviet Pact**.
	• They agreed to:
	   1. sign a 10-year **non-aggression pact** (which Hitler later broke)
	   2. **divide Poland** between them.
	• This pact meant Hitler could invade Poland without risking war on his eastern side.

8. The Polish Corridor	• The **Polish Corridor** separated Germany from one of her provinces, East Prussia. • Hitler demanded the return of the Polish Corridor, but Poland refused. • Britain and France supported Poland, but Hitler believed they were too far away to actually help Poland. • On **1 September 1939**, Hitler invaded Poland.
9. Japanese aggression in the East	• Japan expanded into **China** in the 1930s. The League of Nations failed to stop this. • Japan also invaded **Indo-China** (Vietnam). The US imposed **economic sanctions** on Japan. • Japan attacked the US Pacific Fleet at **Pearl Harbour, Hawaii**. • This event in December 1941 brought the US into the war.
10. American isolation	• America **did not join** the League of Nations after World War I. • Even though America was the most powerful country in the world, she hoped to stay isolated and away from conflict. • However, America was forced to take action because of **Japanese expansion** in Asia.

'Remember... One More Lollypop, and Then You All Go Home!'

An American cartoon criticising the policy appeasement by Dr Seuss (Theodor Geisel) in *PM*, 13 August 1941.

Sample Question

Outline three causes of either World War I or World War II.

There were many causes of World War II. Some of the most significant were: the Treaty of Versailles, the weakness of the League of Nations, and the policy of appeasement.

After World War I, Germany was forced to sign the Treaty of Versailles. Germans greatly resented the severe terms. They could not enter the Rhineland. They lost a piece of land called the Polish Corridor. Union with Austria (Anschluss) was forbidden. Hitler worked to undo many of these terms, which contributed to the outbreak of World War II.

The League of Nations was set up after World War I to promote international co-operation and achieve international peace, but they had a number of weaknesses. The USA did not join, all decisions had to be unanimous, and the League had no army to protect weak countries. As a result of these, the League failed to stop Hitler, Japan or Mussolini from expanding beyond their borders.

Britain and France gave into Hitler's demands because they followed a policy called appeasement. They believed that if they gave into Hitler's demands, then they would prevent war. Hitler saw this as a sign of weakness and continued to make more demands.

Revision Questions

Scan the QR code for more revision questions.

19 World War II, 1939–45 – Course and Impact

aims

After studying this chapter, you should be able to:
- Discuss the course of World War II
- Discuss the immediate and long-term impact of World War II on people and nations (countries).

Key Words

Blitzkrieg	Operation Sea Lion	wolfpack
Luftwaffe	Blitz	convoy
Panzer	Operation Barbarossa	Holocaust
Operation Dynamo	Great Patriotic War	Final Solution
Maginot Line	scorched-earth policy	Operation Overlord
Vichy France	arsenal of democracy	

German Victories, 1939–42

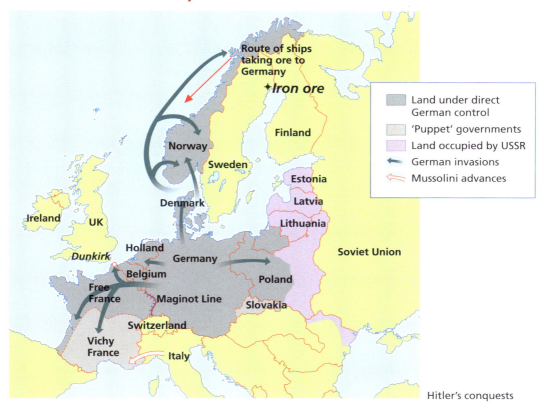

Hitler's conquests

Major Events of World War II

1939	Invasion of Poland
	Phoney War
1940	Denmark and Norway conquered
	Invasion and fall of France
	Dunkirk evacuation
	Battle of Britain
	Blitz (1940–41)
1941	Invasion of Soviet Union – Operation Barbarossa
	Japanese attack on Pearl Harbour
	USA entered World War II
1942	Battle of El Alamein
	Battle of Stalingrad
	Battle of Midway
1943	End of Battle of Stalingrad
	Warsaw Ghetto Uprising
1944	D-Day
1945	Battle of Iwo Jima
	Hitler's suicide
	VE-Day
	USA dropped atomic bombs on Japan
	VJ-Day

What was *Blitzkrieg*?
Blitzkrieg means 'lightning war'. It was a **German war tactic** that combined the use of air power, tanks, infantry and artillery.
1. In Poland, the **German air force (Luftwaffe)** destroyed the Polish air force on the ground.
2. The German **Panzer (tank) units** cut off the Polish army.
3. The **German infantry** defeated the Polish army. Germany also used this tactic in the invasions of France and Soviet Russia.

1. Germany **invaded** Poland on **1 September 1939**. As a result, Britain and France declared war on Germany.
2. Hitler defeated **Poland** in five weeks using *Blitzkrieg* **tactics**, based on speed and surprise. Germany and the **Soviet Union** divided Poland between them, as agreed in the **Nazi-Soviet Pact**.

After this attack, there was no fighting during the winter of 1939–40 in what people called the **Phoney War**; instead, both sides built up their armies.

WORLD WAR II, 1939–45 – COURSE AND IMPACT

Who fought in World War II?	
Allied powers	**Axis powers**
France	Germany
Netherlands	Italy (from June 1940)
Britain	Japan (from December 1941)
Soviet Union (from June 1941)	and other countries
Poland	
USA (from December 1941)	
Belgium	
and other countries	

3. Next, Hitler conquered **Denmark and Norway**. He wanted **Norway** to protect the supply route of **iron ore**, which came from **Sweden** during the winter; this was vital for his **war industries**.
4. Then Hitler attacked **Belgium, Holland and France**. Hitler used *Blitzkrieg* tactics and cut off the British and French armies at **Dunkirk**, in France.
    - In **Operation Dynamo**, the British sent hundreds of boats to **rescue** over 300,000 soldiers from the beaches of Dunkirk.
    - Hitler easily captured the **Maginot Line** (a French defensive line along the border with Germany); then he divided France, ruling part of it directly; the other part was ruled as **Vichy France** under German control (see map on page 119).
        - The government of Vichy France co-operated with the Nazis and rounded up **Jews** and **slave labour** to be sent to Germany.
5. **Churchill**, who replaced Chamberlain as prime minister of Britain, organised British resistance to Hitler in the **Battle of Britain**.
    - Hitler's plan to invade Britain was called **Operation Sea Lion**. But first he had to gain **control of the air** over the English Channel. The **Royal Air Force (RAF)** and the **Luftwaffe** fought for control of the air in the Battle of Britain.

- British **Spitfires** and **Hurricanes** fought intense battles against the German **Messerschmitts** and **Stukas**.
- Britain defeated the Germans with the help of **radar**, which told them where the Germans were going to attack.

6. The Battle of Britain was followed by the **Blitz** in the winter of 1940–41.
   - Cities such as **London** and **Coventry** were attacked; some people evacuated to the countryside, but many stayed in the cities.
   - In London people slept in the **London Underground**.
   - Churchill played an important role in boosting the **morale (spirit) of the people**.
   - The **Blitz ended** when Hitler began preparations for the attack on Soviet Russia in 1941.

Britain had survived to continue the fight against Hitler. This was a **major turning point** in the war.

The **Blitz** was the **aerial bombing** or **attack on British cities** carried out by the **German air force (Luftwaffe)** over the winter of 1940–41.

7. The War in North Africa
I. Hitler sent **Rommel** and the **Afrika Corps** to North Africa to help **Mussolini's Italian army**.
II. Hitler planned to capture the **Suez Canal**, a vital link for shipping to Asia.
III. After advancing as far as Egypt, Rommel was defeated by the British army, led by **Montgomery**, at the **Battle of El Alamein** (1942).
IV. This was a **major turning point in the war**.

8. Operation Barbarossa – the German invasion of the Soviet Union (June 1941): Hitler attacked Soviet Russia because he **hated communists,** and he wanted *lebensraum* (living space in the East for raw materials and food).
   - He attacked towards **Leningrad**, **Moscow** and **Kyiv** with *blitzkrieg* tactics.
   - **Stalin**, leader of Soviet Russia, encouraged the people to fight in what the Russians called the Great Patriotic War.

- He ordered that industries be moved behind the **Ural Mountains**, away from German attack.
- He ordered a **scorched-earth policy** of destroying all crops as the **Soviet Red army** retreated so that the Germans could not use them as they advanced.
- The Germans captured **Kyiv**, but were stopped outside **Leningrad** and **Moscow**.
- The German advance was halted by the **winter snow**.
- **Battle of Stalingrad**: The following year (1942), Hitler ordered an attack on Stalingrad and an advance towards the **oil fields** of the Caucasus.
- There was vicious street fighting, and the German army was trapped in Stalingrad; 100,000 German soldiers had to surrender (February 1943); this was a **major turning point in the war.**

The **scorched-earth policy** was used by the Soviet army when they retreated as the German army advanced in **Operation Barbarossa**. It meant destroying crops, railway lines and bridges so that they would not be of any use to the German army.

9. **America** joined the war when **Japan** attacked the American naval base in **Pearl Harbour** in Hawaii in December 1941.
    - America, under the leadership of **President Roosevelt**, became the arsenal of democracy, supplying Britain and the Soviet Union with food and weapons in its **Lend-Lease programme**.
    - The entry of America (USA) into the war was another **major turning point**.
10. **The War at Sea:** Britain and America won the so-called 'War at Sea' (also known as the **Battle of the Atlantic**), a battle against German **U-boats** (submarines). Fleets of U-boats (wolfpacks) attacked convoys (groups of ships) bringing supplies to Britain.
    - The Allies won the War at Sea because of **increased shipbuilding** and the use of **Ultra**, which cracked the German codes sending messages to their submarines.
11. **The War in the Air:** Britain and America bombed Germany by day and by night to disrupt war production; they bombed major German cities such as **Hamburg** and **Berlin**; about 25,000 people were killed in a raid on **Dresden**.
    - The Germans counter-attacked by using **V1 flying bombs** and **V2 rockets** against Britain, but these came too late to have a major impact.

Leaders during World War II.

Top row (L–R):
Benito Mussolini (Italy),
Adolf Hitler (Germany),
Emperor Hirohito (Japan).

Bottom row (L–R):
Joseph Stalin (Soviet Russia),
Franklin D. Roosevelt (USA),
Winston Churchill (UK).

12. Nazi-controlled Europe

I. By late 1942, Hitler and the Nazis had conquered much of the European continent (on page 119).
II. The **SS** and the **Gestapo** (secret police) enforced Nazi rule.
III. Almost 8 million **slave labourers** were used to keep the German economy producing for the war.
IV. Millions of **Jews** were rounded up as part of Hitler's plan – the Final Solution – to kill all Jews.
V. **Six million Jews** died in the **Holocaust** (see Ch. 20).
VI. Local groups in each of the conquered countries organised **resistance** to the Germans.

The **Holocaust** was the systematic killing of 6 million European Jews by Nazi Germany during World War II.

The **Final Solution** was the Nazi phrase for their policy of the systematic killing of European Jews during World War II.

The Allies Advance, 1942–45

13. The Allies advanced **from the south** through Italy; **Mussolini**, leader of Italy, was deposed by the Italians and he was captured and shot; his body was hung publicly in Milan.
14. The Soviet Union advanced from the east; they defeated the German army in a major tank battle at **Kursk**.

15. **D-Day, Operation Overlord** (the codename for the Allied invasion of France): The Allies planned a **landing on the coast of Normandy** in France. They wanted to open up a **second-front** in the west. They used the coastline's shallow water, sandy beaches and closeness to England to surprise the Germans.
    - General **Eisenhower** commanded the Allied forces; Allied planes bombed the German defences of the **Atlantic Wall**; **paratroopers** dropped behind enemy lines; warships and landing craft landed American, British and Canadian troops on **five beaches** (called **Omaha, Utah, Gold, Juno and Sword**).
    - The Allies built **PLUTO** (Pipeline under the Ocean) to supply oil and **Mulberry Harbours** (floating artificial piers) in order to land trucks and tanks.
    - After taking Normandy, the Allies advanced on **Paris**. They continued their advance on Germany but were slowed down at the **Battle of the Bulge**.
16. **Hitler's suicide:** Hitler, along with his close followers, including his partner, Eva Braun, died by suicide in his bunker in Berlin as the Allied armies closed in on Berlin. Germany surrendered.
    VE (Victory in Europe) **Day** was celebrated on 8 May 1945.

17. The War in the Far East
  I. Japan expanded during the 1930s, invading **China** (1937), and later **Indochina** (Vietnam, Thailand and Cambodia) in 1941.
  II. After the surprise attack on **Pearl Harbour** (December 1941), which brought the USA into the war, Japan next captured British-controlled **Singapore**.
  III. The European war now became a **world war**.
  IV. Japan advanced over **Borneo**, the **Philippines** and other islands in the **Pacific Ocean**.
  V. The **US Navy** halted the Japanese expansion in the **Battle of Midway** (June 1942). This was a **major turning point of the war**.
  VI. The USA, Britain and the Soviet Union pushed back Japan from various directions.
  VII. The USA won another major battle in the **Battle of Iwo Jima** (1945).
  VIII. The Americans decided to use **atomic bombs** against Japan rather than risk an invasion of the country.
  IX. Atomic bombs were dropped on **Hiroshima** and **Nagasaki** (August 1945), killing about 120,000 people.
  X. **Emperor Hirohito** of Japan surrendered. **VJ** (Victory in Japan) **Day** was celebrated on 15 August 1945.

World War II was over.

Why Did the Allies Win the War?

1. **Population and armies:** The Allies had a **larger population** and **larger armies** than Germany, Italy, Japan and others.
   - Allied armies = 28 million; Axis armies = 15.5 million
2. **American wealth:** America – the arsenal of democracy – produced huge amounts of tanks, planes and weapons to keep the Allies (especially Britain and the Soviet Union) going during the war.
3. **Oil production:** The Allies produced **more oil** than the Germans and Japanese.
4. **Victory in battles:** The Allies **won the major battles** of the war – these were **major turning points** in the war – Battle of Britain, Stalingrad, D-Day, Midway, Iwo Jima.
5. **War at Sea:** The Allies won the **Battle of the Atlantic**, so America could continue supplying resources to Europe; the American navy also controlled the Pacific Ocean.
6. **War in the Air:** The Allied air forces **controlled the air** in both Europe and in the Pacific; they bombed cites and supported their armies.

What Were the Impacts of World War II?

Short-term impacts of the war

1. **Death:** 55 million people – civilians and soldiers – died.

Deaths in Allied countries		Deaths in Axis countries	
Soldiers	Civilians	Soldiers	Civilians
18.6 million	25.4 million	5.9 million	5.1 million
Total = 44 million		Total = 11 million	

2. **Destruction:** Cities, industries, roads and railways were destroyed in Europe and Asia.
   - After the war, the USA provided **Marshall Aid** to help the recovery of Europe.
   - America controlled Japan and revived the Japanese economy.
3. **Refugees:** Millions of people were displaced after the war.
   - 11.5 million Germans were expelled from countries in Eastern Europe.
   - Millions of Poles had to leave land taken over by the Soviet Union.
   - Many Jews who survived the concentration camps lived in other camps until they migrated to Israel.
4. **War crimes:** Nazi war criminals such as Goering were tried in the **Nuremberg Trials**. Japanese leaders were tried in **Tokyo Trials** for war crimes.

Long-term impacts of the war

1. **Germany** was **divided** in two between the **Soviet-controlled East Germany** and **Allied-controlled West Germany**. The two were re-united when communism collapsed in 1990.
2. **Japan** was occupied by American troops until 1952. Afterwards, Japan became an ally of America.
3. **Superpowers:** The USA and the Soviet Union became **superpowers** and Europe was weakened. In the 1950s and 1960s, European empires were **decolonised** as countries got their independence in Africa and Asia (see Ch. 24).
4. **Cold War:** Relations between America and the Soviet Union worsened and turned into the **Cold War** after World War II was over; the Soviet Union installed communist governments in Eastern European states (see Ch. 22).
5. European leaders began a drive to **European unity** after the war (see Ch. 27).

Sample Question

Select a battle or event which you consider was a **turning point** in either World War I or World War II, and explain why you consider it a turning point.
Turning point: *The Battle of Britain*
Explanation: *In the Battle of Britain, the Royal Air Force (RAF) defeated the German air force (Luftwaffe). This prevented the Luftwaffe gaining control of the air over the English Channel. This stopped Hitler's plan to invade England (Operation Sea Lion). Now Britain could organise the fight back against Germany.*

Revision Questions
Scan the QR code for more revision questions.

20 The Holocaust

By the end of this chapter, you should be able to:
- Define genocide
- Outline the causes, course and consequences of the Holocaust.

Key Words
genocide
Khmer Rouge
Hutu
Tutsi
Bosniak
anti-Semitism
Nuremberg Laws
pogrom
Kristallnacht
Aryan
Évian Conference
concentration camp
extermination camp
Wannsee Conference
Final Solution
ghetto
Einsatzgruppen
Zyklon B
crematorium
death march

What is Genocide?

Genocide is the deliberate extermination of a group of people.

Examples of genocide

Armenian **genocide**	• Between 1915 and 1917, **1.5 million Christian Armenians** were killed or died during mass deportations by the Turkish government. • The Turkish government denies that this was a genocide.
The Holocaust	• In the Holocaust, **6 million Jewish people** were killed by the Nazis. • **Roma, Sinti, homosexuals** and people with **disabilities** were also targeted during World War II.
The Khmer Rouge in Cambodia	• The **Khmer Rouge** ruled **Cambodia** from 1975–79. • During that time, they killed **2 million people** through execution or starvation.
Rwandan massacre	• In 1994, **800,000 people** were killed by **Hutu** extremists who were targeting the **Tutsi** minority and Hutu political opponents.
Bosnian genocide	• In 1992, the government of Bosnia-Herzegovina declared independence from Yugoslavia. • Bosnian Serb forces attacked Bosnian Muslims (**Bosniak**) and Croatian civilians. • By 1995, 100,000 people had been killed (80% of them were Bosniak).
Darfur genocide	• In 2003, the **Sudanese** government organised a militia which killed **400,000 people** in the **Darfur** region.

THE HOLOCAUST

What Were the Causes of the Holocaust?

- The Holocaust was the deliberate killing of **Jews** before and during World War II.
- There were **seven** main causes of the Holocaust:

1. Rise of the Nazis	• The Nazis targeted the Jewish people (anti-Semitism) and other groups, such as the Roma, when they came to power in 1933. • They passed harsh laws that **discriminated** against Jewish people, e.g. the Nuremberg Laws, and organised violent riots or pogroms (massacres), e.g. Kristallnacht.
2. Nazi propaganda	• 'All Jews have crooked legs, fat bellies, curly hair and a suspicious look. The Jews were **responsible for the [First] World War**. All Jews are … **communists**' – German school textbook.
3. Nazi racial theories	• The Nazis claimed that they were the **Master Race**. They were the superior Aryan race against the 'inferior' Jewish people.
4. Failure of the Évian Conference	• The Évian Conference was held to discuss the problem of Jewish refugees leaving Germany and Austria. Most countries expressed sympathy for the Jews but refused to admit more refugees.
5. Nazi conquest of Europe	• When the Nazis conquered large parts of Europe during World War II, they captured millions more Jews. • Of the 3.3 million Jews living in Poland in 1939, around **3 million** were murdered.
6. Concentration and extermination camps	• A concentration camp was a detention centre for real and perceived enemies of the Third Reich, e.g. Bergen-Belsen. • **Dachau** was the first concentration camp. It was opened in March 1933. • An extermination camp was designed primarily or exclusively for mass murder, e.g. Treblinka.
7. Wannsee Conference	• The Wannsee Conference was a meeting of senior Nazi officials who decided to go ahead with the 'Final Solution [death] to the Jewish Question'.

How Was the Holocaust Carried out?

1. As the German army swept across Europe, millions of Jews came under Nazi rule.
2. Jewish people were rounded up and confined to ghettos or sent on **cattle carts** to **concentration camps**.
3. In the **Warsaw ghetto**, 400,000 Jews were walled into an area of just 3.4 square kilometres.
4. By 1941, Jewish people had to wear a yellow **Star of David** and have 'J' stamped on their ration cards.
5. As the German army advanced into the Soviet Union in 1941, SS **killing squads** called Einsatzgruppen killed thousands of Jews in mass **pogroms**, e.g. **Babi Yar** massacres near Kyiv.

6. The Wannsee Conference in 1942 was organised to find the 'final solution to the Jewish question'.
7. **Adolf Eichmann** organised the **identification, assembly and transportation of Jewish people** from all over occupied Europe to their final destinations at Auschwitz and other extermination camps.
8. **Six** Nazi extermination camps were set up in Poland, including **Auschwitz**.
9. When Jews arrived at these camps, they were separated into two groups: those who could work and those who could not. Infants, the elderly and ill were immediately executed using Zyklon B gas.
10. Mass graves were dug, or bodies were burned in crematoria.
11. Many Jews also died due to diseases and the conditions in both the concentration and extermination camps. The average life expectancy was nine months.
12. The SS made a huge profit from selling Jewish possessions, including the gold fillings from teeth.
13. The camps were also used as sites for **medical experiments**, e.g. **Josef Mengele** often conducted experiments on twins in Auschwitz.
14. Towards the end of the war, **Himmler** ordered the people in the camps be moved towards the centre of Germany to avoid the advancing **Red Army**. These death marches killed thousands more, e.g. of the 60,000 who took part in the death march from Auschwitz, 15,000 died.

What Were the Consequences of the Holocaust?

1. **Six million** Jews were killed.
2. Other minorities, including **homosexual people** and **Roma communities,** also suffered. About 250,000 out of 1 million Roma were killed.
3. The **Nuremberg War Crimes Trials** were held after the war to try Nazi leaders for crimes committed during the Holocaust.
   - Twelve were sentenced to death, e.g. **Hans Frank**.
   - Three were given life sentences, e.g. **Albert Speer**.
   - Three were acquitted, e.g. **Franz von Papen**.
4. Jewish people became **displaced persons** after the war. Many lived in camps because they couldn't return home.
   - Those who tried to return home were subjected to pogroms.
   - Some attempted to emigrate to British-controlled **Palestine**, but were refused entry.
5. Pressure to deal with Jewish emigration led to the foundation of **Israel** in **1948**.

6. The establishment of Israel led to a series of **wars** between Israel and neighbouring Arab states, beginning with the first in **1948–49**.
   - This was followed by further wars in 1956, 1967 (the **Six-Day War**), 1973 (the **Yom Kippur War**) and 1982 (the **Lebanon War**).
7. Over the following decades, ordinary Germans struggled with the **bitter legacy** left by the Holocaust.
8. Starting in 1953, the German government made **payments** to individual Jews and Jewish people to acknowledge the German people's responsibility for the crimes committed in their name.

Exam Question

Here are ten statements about the Holocaust.

(a) One term from the box has been matched with a statement from the table below. Match six other terms from the box with statements from the table below.

Kristallnacht   Final Solution   propaganda   ghetto   genocide
Mein Kampf   ~~Wannsee~~   anti-Semitism   pogrom   Nuremberg

1.	Hostility to or prejudice against Jewish people:	
2.	Hitler wrote about his hatred of Jewish people in a book:	
3.	The organised spreading of information to persuade people to believe a particular point-of-view:	
4.	In 1935, the Nazis introduced laws which said German Jews were no longer German citizens and which banned Jewish people from marrying non-Jews. These laws were called after the city of:	
5.	An organised attack or riot against a religious group:	
6.	In November 1938, the Nazis organised an attack on Jewish synagogues, homes and businesses throughout Germany and Austria. Nearly 100 Jewish people were killed and 30,000 Jews were arrested. This attack is often called:	
7.	An over-crowded, closely-guarded area of a city where Jewish people were forced to live apart from non-Jewish people:	
8.	The crime of trying to completely destroy a group of people based on their religious, national, racial or ethnic background:	
9.	At a conference in January 1942, Nazi leaders decided to kill all Jewish people in Europe, including 4,000 Irish Jews. This conference was held in:	*Wannsee*
10.	The Nazi plan to kill all Jewish people in Europe:	

(b) From your study of the Holocaust, explain why Kristallnacht was a turning point in Nazi persecution of Jewish people.

To receive the maximum number of marks available, ensure your answer includes at **least two points**. Each point should include a key word/term, fact, statistic or explanation.

(c) What evidence about the Holocaust is provided by **three** different types of sources?

To receive the maximum number of marks available, ensure your explanation of the evidence to be found in the source contains a relevant key word/term, fact, statistic or explanation.

(d) What were two consequences of the Holocaust?

Notes on the marking scheme:
Two results: 3 marks + 3 marks
Mark each result on a 3-mark sliding scale:
3m = very good (e.g. '6 million Jews were executed in Europe')
2m = average/good (e.g. 'Millions of Jews were killed')
1m = weak (e.g. 'a lot of Jews were killed')
0m = no attempt/incorrect/irrelevant

Junior Cycle History Exam 2022, Q7

Revision Questions
Scan the QR code for more revision questions.

21 The Impact of World War II on Ireland, North and South

After studying this chapter, you should be able to:
- Describe the impact of World War II on the lives of Irish people in the south of Ireland
- Describe the impact of World War II on the lives of Irish people in Northern Ireland.

Key Words
Irish people
neutrality
The Emergency
censored
shortage
rationing
black market
glimmer men
conscription
Belfast Blitz

When you are asked to **describe the impact of war on the lives of Irish people**, you should write about the **impact of World War II**, and you should refer to the lives of people **both in Northern Ireland and in the south of Ireland**.

In the 1937 Constitution, the name of this state is Éire or Ireland. The state is referred to in this chapter as the south of Ireland, to explain the different experiences of Irish people in the two parts of the island of Ireland.

Irish people are people living on the island of Ireland, both north and south of the border.

Ireland in 1939

In September 1939, when World War II began, Northern Ireland and the south of Ireland went **different** ways.
- The **south of Ireland (Éire)**, even though it was part of the British Commonwealth, remained **neutral** in World War II because it wanted to stay **independent** and also because it was a **small country**. As a **neutral country**, Éire would not fight in the war or help either side. This was a policy supported by most people.
- **Northern Ireland**, as part of the United Kingdom (UK), was **directly involved** in the war.

Being **neutral** meant not supporting or helping either side in a conflict or war.

The Emergency was the name given to the years of World War II (1939–45) in the south of Ireland.

What Was Life Like in the South of Ireland during World War II?

The Taoiseach, **Éamon de Valera**, passed the **Emergency Powers Act**, which gave the government great power to control the country. The years of World War II (1939–45) were known as '**The Emergency**'.

The **defence forces** were increased in case the country was invaded during the war. The number of part-time (**Local Defence Force** – LDF) and full-time (Irish Army) soldiers grew from about 25,000 to almost 200,000.

Over 80 **'ÉIRE' signs** were carved into headlands around the coast to warn Allied and German bombers they were flying over a neutral country. **Newspaper** and **radio reports** were **censored** (controlled) by the government so that they would not favour either side and the south of Ireland would maintain its neutrality.

An 'ÉIRE' sign at Crohy Head, Co. Donegal

However, **secretly** the Irish government **favoured** the Allied forces.
- Allied planes were allowed to fly from Northern Ireland over **Donegal** on their way to patrolling the North Atlantic.
- Irish **weather reports** were sent secretly to the Allies.
- Surviving Allied pilots who crash-landed in the south of Ireland were quietly sent to Northern Ireland, while surviving German pilots were interned (imprisoned) in the **Curragh camp**.
- Leaders of the **IRA** (Irish Republican Army), who tried to get help from Germany, were also interned in the Curragh camp.

Impact on the economy – Shortages and rationing

Seán Lemass, Minister of Supplies, bought and chartered ships to bring supplies to the south of Ireland. But there were severe **shortages** (scarcity).
- Imports of fertiliser for the land and maize for animal feed were stopped.
- Petrol and coal imports were cut.

Rationing (controlled distribution) of tea, sugar, clothes and footwear was introduced.
- People were issued with **ration cards**.
- However, eggs, potatoes and meat were in good supply.
- Some people grew vegetables in their gardens.
- People also bought supplies on the **black market** (illegal trade).
- Turf replaced coal on the trains, but journeys took a long time.

Electricity and gas were also rationed.
- Inspectors (**glimmer men**) checked out the use of gas in the houses.
- The rationing of electricity cut production in **factories**, so workers were laid off and **unemployment** increased.

Overall **living standards fell** – prices of goods increased (**inflation**), but wages were not increased.
- Some men and women **emigrated** to England to get work in **war industries** or in the **British army**.

Direct impact of the war

The south of Ireland felt very little direct impact of the war.

Germany planned **Operation Green** (the code name for the invasion of Ireland), but decided Ireland was too far away to invade.

However, German bombers did bomb the village of **Campile** in Co. Wexford in August 1940, killing three people. They also bombed the **North Strand** in Dublin in May 1941, killing 34 people.

What Was Life Like in Northern Ireland during World War II?

In contrast to the south, Northern Ireland was **directly involved** in the war.

1. **Industry:** Ships, planes, parachutes and shells were all produced for the war.
   - **Harland & Wolff** produced warships and tanks
   - **Short & Harland** produced Stirling bombers and Sunderland flying boats
   - Engineering works produced shells
   - **Unemployment** was reduced from a pre-war level of 25% to 5%.
2. **Agriculture:** Food supplies were shipped from Belfast to Britain every day – milk, eggs, meat.
3. **Conscription** (forced enlistment in the army) was **not** introduced to Northern Ireland because of fear of nationalist opposition. However, almost **40,000 people volunteered** for service in the British armed forces.
   - A **Victoria Cross** was awarded to **James Magennis**, Royal Navy, a Belfast Catholic.
4. Northern Ireland also contributed to **patrolling** the North Atlantic to protect shipping from U-boat attack – patrol boats and planes used Northern Ireland as a base.
5. Later, the **USA** brought 120,000 soldiers and sailors to Northern Ireland to prepare for **D-Day**.

What was the Belfast Blitz, April–May 1941?

1. **Belfast** was badly defended early in the war. The Northern Ireland government believed that the city was too far away from Germany to be attacked.
2. However, the city was bombed **four times** in April and May 1941 in the **Belfast Blitz**. Shipbuilding was disrupted, but the worst effects were the numbers of civilians who were killed.
   - 1,100 people were **killed**.
   - Half the houses were destroyed.
   - Poverty in the back streets of the city was exposed.
   - About 100,000 people were made **homeless**.
3. The government in the south of Ireland sent **fire brigades** on two occasions to help Belfast.
4. **People left the city** – some came south, some went to other towns in the North and some went to the countryside around Belfast every night.
5. Victory in Europe (VE Day) was celebrated in Belfast and other parts of Northern Ireland.

Differences between North and South

The north and south of Ireland had very different experiences during World War II. The two parts of the island were driven **further apart** because of the **different wartime experiences**.

THE IMPACT OF WORLD WAR II ON IRELAND, NORTH AND SOUTH

Exam Question

Historian Gillian O'Brien gives the following advice about setting up museum exhibitions:

> Objects and documents are vital, but photographs, film, and oral testimony can be fascinating too.

Suggest **three** examples of objects, documents and/or other presentation methods you would use to set up a museum exhibition about Ireland, north and south, during World War II. Justify each choice.

(i) *Ration cards: People in the south of Ireland (Éire) had to use ration cards during World War II to buy tea and sugar. The cards would show how rationing was used because of shortages during the war.*

(ii) *Photographs of American soldiers based in Northern Ireland: Photographs of American soldiers would remind people about the important role Northern Ireland played as these soldiers got ready for D-Day.*

(iii) *Pages of a newspaper published in the south of Ireland: The pages of a newspaper would show how life went on in the south of Ireland (Éire) in spite of war in Europe. There would be reports of matches, shows and advertisements for clothes.*

Junior Cycle History Exam 2022, Q8(g)

Revision Questions

Scan the QR code for more revision questions.

22 The Cold War

After studying this chapter, you should be able to:
- Recognise the importance of the Cold War in international relations.

Who were the superpowers?
The **superpowers** were the **USA** and the **USSR** (Soviet Union) because they were so much more powerful than Britain, France and other countries.

Key Words
superpower
Cold War
international relations
capitalism
communism
Truman Doctrine
policy of containment
Marshall Plan
Iron Curtain
arms race
Space Race
blockade
rationing
Operation Vittles
airlift
NATO
nationalise

What Was the Cold War?

The **Cold War** was a period of hostility between **the USA**, and its allies, and **the USSR**, and its allies, which began after World War II. The Cold War dominated **international relations** from the end of World War II until the communist system collapsed in the Soviet Union in 1990.

International relations concerns the relations between countries, particularly through their foreign policies.

What Caused the Cold War?

1. **Political differences**: The USA believed in **democracy** and **private industry** (**capitalism**), while the Soviet Union believed in **dictatorship** and **government ownership** of business and industry (**communism**).
2. **Disagreements during World War II**: America had the secrets of the atomic bomb and would not share them with the Soviet Union.
3. **Post-war disagreements**: After the war, **Stalin** said he installed communist governments in Eastern European countries to act as a **buffer** (defence) **zone** against the West and to protect the Soviet Union. However, America believed Stalin was trying to increase the number of countries under his control.

THE COLD WAR

4. The **Truman Doctrine**: In the **Truman Doctrine**, President **Truman** of the USA said he would help countries resisting the spread of communism; this became the basis for the US **policy of containment** to stop the spread (expansion) of communism.
5. The **Marshall Plan**: In the **Marshall Plan**, America offered to help Europe's economy recover after the war. However, Stalin prevented Eastern European countries from getting help from the Marshall Plan (also known as the European Recovery Program).

The **Iron Curtain** refers to the **border** or dividing line between European countries. The term comes from a speech made by Winston Churchill, who said that there was an 'iron curtain' dividing Europe. Democratic countries were in the west of Europe, and communist countries were in the east. The Iron Curtain ran from the Baltic Sea in the north to the Adriatic Sea in the south.

Major Events of the Cold War 1945–90

1945	USA drops atomic bombs on Hiroshima and Nagasaki
1945	Soviet Union controlled countries in Eastern Europe
1946	Churchill's Iron Curtain speech
1947	Truman Doctrine
	Marshall Plan – European Recovery Program
1948–49	**Berlin Blockade and airlift**
1950–53	**Korean War**
1957	Sputnik in space
1961	Bay of Pigs
	Berlin Wall built
1962	**Cuban Missile Crisis**
1964–73	Heavy American involvement in Vietnam War
1985	Gorbachev in power in USSR
1989	Fall of the Berlin Wall
1990	German unification
1991	Soviet Union collapsed; **end of the Cold War**

Political leaders in the era of the superpowers

Harry S. Truman, president of the **USA** during the Berlin Blockade and the Korean War

Joseph Stalin, leader of the **Soviet Union** during the Berlin Blockade and the Korean War

Mao Zedong (Mao Tse-Tung), leader of communist **China** during the Korean War

John F. Kennedy, president of the **USA** during the Cuban Missile Crisis

Nikita Khrushchev, leader of the **Soviet Union** during the Cuban Missile Crisis

Fidel Castro, leader of **Cuba** during the Cuban Missile Crisis

Danger of Nuclear War

The Cold War resulted in an **arms race** between the USA and the Soviet Union. Both sides developed hydrogen bombs (H-bombs) and ICBMs (Intercontinental Ballistic Missiles), which could reach the opposing country. The international tension created by the Cold War and the **arms race** brought the world to the brink of a nuclear war.

The **arms race** refers to the competition between the USA and the USSR (Soviet Russia) to develop more powerful armaments to maintain superiority over the other side.

The Space Race

The USA and the Soviet Union competed in the **Space Race** – they both wanted to be the first nations to launch satellites and people into space, and to get the first person on the Moon (see Ch. 24).

Conflicts during the Cold War

The international tension created by the Cold War led to **local conflicts** which brought the world to the brink of a **world war**. In these local conflicts, the USA and the USSR supported opposing sides.

THE COLD WAR

The Berlin Blockade 1948–49

1. After World War II, **Germany** was divided into **four zones** and **Berlin** was divided into **four sectors**. These were controlled by the USA, Britain and France on one side, and the Soviet Union on the other.
2. The **USA** wanted to revive the German economy. They wanted a strong democratic government.
3. The **Soviet Union** disagreed and took **reparations** (damages, compensation) from their part of Germany.
4. **President Truman** of the USA wanted to use **Marshall Plan** funds to revive the German economy. The USA and their Allies launched a **new currency** – the **Deutschmark**.
5. **Stalin**, leader of communist Russia, organised a blockade – he cut off all road, rail and canal links to West Berlin in June 1948.

The Berlin airlift

- Berlin suffered because there were shortages, so rationing (limiting the amount given to people) was used.
- Industry suffered, and 120,000 people lost their jobs.
- The USA and its allies organised Operation Vittles – an airlift to fly supplies into Berlin.
- Large cargo planes used **three air corridors** to fly into three airports in West Berlin.
- At the peak, they were flying in every 90 seconds with 8,000 tons of goods a day.
- The goods included food, medical supplies, petrol and coal.

- The **spirit of the people** in West Berlin was kept up by huge public meetings.
- Stalin realised that he was not going to win – he wanted Truman to drop the currency or leave Berlin. Stalin lifted the Blockade.

How was the Berlin Blockade important in international relations?
- The USA won the **first victory** in the Cold War battle with the Soviet Union.
- After the Blockade was lifted, **NATO (North Atlantic Treaty Organisation)** was formed to defend its members against potential (possible) Soviet attacks. It included the USA, Canada and 10 Western European countries.
- In response, Stalin and the Soviet Union created the **Warsaw Pact**, a defence treaty between the Soviet Union and seven countries in Eastern Europe (1955). The major countries were now divided into **two armed groups**.
- Berlin remained a **source of tension** during the Cold War, especially as East Germans left their side to get work in the more prosperous West. Eventually the Soviet and East German governments built the **Berlin Wall** (1961), which became a **symbol** of the conflict between **'East'** (the Soviet Union and its allies) and **'West'** (the USA and its allies). Germany remained **divided** until the Cold War ended in 1990.

The Korean War 1950–53

1. After World War II, **Korea** was divided along the **38th parallel**.
   - **North Korea** was a **communist** country, supported by the Soviet Union.
   - **South Korea** was a **capitalist** country, supported by the USA.
2. In 1950, North Korea **invaded** South Korea.
   - The North Korean army took over most of the country, almost as far south as **Busan**.
3. President **Truman** of the USA moved to help South Korea. He believed in a **policy of containment** to stop the spread of communism.
4. The **United Nations** organised armies from the USA and 15 other countries to help the South Koreans.
   - The UN forces, led by **Douglas MacArthur**, pushed the North Koreans back.
5. The communist government in China, led by **Mao Zedong**, then joined the war, backing North Korea.
   - They drove the UN forces down south.

Korea after World War II

The **policy of containment** was the plan of the USA to prevent the spread of communism after World War II.

THE COLD WAR

6. Truman fired MacArthur because MacArthur wanted to attack China; he also proposed using the atomic bomb.
7. The war dragged on until 1953. By this time, Truman had been replaced as president by **Eisenhower**, and Stalin had been replaced by **Khrushchev**.
   - **Peace** was agreed and both sides held onto **a border similar to the pre-war border,** on or close to the 38th parallel.
   - There were 54,000 American soldiers killed, 400,000 South Koreans, about half a million North Koreans and between 200,000 and 500,000 Chinese.

How was the Korean War important in international relations?
- The **United Nations** had played an important role in supporting South Korea.
- America got a **new ally** in Japan, which helped out by supplying materials for the war.
- The **USA made alliances** with other countries in Asia in order to **contain communism** in China.

The Cuban Missile Crisis 1962
1. Fidel **Castro**, a communist leader, overthrew **Batista**, the dictator of Cuba.
   - Castro **nationalised** (took under government ownership) American businesses and the US refused to buy **sugar** from Cuba.
   - Cuba got help from the Soviet Union, led by **Khrushchev**.
2. **President Kennedy** of the USA gave the go-ahead for the **Bay of Pigs** invasion, which failed to overthrow Castro.
3. Then a **U2 spy plane** photographed Soviet missile bases being built in Cuba.
   - These bases would bring major **US cities** such as Washington DC and New York City within the range of Soviet nuclear missiles.
4. Kennedy decided to **blockade** (cut off supplies from) Cuba until the missiles were removed.
   - The world was on the brink of **nuclear war**.
5. Then the USA and the Soviet Union came to an **agreement**.
   - **Khrushchev** said he would **dismantle** the missiles in Cuba if the USA promised not to invade the island.
   - **Kennedy** accepted this.

How was the Cuban Missile Crisis important in international relations?
- Both sides agreed that they would **never risk** a nuclear war again.
- A **telephone hotline** was set up between **Washington** and **Moscow** so that both leaders would be in **direct communication**.

- The USA and the Soviet Union agreed to sign a **Nuclear Test Ban Treaty** which stopped above-ground nuclear tests.
- The USA **dismantled missiles** which it had in Turkey.

The Vietnam War

The Vietnam War was another example of a **local conflict** affected by the **Cold War**. The **USA** became involved in Vietnam because of the **policy of containment**. North Vietnam, a communist country, was helped by the Soviet Union and China. It attacked South Vietnam, which was helped by the USA (see Ch. 24).
- The USA was **criticised** in many countries for its involvement in the war.
- The Vietnam War resulted in a **defeat** for the USA and the policy of containment.

The Collapse of Communism in the Soviet Union and the End of the Cold War

1. The Cold War led to the collapse of communism in the Soviet Union.
2. The **Soviet economy** could not afford to maintain the huge spending on the **arms race** and the **Space Race**.
3. A new leader of the Soviet Union, **Gorbachev**, promised that the Soviet Union would **not support** communist governments in Eastern Europe.
    - This led to the **collapse of communism** in those countries.
    - The **Berlin Wall** was demolished.
    - West and East Germany were **united** in **one country**.
4. **Communism in the Soviet Union** collapsed, and the country broke up into independent republics.
5. **The Cold War was over.**
    - Many Eastern European countries now joined countries in Western Europe as part of an **enlarged European Union** (see Ch. 27).

Mikhail Gorbachev

THE COLD WAR

Sample Question

The image on the right shows the cover of an American comic-book published in 1960. This was a time during the Cold War when many Americans feared that the spread of communism around the world would threaten their freedom and their way of life.

1. State which country you think is represented by:
   (i) The iceberg: *Soviet Union (USSR)*
   (ii) The boat: *USA*
   What are the reasons for your answers to (i) and (ii) above?

(i) The symbol on the iceberg is the hammer and sickle of the Soviet Union. Also the colour is red, which is a symbol for revolution.
(ii) The letters 'USA' are printed on the side of the boat. Uncle Sam, who represents the USA, is sitting on the boat. The colours of red, white and blue represent the USA flag.

2. The various countries named on tombstones were communist countries in 1960. Why do you think the cartoonist uses the image of tombstones to represent them?

The cartoonist uses tombstones because they represent dead countries under the control of communism and the Soviet Union.

3. What message do you think the cartoonist is trying to get across about the Cold War?

The message of the cartoonist is that the USA is in danger of crashing into the communist iceberg and this could lead to the collapse or sinking of the USA, or maybe to a world war.

Sample 15 NCCA Junior Cycle History Assessment Items, www.curriculum.ie

Revision Questions
Scan the QR code for more revision questions.

23 The Changing Experience of Women in 20th-Century Ireland

After studying this chapter, you should be able to:
- Explain how the experience of women changed in 20th-century Ireland.

Women at Work

The early 20th century

Key Words
domestic servants
marriage bar
Irish Women's Liberation Movement
Contraceptive Train
Irish Women's Franchise League
Cumann na mBan

1. At the start of the 20th century, women were seen as **second-class citizens**:
   - They could **not vote**.
   - Their education was **limited**.
   - They were expected to **marry** and have children.
   - When married, they were largely **dependent** on their husbands.
   - Women in rural areas often did **farm work**.
2. Single women often became **domestic servants**. By 1911, **one in three** working women were servants.
3. After the Irish Free State was established in 1922, the situation for women in the south of Ireland remained largely unchanged for the next 40 years.
4. In **1926**, the average pay for women was only **70%** of a man's pay. This meant trade unions often worked to **protect male employees** from cheaper female competition.
5. The proportion of women emigrating was significantly **higher** than men – **1,298 women emigrated for every 1,000 men**.
6. A '**marriage bar**' was brought in in 1932. This meant women working in the civil service had to give up their jobs when they got married.
7. **Contraceptives were banned** in 1935. This meant many women were often left caring for large families at home.
8. The **1937 Constitution** recognised a woman's special role 'within the home'. It also **banned divorce**.
9. By **1958**, the ban on married primary school teachers had been lifted.

The 1960s onwards

1. The **Irish Women's Liberation Movement (IWLM)** was founded in Dublin in 1970.
   - It drew inspiration from people like **Betty Friedan**, who wrote *The Feminine Mystique*, demanding more from life than 'marriage, motherhood and homemaking'.
   - The IWLM published *Chains or Change* in 1971. This was a critical analysis of the position of women in Irish society at the time.

Members of the IWLM about to board the Contraceptive Train

   - The Movement got a lot of publicity following appearances on the *Late Late Show* and because of the **Contraceptive Train** to Belfast. This was when members of the IWLM travelled to Belfast by train to buy contraceptives in protest against the law prohibiting their sale in the Republic.
2. The **Commission for the Status of Women** issued a report in 1972, encouraging the elimination of all forms of inequality.
3. This report led to the **marriage bar being lifted**. It also contributed to laws that required **equal pay for equal work**.
4. Ireland joined the EU in **1973**. They often forced the introduction of equality laws.
5. The **Social Welfare Act 1973** provided **social welfare allowances** for single mothers. They were given **£8 per week** and £2 per week extra for each additional child.
6. In 1974, the **Anti-Discrimination (Pay) Act** was introduced.
7. The **Employment Equality Act 1977** outlawed discrimination on the basis of sex or marital status.
8. In 1979, contraceptives were allowed for married couples over 18.
9. By 1999, **51.2%** of women were employed outside of the home.
10. In 2000, the **Equal Status Act** prohibited gender-based discrimination, along with other forms of discrimination such as race, marital status and religion.

Women and Education

The early 20th century

1. Women's role in education was **limited**.
2. More girls continued their education in **convent secondary schools**, but the number of women in colleges remained small – about **300 women to more than 3,000 men**.
3. This did not change significantly until the 1960s.

The 1960s onwards

1. Since the introduction of free second-level education in 1967, 'girls have demonstrated consistently higher rates of school completion. Boys account for almost two-thirds of the pupils who leave second-level education before the Leaving Certificate'. (**www.education.ie**)
2. There are still issues, but 'boys far outnumber girls in the take-up of "practical subjects," such as engineering, technical drawing, and construction studies and girls far outnumber boys in home economics, music, art and European languages'. (**www.education.ie**)

Women and Politics

The early 20th century

1. At the start of the 20th century, women **could not vote** or be elected to parliament.
2. Hanna Sheehy-Skeffington founded the **Irish Women's Franchise (voting) League** in 1908 to campaign for the vote.
3. **Redmond** (Home Rule leader) and **Carson** (unionist leader) **opposed** votes for women.
4. They worried female suffrage would be a **distraction**. The unionists, though, committed themselves to giving votes to women if they set up a Provisional Government.
5. During World War I, many women got jobs in factories, offices, banks and hospitals.
6. As Ireland was part of the UK at that time, Irishwomen **over the age of 30** voted for the first time in 1918 due to the role they played in World War I.
7. Irish women were also involved in the independence movement.
8. **Cumann na mBan** was founded in 1914 'to assist in arming and equipping a body of Irishmen for the defense of Ireland'.
9. In the Irish Free State, women **over the age of 21** got the vote in 1922, but Ireland remained conservative until the 1960s.

Countess Markievicz
- **Countess Markievicz** was the most famous member of **Cumann na mBan**.
- She was also active in the **Irish Citizen Army** and **Sinn Féin**.
- She was second-in-command in the **College of Surgeons** during the 1916 Rising.
- She was sentenced to death but not executed because she was a woman.
- She was not happy about this: 'I do wish your lot had the decency to shoot me!'
- She was the first woman **elected to Westminster**, but she refused to take her seat (**absenteeism**).
- Markievicz was also the **first female TD**.

10. Many thought that 'a woman's place was in the home'. This belief was reflected in most Western countries at the time.
11. Following the **1927 Juries Act**, women were not eligible for jury service unless they applied.
12. In 1951, a healthcare scheme which proposed free healthcare for mothers and their children, called the **Mother and Child Scheme**, was proposed but never introduced. It was so controversial that the Minister for Health, **Dr Noël Browne**, resigned.

The 1960s onwards

1. More women became involved in **politics in the south of Ireland**.
   - **Máire Geoghegan-Quinn** was Minister for Justice.
   - **Gemma Hussey** was Minister for Education.
   - **Mary Harney** was the first leader of a political party in the South (Progressive Democrats) and the first female Tánaiste.
   - **Mary Robinson** became Ireland's first female president in 1990.
2. Women also took an active role in **Northern Irish politics**.
   - **Angela McCrystal** was involved in the **Homeless Citizens League**, highlighting discrimination in housing against Catholics.
   - **Patricia McCluskey** and **Brid Rodgers** were involved in the **Campaign for Social Justice**, which campaigned for civil rights in Northern Ireland. Both were also involved in the **Northern Ireland Civil Rights Association (NICRA)** with **Bernadette Devlin**.
   - Devlin was one of the leaders of the **People's Democracy March** from Belfast to Derry (1969), which was attacked by loyalist groups. Devlin was also **elected as an MP** at 21.
   - **Dolours and Marian Price** were imprisoned for the bombing of the Old Bailey that injured 200 people.
   - **Mairéad Corrigan** and **Betty Williams** founded the **Community for Peace People**, for which they won the **Nobel Peace Prize** in 1976.
   - **Anne Dickson** became the first female leader of a major political party in 1976, when she became the leader of the **Unionist Party of Northern Ireland**.

Mairéad Corrigan and Betty Williams

Sample Question

What changes have occurred in the experience of women in 20th-century Ireland?

There were many changes in the experience of women in 20th-century Ireland. In 1932, A 'marriage bar' was introduced. This meant women working in the civil service had to give up their jobs when they got married.

The Commission for the Status of Women issued a report in 1972, encouraging the elimination of all forms of inequality. This report led to the marriage bar being lifted. It also contributed to laws that required equal pay for equal work.

Contraceptives were banned in 1935. This meant many women were often left caring for large families at home. In 1979, contraceptives were allowed for married couples over 18.

At the start of the 20th century, women could not vote or be elected to parliament. As Ireland was part of the UK at that time, Irishwomen over the age of 30 voted for the first time in 1918 due to the role they played in World War I. In the Irish Free State, women over the age of 21 got the vote in 1922.

Revision Questions

Scan the QR code for more revision questions.

24 The 1960s – An Important Decade in World History

After studying this chapter, you should be able to:
- Debate the idea that the 1960s was an important decade in European and world history
- Examine the role of key personalities, issues and events.

Key Words

decade
personality
issues
events
Cold War
international relations
nuclear war
assassination
Space Race
Vietnam War
civil rights
passive resistance
decolonisation
Women's Liberation Movement
discrimination
youth culture
counterculture
vernacular
modernised

Timeline of the 1960s in European and World History

1960	Independence for many African and Asian countries
1961	Yuri Gagarin (Soviet Union), first man in space
1962	The **Cuban Missile Crisis**
	Vatican II began
1963	*The Feminine Mystique* published
	Martin Luther King's 'I Have a Dream' speech
1964	**Civil Rights Act (USA)**
1965	US ground troops in Vietnam
	Voting Rights Act (USA)
1968	Student revolt in Paris
1969	**First moon landing**

Why Was the 1960s an Important Decade in European and World History?

The 1960s was an important **decade** (10 years) in **European and world history** because of the role of relevant **personalities** (prominent people), **issues** (problems, concerns) and **events** (incidents, happenings), which had a huge **impact** (effect) on the lives of people.

Key personalities	Key issues	Key events
• **President John F. Kennedy** • **Martin Luther King** • **Muhammad Ali** • **Betty Friedan** • **Elvis Presley** • **Pope John XXIII**	• Cold War • Civil Rights • Women's rights • Decolonisation • Space Race • Modernisation	• Cuban Missile Crisis • Vietnam War • Vatican II • Civil rights marches • Landing on the Moon • Youth demonstrations • Independence for African and Asian countries

The Cold War

The **Cold War** was a battle for **world dominance** between the two **superpowers**, the USA and Soviet Russia, which resulted in a time of hostility and tension in **international relations**, without actual fighting between the two (see Ch. 22).

Key events of the Cold War in the 1960s

- The building of the Berlin Wall
- The Cuban Missile Crisis
- The Space Race
- The Vietnam War

Why was the Cold War important?

- It brought the world to the brink of a **nuclear war** (a war using atomic and hydrogen bombs), especially during the **Cuban Missile Crisis** (see page 143).
- It forced **other countries** to support either the USA or the Soviet Union.
- It resulted in **spending enormous sums of money** on military equipment.

President John F. Kennedy
- Elected president in 1960
- Committed USA to land men on the Moon in the 1960s
- Led the USA during the Cuban Missile Crisis
- Sent US special advisers to Vietnam to train local South Vietnamese Army
- **Assassinated** (murdered) in 1963

An **assassination** is the murder of political leaders for political reasons.

The Cuban Missile Crisis

Key events of the Cuban Missile Crisis

1. **Castro**, the Cuban communist leader, gave permission to the **Soviet Union** to construct **missile sites** in the country.
2. A US **U2 spy plane** photographed the missile sites being constructed.
3. The USA, led by **President Kennedy**, **blockaded** Cuba until the missile sites were removed.
4. The Soviet Union **agreed** to remove the missile sites.

Why was the Cuban Missile Crisis important?

- The Cuban Missile Crisis brought the world to the **brink of a nuclear war**.
- The USA and the Soviet Union agreed to **a telephone hotline** between Washington and Moscow to reduce the danger of a nuclear war.

- The USA and the Soviet Union also agreed to a **Nuclear Test Ban Treaty** which stopped **above-ground nuclear tests**.

A **nuclear war** is a war using atomic and hydrogen bombs, which would cause massive destruction and loss of life.

The Space Race

The Space Race was part of the Cold War. It was a race between the USA and the Soviet Union to land the first people on the Moon, and to return them safely to earth.

Key events of the Space Race in the 1960s

1. The USSR (Soviet Union) sent the **first man**, **Yuri Gagarin**, into space.
2. **President Kennedy** made his **speech**, which committed (promised) that the USA would land the first people on the Moon by the end of the 1960s.
3. The Soviet Union sent the **first woman**, **Valentina Tereshkova**, into space.
4. The USA sent **Apollo 11** to the Moon, and **Neil Armstrong** and **Buzz Aldrin** were the first people to land on the Moon.

What was the importance of the Space Race?

- The USA **won** the Space Race. It was a victory for **US technology** to get the first people on the Moon.
- The USA and the USSR (Soviet Union) invested **enormous sums of money** in **space exploration**.
- The **technology** developed for space exploration **benefited other areas** of life, e.g. CAT and MRI scanners for hospitals, freeze-dried food.

The Vietnam War

The Vietnam War was a war between communist North Vietnam, supported by communist guerrilla groups called the **Viet Cong**, against South Vietnam, supported by the **USA**.

Key events of the Vietnam War in the 1960s

1. **President Kennedy** increased help to South Vietnam.
2. As a result of the **Gulf of Tonkin incident** when US claimed North Vietnamese boats attacked US ships, **President Johnson** increased **US direct involvement** in the Vietnam War.
3. There was a **huge increase** in US troops in Vietnam in 1965.
4. There were huge **anti-war demonstrations** in the USA in 1967 and later years.

5. In the **Tet Offensive** in 1968, North Vietnamese troops and Viet Cong guerrillas attacked many areas of South Vietnam.
6. **Nixon** was elected president of the USA and he promised to end the Vietnam War.
7. The USA **left Vietnam** in 1973.

Why was the Vietnam War important?
- The Vietnam War showed up the **deep divisions** in US society.
- The Vietnam War resulted in almost **60,000 US deaths**, and many hundreds of thousands of North Vietnamese and South Vietnamese deaths.
- The **US military technology** failed to defeat a **guerrilla campaign** supported by the people.
- The **US policy of containment failed** because communist North Vietnam took over South Vietnam.

Muhammad Ali
- Heavyweight boxing champion of the world
- Converted to Islam and changed his name from Cassius Clay to Mohammad Ali
- Refused to serve in the Vietnam War
- Promoted civil rights for Black Americans

Civil Rights in the USA

The **civil rights** campaign in the USA was a campaign to win **equal rights for Black Americans** and other minority groups. It achieved key victories in the 1960s under the leadership of **Martin Luther King**.

Key events of the civil rights campaign in the USA in the 1960s

1. In 1963, **Martin Luther King** made his 'I Have a Dream' speech as part of the **March on Washington**.
2. The **Civil Rights Act** of 1964 outlawed discrimination based on race, colour, religion, sex or national origin.
3. Martin Luther King led the **Selma to Montgomery march**.
4. The **Voting Rights Act** of 1965 banned efforts to impose voting restrictions (controls) on Black Americans.
5. The **assassination** of Martin Luther King (1968) led to **riots** in US cities.

Martin Luther King
- Baptist minister
- Rose to fame over leadership of Montgomery Bus Boycott, where Black Americans protested their treatment on public buses
- Believed in **passive resistance** (peaceful, non-violent protest) to achieve civil rights for Black Americans
- Made the famous **'I Have a Dream'** speech in Washington
- Achieved Civil Rights Act (1964) and Voting Rights Act (1965)

Why was the civil rights campaign in the USA important?

- Martin Luther King showed that a campaign of **passive resistance** could win support for civil rights.
- It showed that **racism** was widespread in the southern states of the USA.
- It showed how the **deep divisions** in the USA were over race.
- It inspired other campaigns such as the **women's liberation movement**, and the **civil rights campaign** in Northern Ireland (see Ch. 26).

Decolonisation in Africa and Asia

Decolonisation was the process whereby the European countries that had large empires in Africa and Asia withdrew from those colonies, which got their independence. In Africa alone, 32 countries got their independence in the 1960s.

Key events of decolonisation in the 1960s

1. The **European empires** of Britain, France and Germany were weakened by World War II.
2. After World War II, the USA and the Soviet Union were **opposed** to maintaining the European empires.
3. Most of the African and Asian countries were **decolonised** after World War II – the largest number of Asian countries achieved independence in the 1940s; the majority of African countries achieved independence in the 1960s.

African and Asian countries achieving independence			
Decade	Number of Asian countries	Number of African countries	Total
1940s	11	1	12
1950s	4	8	12
1960s	7	32	39
After 1960s	7	10	17

Why was decolonisation in Africa and Asia important?

- Many countries in Africa and Asia got their **independence** – 39 in the 1960s.
- Some countries, particularly in Africa, were divided by **civil wars** after independence, e.g. Democratic Republic of the Congo.
- Many native people **emigrated** to Britain and France from their former colonies, e.g. from India and Pakistan to Britain.

The Women's Liberation Movement

The **Women's Liberation Movement** began in the 1960s in the USA to overcome discrimination against women, to achieve equal rights and opportunities for women.

Key events of the Women's Liberation Movement

1. Prior to the 1960s, **a woman's place** was seen as being in the home, as a mother and housekeeper. Women were treated as second-class citizens.
2. In 1963, **Betty Friedan** published *The Feminine Mystique*, which criticised the traditional role of women. She said suburban women were **bored and lacked fulfilment** (achievement, satisfaction) in life.
3. Friedan was one of the founders of the **National Organisation for Women** (NOW), to end discrimination against women in pay and job opportunities.
4. The women's movement objected to the **Miss America pageant** in 1968.
5. It demanded **changes** in relation to maternity leave, childcare centres, equal education and equal pay and job opportunities.

Why was the Women's Liberation Movement important?

- The **women's movement** spread from the USA to many countries, including Ireland. It had great success in **changing laws and ideas** which discriminated against women.
- **Laws** in relation to equal pay and opportunities, discrimination against women, maternity leave, contraception, abortion and marriage were changed in many countries, especially in North America and Europe.
- **Women's role in history** was re-examined, and women's studies courses were taught in universities.

Betty Friedan
- Wrote **The Feminine Mystique** in 1963
- She said women were dependent on their husbands, and that they were frustrated
- She said women should be given a chance to develop their talents
- She founded the **National Organisation for Women** (NOW)
- She campaigned to achieve equal opportunities for women

Youth Culture and Revolution

In the late 1950s and especially in the 1960s, a **youth culture** developed which created a gap between youth and adults, called the **generation gap**. Youth culture differed from

THE 1960S – AN IMPORTANT DECADE IN WORLD HISTORY

the traditional values of adult culture. There were differences in music, clothes, hair style and general behaviour.

Key events of youth culture

1. In the USA, **Elvis Presley** led a rock 'n' roll revolution, which influenced lifestyles and fashion, and contributed to the generation gap between youth and adult life.
2. The **hippies** were part of the **counterculture** (cultural movement opposed to the establishment) of the 1960s. They believed in communal living, experimented with recreational drugs and followed different music.
3. In Britain, the **Beatles** and **Rolling Stones** were leaders in the new music.
4. The **Mods** and the **Rockers** each had their own style of clothes, hair, music, places to hang out.
   - There were **clashes** between the two groups.
5. **Middle-class youths** benefited from university education. They criticised aspects of current society – the Cold War, the nuclear arms race and the Vietnam War.
6. In 1968, they staged many **demonstrations** in the USA and France against the running of the government and education in their universities.

Elvis Presley
- US rock 'n' roll star
- Became popular in the late 1950s
- He had huge hits in the 1960s: 'It's Now or Never', 'Are You Lonesome Tonight?'
- Starred in 27 movies in the 1960s

Why was youth culture and revolution important?

- It highlighted **differences** between younger people and adults.
- It created a **new market** for clothes and music.
- Youth culture influenced **future ideas** on fashion.
- It created a **sexual revolution** of more widespread premarital sex, aided by the introduction of the contraceptive pill in 1960.

Vatican II

Vatican II was a council meeting of the **cardinals of the Catholic Church** to reform the teachings and organisation of the Church. It was called by **Pope John XXIII**, and was held between 1962 and 1965.

Pope John XXIII
- He organised a Council of the Catholic Church, Vatican II
- He died during the Council, but the Council led to important changes in the Catholic Church

Key events of Vatican II

1. The Council agreed that there would be **greater lay participation** in the running of the Catholic Church.
2. The **Mass** was now said in the language of the people (vernacular), rather than in Latin.
3. The Catholic Church **improved relations** with other Christian churches, and with Jews.
4. Pope John XXIII died during the Council. He was succeeded by **Pope Paul VI**.

Why was Vatican II important?

- Vatican II made changes so that the Catholic Church would be modernised (updated, reformed).
- It gave a **greater role** to the laity in the church.
- It opened the Catholic Church to more **Third World influences**.

Sample Question

1. You studied the 1960s as an important decade in Irish, European and/or world history. Give the name of **one** personality, issue **or** event you studied from the 1960s.

   Martin Luther King

2. Briefly, why is this personality, issue or event considered **historically significant**?

   Martin Luther King is historically significant because his campaigns led to improvements in the conditions of Black Americans who were discriminated in the USA in the 1960s. He made a famous speech, 'I Have a Dream', which inspired many people. He led protests by Black Americans which caused the passing of the Civil Rights Act (1964). This act outlawed discrimination based on race, colour, religion, sex or national origin. He also led the Selma to Montgomery march. This contributed to the passing of the Voting Rights Act (1965), which banned efforts to impose voting restrictions (controls) on Black Americans. His assassination in 1968 led to riots in many American cities.

Revision Questions

Scan the QR code for more revision questions.

25 The 1960s – An Important Decade in Irish History

After studying this chapter, you should be able to:
- Debate the idea that the 1960s was an important decade on the island of Ireland
- Identify important people, issues and events from 1960s Ireland.

This learning outcome mentions the 'island of Ireland', which means the Republic of Ireland and Northern Ireland.

Key Words
protectionism
emigration
First Programme for Economic Expansion
community and comprehensive schools
Swinging Sixties
Vatican II
lay participation
ecumenism
unionists
nationalists
gerrymandering
Northern Ireland Civil Rights Association (NICRA)
'One man, one vote'
discrimination
Battle of the Bogside
Troubles

An Overview of the 1960s on the Island of Ireland

The 1960s in Ireland were characterised by certain personalities, issues and events.

Key people	Key issues	Key events
• Seán Lemass • Jack Lynch • Seán Ó Riada • Donogh O'Malley • T.K. Whitaker • Terence O'Neill • Ian Paisley • Gay Byrne	• **New economic policies**, like the **First Programme for Economic Expansion**, were introduced to tackle the unemployment and emigration of the 1950s. • Economic changes led to important **social changes**, such as the opening of shopping centres and the growth of the tourism industry. • Entertainment changed with the **ballad boom** and **revival of traditional Irish music**. • The **civil rights campaign** in Northern Ireland.	• **Teilifís Éireann** (RTÉ) was established. The emergence of TV led to a decline in cinema. • **Free second-level education** was introduced. • **Vatican II** took place. • **JFK** visited Ireland. • The **NICRA** was set up. • Lemass and O'Neill met. This was the **first official meeting** between the leaders of the two states since partition.

What Important Economic Changes Occurred in the 1960s?

1. There was **high unemployment** and **high emigration** in Ireland in the 1950s and the **population fell**.
2. Government policy focused on **protecting home industry** by **taxing imports** (**protectionism**).
3. **Emigration** averaged **40,000** a year. Workers' **income fell** and there were fewer people working.
4. **Seán Lemass** became **Taoiseach** in 1959. He promised **economic reform** and introduced the **First Programme for Economic Expansion**, which was created by **T.K. Whitaker**.
   - Whitaker encouraged **exports**.
   - The Programme also gave **tax concessions** and **grants** to **attract foreign industry** to set up factories in Ireland.
5. This brought British and American companies to Ireland.
6. **Employment rose** and **emigration fell**. Ireland's **population began to increase** from 1961 onwards. The population of the Republic of Ireland increased from **2.8 million** in 1961 to **2.9 million** in 1971.
7. People were **better off** and the **standard of living rose**.

What Important Changes Happened in Education in the 1960s?

Education changes in the 1960s

1. The first **community and comprehensive schools** were built. These combined academic subjects of secondary schools and practical subjects of vocational schools.
2. This gave many children the opportunity to **escape poverty**.
3. The Minister for Education, **Donogh O'Malley**, introduced free **secondary education** and **free transport** in 1969.
4. The numbers attending secondary school **increased** rapidly.
5. At the time, fewer than 50% of children were still in school at the age of 15. Now, more than **90%** of the population completes the Leaving Certificate.

THE 1960S – AN IMPORTANT DECADE IN IRISH HISTORY

What Important Social Changes Occurred?

During the '**Swinging Sixties**', people were better off, which changed the way they lived. **Shopping centres** were built. They encouraged weekly rather than daily shopping and **undermined** local grocery shops.

More **tourists** came to Ireland and more Irish people holidayed abroad.

In the 1960s, the Catholic Church was a hugely influential power in Irish life. For example, the Mother and Child Scheme from page 149 failed in part due to opposition from the Church. The Catholic Church brought in many reforms after **Vatican II**.

- The **Latin Mass** was now said in **English** or **Irish**.
- The priest now **faced the people**.
- There was greater **lay participation** (non-members of the clergy who participate in the Church).
- Relations with other religions were improved (**ecumenism**).

Teilifís Éireann (RTÉ) started broadcasting in **1961**.

The Late Late Show, presented by **Gay Byrne**, and *7 Days* openly discussed many controversial topics for the first time.

When **John F. Kennedy** visited Ireland in 1963, he said *'you have modernised your economy … diversified your industry … and improved the living standards of your people'.* JFK's visit was significant because he was **American's first president** of Irish Catholic descent.

What Important Changes Occurred in Entertainment in the 1960s?

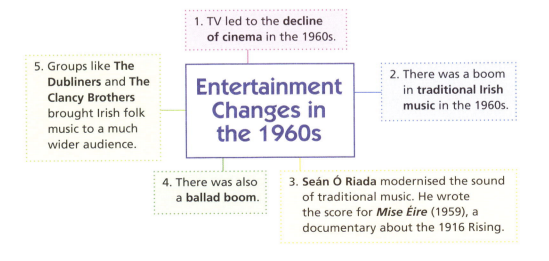

What Important Changes Occurred in Northern Ireland?

1. **Terence O'Neill** took over as **prime minister** of Northern Ireland in 1963. His main goals were *'to make Northern Ireland economically stronger and prosperous ... and to **build bridges** between the two traditions in our community'*.
2. **Traditional industries** like shipbuilding and linen were in serious **decline**. The O'Neill government attracted **new industries** to the North, e.g. **Ford**, **Goodyear** and **Imperial Chemicals**. But they were mostly located in the **Protestant**, **eastern part of Ulster**.
3. O'Neill tried to **improve relations** with Catholics. This is significant because he took over from a prime minister who *'never crossed the border (with the South), never visited a Catholic school, and never received or sought a civic reception from a Catholic town'*.
    - O'Neill **met the Catholic Cardinal Conway**, Archbishop of Armagh.
    - He **visited Catholic schools**.
    - However, he also allowed a new university to be built in **Coleraine**, a mainly Protestant town, rather than in the larger, mainly Catholic **Derry/Londonderry**.

> **exam focus**
> For more on the Troubles, see Chapter 26.

Why Were the 1960s Important for North-South relations?

Seán Lemass met Terence O'Neill in Belfast and Dublin in **1965**. This was the **first official meeting** between the leaders of the two states **since partition** in 1920. Relations between North and South worsened towards the end of the 1960s as the Troubles began (see Ch. 26).

Why were the 1960s important for relations between nationalists and unionists in Northern Ireland?

1. Throughout the 1960s, **tensions** began to grow in Northern Ireland.
2. More extreme unionists were worried about O'Neill's efforts to improve relations with Catholics. They formed the UVF (Ulster Volunteer Force) in 1966.
3. **Rev. Ian Paisley**, leader of the **Free Presbyterian Church**, was very **critical** of O'Neill's efforts to improve relations.
4. Catholics/nationalists in Northern Ireland faced many different types of discrimination:

- Only **property owners** could vote in local elections – this **favoured Protestants**.
- Gerrymandering, the manipulation of constituency boundaries, was used to ensure unionists **controlled councils** in nationalist areas.
- The allocation of jobs in the **civil service** and **local councils** favoured Protestants.
- **Housing allocation** by local councils favoured Protestants.

5. This discrimination led to the formation of the Northern Ireland Civil Rights Association (NICRA) in 1967.
6. They demanded:
    - 'One man, one vote' in local elections.
    - An end to **gerrymandering**.
    - An end to discrimination in housing and jobs.
7. There were marches and rioting in Belfast and Derry. In October 1968, a civil rights march in Derry was stopped by the **RUC** (police). TV cameras captured the **brutal treatment** of civil rights leaders by the police.
8. The British government forced O'Neill and his government to bring in reforms in housing and local elections, but this did not stop the demonstrations.
9. O'Neill faced **opposition** from extreme unionists (**Paisley**) who demanded that he should not give in to Catholics.
10. O'Neill was forced to **resign** in 1969 when he lost the support of his own party.
11. Conflict between nationalists and unionists continued to worsen with the Battle of the Bogside and the Troubles, which broke out in 1969 (see Ch. 26).

Important Leaders from Ireland, North and South, during the 1960s

	Seán Lemass	Terence O'Neill
Background	• Involved in the 1916 Rising, War of Independence and Civil War • **Minister for Industry and Commerce** in the 1930s • Minister for Supplies during World War II • Elected as **Taoiseach** when Éamon de Valera was elected president of Ireland in **1959**	• Became **prime minister of Northern Ireland** in **1963**
Career highlights	• Introduced the **First Programme for Economic Expansion** (1958–63), which was very successful • Met **Terence O'Neill**, prime minister of Northern Ireland, on two occasions in 1965	• **Attracted foreign industry** to Northern Ireland, e.g. **Ford** • Worked to **improve relations** with Catholics/nationalists; he met Cardinal Conway and visited Catholic schools • **Met Taoiseach Seán Lemass** in 1965 and **Jack Lynch** in 1967
Opposition/ career lows	• The **Second Programme for Economic Expansion** was introduced in 1963 and was not as successful	• Opposed by **extreme unionists**, led by **Rev. Ian Paisley** • Approved the creation of a new university in **Coleraine**, rather than Derry/Londonderry • **Disappointed Catholics** due to the lack of reforms introduced • Tensions between Catholics/nationalists and Protestants/unionists continued to grow throughout the 1960s, ultimately leading to the outbreak of **the Troubles** in 1969
End of career	• Lemass **resigned** as Taoiseach in **1966**, 50 years after he took part in the 1916 Rising	• **Forced to resigned** as prime minister in **1969** when he lost support from his own party due to his handling of the civil rights movement in Northern Ireland

Exam Question

(e) You studied the 1960s as an important decade in Irish, European and/or world history. Give the name of one personality, issue or event you studied from the 1960s.

The outbreak of the Troubles

(f) Briefly, why is this personality, issue or event considered historically significant?

The Troubles were a 30-year-long period of violence in Northern Ireland that broke out in 1969. About 3,500 people were killed in Northern Ireland during the Troubles. More than 42,000 people were injured.

(g) Suggest three examples of objects, documents and /or other presentation methods you would use to set up a museum exhibition about this personality, issue or event from the 1960s. Justify each choice.

Object: *Footage from the October 1968 civil rights march*
Justification: *In October 1968, a civil rights march in Derry was stopped by the RUC (police). TV cameras captured the brutal treatment of civil rights leaders by the police. This footage would show just how badly civil rights protesters were treated.*

Object: *'One man, one vote' poster*
Justification: *The Northern Ireland Civil Rights Association (NICRA) was set up in 1967 in response to the discrimination that many Catholics in NI faced. They campaigned for 'one man, one vote' in local elections.*

Object: *Gerrymandering diagram*
Justification: *Gerrymandering refers to the manipulation of constituency boundaries and was used to ensure unionists controlled councils in nationalist areas. The NICRA campaigned for an end to gerrymandering. A diagram could be used to help people understand or visualise what this was.*

Junior Cycle History Exam 2022, Q8

Revision Questions

Scan the QR code for more revision questions.

26 The Troubles in Northern Ireland

After studying this chapter, you should be able to:
- Identify the causes, course and consequences of the Northern Ireland Troubles
- Identify the impact of the Northern Ireland Troubles on North-South relations
- Identify the impact of the Northern Ireland Troubles on Anglo-Irish relations.

Key Words
causes
identities
nationalists
parliamentary means
physical force tradition
unionists
border
partition
sectarianism
gerrymandering
discrimination
Royal Ulster Constabulary (RUC)
loyalists
paramilitary organisations
internment
direct rule
political prisoner
decommissioning arms
consequences
North-South relations
Anglo-Irish relations

The **causes** explain **why** events happened.

What Were the Causes of the Troubles?

Long-term causes

1. British conquest and colonisation
2. Separate communities
3. The struggle for independence
4. Partition

1. British conquest and colonisation

In the 16th and 17th centuries, the kings and queens of England brought Protestant **planters** (settlers) from England and Scotland to Ireland. They took over land once owned by Gaelic and Anglo-Irish lords. The most important of these plantations was the Plantation of Ulster. The Protestant planters developed **different identities** from the local Catholics (see Ch. 9).

2. Separate communities

Two separate communities developed in Northern Ireland, with **different identities** (characteristics of a group).

- **One community** was the **Protestant unionist community**, which wanted to retain its links with Britain. They had their own areas for living (ghettoes), their own schools and sports.
- The **other community** was the **Catholic nationalist community**, which wanted some form of independence from Britain. They also lived in their own areas, and went to their own schools and played their own sports.

Areas in Northern Ireland with majority Protestants and majority Catholics in 1960s

3. The struggle for independence

From the late 18th century onwards, **nationalists** developed an **independence movement** in Ireland to win independence from Britain.

- Some wanted to win independence by **parliamentary (peaceful) means**.
- Others wanted to win independence by **physical force** (armed rebellion) (see Ch. 11).

Nationalists were opposed by **unionists**, who wanted to retain the **Act of Union** (1800), which brought in direct rule of Ireland from the parliament in Westminster. The unionists were strongest in **Northern Ireland**.

4. Partition

In the early 20th century, the unionists resisted the demand for Home Rule for Ireland. As a result, the British government passed the **Government of Ireland Act 1920**, which set up a parliament in Belfast to deal with the internal affairs of Northern Ireland. This created the '**border**' or **partition** between Northern Ireland and the south of Ireland (Irish Free State, Éire, and later the Republic of Ireland). The **Unionist Party** controlled Northern Ireland for the next 50 years.

Short-term causes

1. Discrimination
2. Gerrymandering
3. Civil rights campaign
4. The Day the Troubles Began

1. Discrimination

The unionists maintained power by **discriminating** against (treating unfairly) Catholics and nationalists. The unionists controlled jobs and housing in local councils. They favoured fellow Protestants in allocating jobs and houses. This **sectarianism** (prejudice, discrimination against another group) caused **tensions** between the two communities.

2. Gerrymandering

In a process called **gerrymandering**, the unionists rigged (arranged) the voting system in local elections. They ensured that that there was a majority of unionist councillors in local councils even though Catholics were a majority in the local population. For example, in Derry/Londonderry there was a Catholic/nationalist majority, but the unionists controlled the city council.

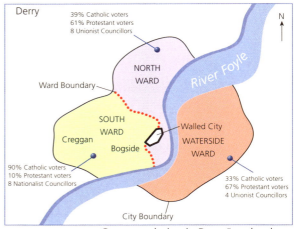

Gerrymandering in Derry/Londonderry

3. Civil rights campaign

The **Northern Ireland Civil Rights Association (NICRA)** was founded in 1967 to end **discrimination** against Catholics and nationalists. They demanded:
- **'One man, one vote'** in local elections
- An end to gerrymandering
- An end to discrimination in housing and jobs.

They organised marches and demonstrations in Derry and Belfast. These civil rights marches led to clashes with the **Royal Ulster Constabulary (RUC)**. The leaders of NICRA included **Gerry Fitt** and **John Hume**.

Terence O'Neill, prime minister of Northern Ireland, wanted to improve relations with **Catholics** by visiting Catholic schools.
- More **extreme Protestants** (**loyalists**) were opposed to O'Neill.
- Catholics and nationalists were disappointed that O'Neill was not bringing in more reforms to end discrimination.

This **increased tension** between Catholics and Protestants.

4. The Day the Troubles Began

Saturday, 5 October 1968, is marked as the **Day the Troubles Began**. On that day, a civil rights march in Derry was stopped by the **Royal Ulster Constabulary (RUC)**.
- The RUC used batons and water cannons to disperse the marchers.
- Television news beamed pictures of the RUC attacks across the world.

After that, O'Neill was forced by the British government to bring in more reforms. However, the demonstrations continued.

The **loyalist opposition** within his own party, the Unionist Party, forced O'Neill to resign after he brought in reforms for nationalists.

Timeline of the Troubles

1968	The Day the Troubles Began – NICRA march in Derry	1974	Ulster Workers' Council strike Dublin-Monaghan Bombings
1969	**Battle of the Bogside**	1980	Hunger strike began
	Provisional IRA formed	1981	Ten hunger strikers dead
1971	Internment	1985	**Anglo-Irish Agreement**
1972	Stormont abolished; **direct rule from Westminster**	1993	**Downing Street Declaration**
		1994	Temporary IRA ceasefire
	Worst year of the Troubles for deaths	1998	**Good Friday Agreement**
		2001	IRA began decommissioning arms
1973	**Sunningdale Agreement**		

The Troubles Worsen – The Battle of the Bogside

There were **clashes** between Catholics/nationalists and the RUC in Derry after an **Apprentice Boys** (Protestant organisation) march in **August 1969**.

- This led to the **Battle of the Bogside**, when RUC tried to get into a Catholic area.
- There were also **riots** in Belfast, as Catholics barricaded the streets.
- Taoiseach **Jack Lynch** said on television that the Irish government *'can no longer stand by and see innocent people injured and perhaps worse'*.
- The **British army** was brought in to replace the RUC. Nationalists initially welcomed their arrival.

Paramilitary Organisations

The Provisional IRA (Irish Republican Army)

The **Provisional IRA** ('Provos') was formed in 1969 when it split from the Official IRA, which was moving away from violence.

- The Provisional IRA demanded a united Ireland. It supported the **physical force tradition** – it believed that armed rebellion (violence) would force Britain to withdraw from Northern Ireland. It was represented by the political party, **Sinn Féin**.

The Provisional IRA organised attacks on the British army and RUC. They also organised a bombing campaign in Northern Ireland and Britain, which resulted in the deaths of many people.
- Bombings increased from 170 in 1970 to over 1,800 in 1972 (the worst year).
- On **Bloody Friday** (21 July 1972), the IRA exploded **35 bombs** across Northern Ireland, **killing nine people** and injuring 130.

UVF and UDA

On the unionist side, **paramilitary organisations** (organised like an army) included the **Ulster Volunteer Force** (UVF) and the **Ulster Defence Association** (UDA). They were supported by the more extreme unionists called **loyalists**.
- The **UVF** was responsible for the **Dublin-Monaghan bombings**, which killed 34 people (May 1974).

Loyalists are extreme unionists who support the union with Britain and are prepared to use violence.

Political Parties – The SDLP and DUP

New political parties were formed in Northern Ireland.
- The **Social, Democratic and Labour Party** (SDLP) was founded in 1970. It was the **largest nationalist party** at that time. One of its leaders was **John Hume**, who later became the most important person in promoting the peace process.
- On the unionist side, the **Rev. Ian Paisley** founded the **Democratic Unionist Party** (DUP) in 1971. The DUP opposed the Unionist Party of Northern Ireland and demanded strong action be taken against the IRA.

Internment

The unionist government of Northern Ireland led by **Brian Faulkner** brought in **internment** (imprisonment without trial), which was aimed at rounding up IRA leaders. In August 1971, 342 people were arrested and held without trial. However, many innocent people were arrested, and many leaders of the IRA escaped arrest.
- Internment resulted in **huge protests** from nationalists, north and south of the border.
- It also led to increased bombings and shootings, and increased support for the IRA.

Bloody Sunday

One of the protests was an **anti-internment march** in Derry in January 1972. The crowd was shot at by British troops, killing 14 people. This was called **Bloody Sunday**.
- This led to huge protests by nationalists all over Ireland, including in Dublin where the **British embassy** was burned down.

Direct Rule

Soon after this the British government abolished the **parliament in Stormont** and established direct rule from Westminster. The unionist government had failed to solve the problems of Northern Ireland.

Attempts at Peace – The Sunningdale Agreement, 1973

The first major attempt to bring peace to Northern Ireland came with the **Sunningdale Agreement**, 1973. This was an agreement between the British and Irish governments, and political parties in Northern Ireland.
- It proposed a **power-sharing government** in Northern Ireland where unionists and nationalists would **rule together**.
- The **Unionist Party** led by Brian Faulkner and the **SDLP** led by Gerry Fitt formed the first power-sharing government.
- There was also a **Council of Ireland** to organise cross-border co-operation.

The Ulster Workers' Council Strike

The power-sharing government **collapsed** within five months, as the loyalists organised a **general strike** against it in May 1974. The strike was called by the **Ulster Workers' Council** (UWC), which feared that the Sunningdale Agreement would lead to a united Ireland.
- The power-sharing government was replaced by direct rule from Westminster.
- The first major attempt at bringing peace to Northern Ireland had failed.

Hunger Strikes

There was further trouble during the **Hunger Strikes** (1980–81).
- IRA prisoners demanded political prisoner status (imprisoned for political activities, not criminal) in the **Maze Prison**.
- When the British government, led by **Margaret Thatcher**, refused, some of the prisoners, led by **Bobby Sands**, went on **hunger strike** (refused to eat).

Between May and August 1981, **10 hunger strikers died** as the British government refused to give in. The IRA then called off the hunger strike.

Attempts at Peace – The Anglo-Irish Agreement, 1985

As the violence continued, the British and Irish governments negotiated the **Anglo-Irish Agreement** (1985).
- The Agreement was signed by the British prime minister, **Margaret Thatcher**, and the Taoiseach, **Garret Fitzgerald**.
- The Agreement gave a **greater say by the South** in the affairs of Northern Ireland.

This agreement led to **huge protests** by the Unionist Party and the DUP. Unionists believed this was a step towards a united Ireland.
- The Anglo-Irish Agreement laid the **foundation for future progress** in the peace process.

Further Peace Moves – The End of the Troubles

But it took many more years before the Troubles came to an end and peace was brought to Northern Ireland.

1. A further step on the road to peace was the **Downing Street Declaration** (1993), which was agreed by **John Major**, British prime minister, and **Albert Reynolds**, Taoiseach. The Declaration stated that:
   - The British government said that Irish unity was a matter for the Irish people.
   - The Irish government said that unity could only come about with the consent of the people, North and South.
   - The Declaration led to an IRA ceasefire in 1994, though the ceasefire was broken for a while later.

2. **Hume-Adams talks:** There were secret discussions between John Hume and Gerry Adams, leader of the IRA. Hume persuaded Adams that the IRA should give up its arms and work through its political party, Sinn Féin.

3. **The Good Friday Agreement, 1998**
   The USA, under **President Clinton**, got more seriously involved in peace-making in Northern Ireland.
   - Clinton sent a representative, **George Mitchel**, to conduct negotiations between the different groups. These negotiations produced the **Good Friday Agreement**.
   - It was agreed that:
     - There would be a **power-sharing government** in Northern Ireland.
     - Northern Ireland would remain part of the UK until people North and South agreed otherwise.

- All the parties to the Agreement would work towards **decommissioning arms** (arms put beyond use, destroyed).
- A separate **referendum** was held both North and South, both of whom supported the Agreement.
- Within a few years, the **Provisional IRA** and **loyalist paramilitaries** decommissioned their arms.
- **This brought the Troubles to an end.**
- A **Northern Ireland Assembly** and **Executive** were formed in which unionists and nationalists shared power.
  - Power was first shared mainly between the **Unionist Party** and the **SDLP**.
  - Later events in Northern Ireland led to the further rise of the **DUP** and **Sinn Féin**, which became the strongest unionist and nationalist parties, respectively.

What Were the Consequences of the Troubles?

'Consequences' = 'effects' = 'results' = 'impact' = **showing historical change**

1. Deaths during the Troubles

Over **3,500 people were killed** in Northern Ireland during the Troubles (1969–98). Over half of these were killed by republican paramilitary groups, especially the Provisional IRA. A majority of those killed were **civilians**.
More than 47,000 people were injured.

Who was responsible for the killings in the Troubles?	
Republican paramilitary groups (mainly Provisional IRA)	2,057
Loyalist paramilitary groups	1,027
British security forces	363
Persons unknown	80
Irish security forces	5
Total	3,532

Source: **cain.ulster.ac.uk**

2. Destruction during the Troubles

There was great destruction in Belfast, Derry and other northern towns, largely caused by IRA car bombs. Roads and bridges were either blocked or blown up along the border.

3. Political consequences of the Troubles

- The unionists were forced to **share power** with the nationalists.
- The **Irish government** got a greater say in the affairs of Northern Ireland.
- The **US government** became involved in the peace process.
- **Power changed hands** within the unionist and nationalist communities.
    - The DUP became the dominant unionist party instead of the Ulster Unionist Party.
    - Sinn Féin became the dominant nationalist party instead of the SDLP.

4. Economic consequences of the Troubles

During the Troubles, **serious economic damage** was done to Northern Ireland. The **economic advantages** that the North enjoyed over the South before the Troubles began were wiped out by the IRA campaign of violence.
- Businesses were wrecked by the bombings.
- Foreign investment did not want to set up in Northern Ireland.
- There was rising unemployment, which rose from 4.5% in 1973 to almost 17% in 1986.

5. The impact of the Troubles on North-South relations

1. **North-South relations** improved in the 1960s prior to the Troubles. The northern prime minister, **Terence O'Neill**, met the southern Taoiseach, **Seán Lemass**, on a couple of occasions.
2. However, there was rising tension during the civil rights campaign and later the Troubles.
    - Nationalists moved south after attacks on Catholic ghettoes in Belfast and Derry by loyalists.
    - Taoiseach Jack Lynch said on television that the Irish government *'can no longer stand by and see innocent people injured and perhaps worse'*.
    - Unionists claimed that the government of the South was not doing enough to stop the IRA.

3. Gradually, the **Irish government's view** of the northern conflict **changed**.
   - Instead of believing that partition was the cause of the Troubles, the Irish government moved to **improve relations** between the communities in Northern Ireland.
   - They also believed that a united Ireland could only come with the **consent** of the people of Northern Ireland.
4. Relations between North and South improved or worsened depending on events in Northern Ireland (e.g. Bloody Sunday) or in the South (e.g. UVF car bombings in Dublin and Monaghan) during the Troubles.
5. Gradually, negotiations during the **Sunningdale Agreement** (1973), **the Anglo-Irish Agreement** (1985) and the **Good Friday Agreement** (1998) improved relations between North and South, even though the southern government got a greater say in the affairs of Northern Ireland.

6. The impact of the Troubles on Anglo-Irish relations

Relations between the British and Irish governments (Anglo-Irish relations) improved after the beginning of the Troubles.
- The British government realised that the Irish government was needed to ensure that northern nationalists would trust any agreement for peace in Northern Ireland.

Relations between the two governments were strengthened as they negotiated each of the agreements that led to peace.
- The Sunningdale Agreement (1973)
- The Anglo-Irish Agreement (1985)
- The Downing Street Declaration (1993)
- The Good Friday Agreement (1998)

Sample Question

John Hume, a leading figure in the Northern Ireland campaign for civil rights and in the Northern Irish peace process, said:

All conflict is about difference, whether the difference is race, religion or nationality. Difference is not a threat, difference is natural. Difference is an accident of birth and it should never be the source of hatred or conflict. The answer to difference is to respect it.

What were **three key differences** between Unionists and Nationalists during the time of the Troubles in Northern Ireland?

Unionists were mainly descendants of English and Scottish planters who came to Northern Ireland during and after the Ulster Plantation. They lived separately from the nationalists, who were descendants of the native Irish who were expelled from their land during the Ulster Plantation. Unionists and nationalists largely lived in separate areas.

Unionists were mainly Protestants who supported the union with Britain. They were opposed to a united Ireland. Nationalists were mainly Catholics who wanted independence from Britain. They wanted to unite Northern Ireland with the Republic of Ireland.

Unionists led by the Unionist Party were in control of the government in Northern Ireland. They discriminated against Catholics in voting, jobs and housing. Catholics were the minority in Northern Ireland. They began the civil rights campaign to get one man, one vote, to end gerrymandering in elections and discrimination in housing.

Revision Questions
Scan the QR code for more revision questions.

27 The European Union and Ireland's Links with Europe

After studying this chapter, you should be able to:
- Evaluate the role of the EU in promoting international co-operation
- Identify what countries joined the EU and when
- Evaluate the role of the EU in promoting justice and human rights
- Analyse the evolution and development of Ireland's links with Europe.

If you are asked about **a movement or organisation like the European Union or United Nations**, you should write about the **European Union**.

The Origins of the EU and the Desire for European Unity

Key Words
European unity
common market
Four Freedoms

The destruction and suffering in Europe after World War II led many Europeans to think that the best way to solve Europe's problems was through **European unity**. This meant European countries working together to secure lasting peace.

There were many reasons for European unity.

What were the reasons for European unity?

1. **Revive European economies** after World War II.
2. Prevent future European wars.
3. Nationalism was a major cause of both world wars. European unity would replace nationalism with **international co-operation**.
4. **Strengthen Europe** against the USA and USSR.
5. Control German aggression.
6. Unite against the fear of the spread of **communism** from the USSR.

- The **Treaty of Rome** (1957) established the **European Economic Community (EEC)** in 1958.
- **France**, **West Germany**, **Belgium**, **the Netherlands**, **Luxembourg** and **Italy** were the original six members of the EEC.
- The aims of the EEC were:
    1. To promote economic activity
    2. To raise living standards
    3. To bring member states closer together.

How Did the Expansion of the EEC Promote International Co-operation?

1. Over the next 30 years, the EEC **expanded** as new countries joined, e.g. **Britain**, **Ireland** and **Denmark** in 1973.
2. Since the **Maastricht Treaty**, the name **European Union (EU)** has been used.
3. By the 1990s, there were **15** countries in the European Union.
4. The collapse of communism and the Soviet Union in 1990–91 provided the opportunity for many Eastern European countries to join the EU.
5. In 2004, 10 new countries, mostly from Eastern Europe, joined the EU.
6. International co-operation in Europe was **improved** with this enlargement.

How Does the EU Promote International Co-operation?

1. The EEC established a **common market** to achieve its aims. A common market is a free trade area with relatively free movement of goods and services.
2. All **tariffs** (taxes) and **quotas** between member states would be **abolished**.
3. The EEC was based on the **Four Freedoms** (free movement of goods, persons, services and capital).
4. It also followed **common policies** in **agriculture** and **transport**, e.g. **Common Agricultural Policy**.
5. **Common standards** in metric scales, decimal currency, VAT and euros were introduced.
6. Joint **research projects** were launched, e.g. addressing climate change.
7. Different **languages** of member states were recognised.

How Did Greater Powers for the EU Promote International Co-operation?

As the EEC grew, it changed its name and its powers.
The European Community (EC), and later the EU, negotiated the **Single European Act**, the **Treaty of European Union** and the **Treaty of Lisbon**.

- **The Single European Act** (1987) created a **single European market**.
- **The Treaty of the European Union/Maastricht Treaty** (signed in 1991 and came into effect in 1993) set out plans for the **euro**, gave greater powers to the European Parliament and stated that member states should **co-operate** in combatting **fraud** and **drug trafficking**. This treaty took powers from national parliaments and gave it to the EU.
- **The Treaty of Lisbon** (2009) increased the powers of the European Parliament and created a full-time president of the EU. It also made the **Charter of Fundamental Rights** legally binding.

How Do the Institutions of the EU Promote International Co-operation?

The EU works to get agreement from all countries on new policies, regardless of their size.

1. The **European Council** is composed of the heads of government of all EU countries. It meets four times a year. It decides overall guidelines for EU policy.
2. The **European Parliament** is made up of **MEPs** who are elected by the people. They propose new ideas and vote on the budget. They supervise the **Council of Ministers**.
3. The **Council of Ministers** decides EU laws and budget. It's made up of **one minister** from each EU country. They represent the interests of their country.
4. The **European Commission** is made up of commissioners nominated from each EU state. It is composed of **civil servants** of the EU who carry out EU policy. They operate in **Brussels**.
5. The **Court of Justice** has 28 judges and is based in Luxembourg. They can fine countries that break EU law.

Quick recap	
Name of organisation	European Union (EU), formally known as the European Economic Community (EEC)
What date was the EU established?	1957
Who were the original members?	France, West Germany, Belgium, the Netherlands, Luxembourg and Italy
What was their aim?	European unity
What year did Ireland join?	1973
How does the EU promote international co-operation?	• **A common market** was established. • The **Four Freedoms** allowed the free movement of goods, persons, services and capital. • Common policies were introduced, e.g. **CAP** (Common Agricultural Policy). • Common standards were introduced, e.g. the **euro**. • **Joint research projects** were introduced. • The **Single European Act** (1987) created a single European market. • The **Maastricht Treaty** stated that member states should co-operate in combatting fraud and drug trafficking. • EU institutions such as the **European Council**, **European Parliament** and **European Commission** are made up of representatives from each country in the EU.
How does the EU promote justice?	• People can appeal decisions made in national courts to the **Court of Justice of the European Union**. • The EU wants a **common legal and judicial culture** across all states; this has become more necessary with the growth of cross-border online sales.
How does the EU promote human rights?	• The **Treaty of Lisbon** (2009) made the **Charter of Fundamental Rights** legally binding. • The EU set up the **European Agency for Fundamental Rights** (FRA) to protect the rights of people living in the EU. • It also developed an **Action Plan on Human Rights and Democracy**. • Trade agreements with non-EU countries include a **human rights clause**. • **Sanctions** are imposed on countries that breach human rights laws. • During the migrant crisis of 2015–16, the EU **relocated refugees**, developed **border patrols** and worked with **Turkey** to stop the flow of migrants across the sea to Greece.

THE EUROPEAN UNION AND IRELAND'S LINKS WITH EUROPE

Ireland's Links with Europe

1. Early Christian Ireland
431

- In 431 AD, Pope Celestine sent **Palladius** to Ireland as a **missionary**.
- Missionaries like **St Patrick** were responsible for converting the country to Christianity.
- In later centuries Irish missionaries like **St Colmcille** were responsible for carrying Christianity to other parts of Europe, e.g. **Scotland**.

2. The Normans
1169

- **The Normans**, from Normandy in France, invaded Ireland from Britain.
- They initially conquered **Waterford** and **Wexford** before spreading out through the rest of Leinster.
- They brought their land system (**the Feudal system**) with them.
- They also brought **castles** and **stone-walled towns**, e.g. **Kilkenny**, **Trim** and **Youghal**.

3. The Reformation
1500s

- The Protestant **Reformation** began in Germany when **Martin Luther** criticised the Catholic Church.
- It spread to Ireland in the 16th century through the **Tudor kings and queens** who changed the laws and who sent **Protestant planters** to Ireland.
  - **Henry VIII** closed all the monasteries and **confiscated their property**, e.g. Quin Abbey, Co. Clare.
  - **Presbyterian planters** from Scotland came to Ulster during the Ulster Plantation.

4. The Nine Years' War
1594–1603

- Prior to the Ulster Plantation (1609), **Hugh O'Neill** and **Hugh O'Donnell** rebelled against Queen Elizabeth's efforts to impose English laws and religion in Ulster.
- They got help from **Philip II of Spain**, who sent ships to **Kinsale, Co. Cork**.
- These troops were defeated, but future rebellions would continue to look to Europe for help.
- After their defeat, the Ulster chiefs headed for Europe. This was called the **Flight of the Earls**.

5. 1798 Rebellion
1798

- Ideas of the **French Revolution** (liberty, equality and fraternity) were popular in Ireland in the 1790s.
- **Wolfe Tone** and the **United Irishmen** looked to France for help.
- The French sent ships and soldiers on three occasions, to **Bantry Bay**, **Killala** and **Lough Swilly**.

6. 1916 Rising
1916

- Leaders of the **1916 Rising** got arms and ammunition from **Germany**, who were fighting Britain in World War I.
- In the **1916 Proclamation**, the leaders said they were supported by **'gallant allies in Europe'**.
- The *Aud*, which was carrying the arms, was captured off the Kerry coast. This was one of the main reasons that the Rising was largely confined to Dublin.

7. World War II
1939–45

- During World War II, Ireland was **split in two**. North and South played different parts in the war.
- The South stayed **neutral**, while the North took an **active role** in the war.
- Both parts of the country were bombed, but the North suffered much greater damage, e.g. during the **Belfast Blitz**.

8. Ireland and the EEC (EU)
1973–present day

- The Republic of Ireland applied to join the **EEC** in the early 1960s, along with the United Kingdom and Denmark.
- French president de Gaulle vetoed the British application and the Irish application fell as well.
- A referendum held in **1972** showed a huge majority in Ireland were in favour of joining the EEC. However, some groups, like **commercial fishermen**, were opposed to joining.
- Ireland, the UK and Denmark joined the EEC on **1 January 1973**.

THE EUROPEAN UNION AND IRELAND'S LINKS WITH EUROPE

- Why did Ireland join the EEC?
    1. **More jobs** in industry.
    2. Foreign companies would **invest** in Ireland to have access to the EU market.
    3. Reduce Ireland's dependence on the British market.
    4. Britain (and Northern Ireland) was joining, so Ireland had to join as well.
    5. Irish agriculture would benefit from **CAP** (**Common Agricultural Policy**).

Sample Question

What is the role of the EU in promoting justice and human rights?

The Treaty of Rome, which founded the EEC, was concerned with economic matters and made **no reference to human rights**. In 2000, the **European Charter of Fundamental Rights** was agreed, but it did not become legally binding until 2009. The Charter outlined the civil, political, social and economic rights of EU citizens.

The EU set up the **European Agency for Fundamental Rights (FRA)** to protect the rights of people living in the EU. It has also developed an **Action Plan on Human Rights and Democracy**. The EU has a special representative for Human Rights whose job is to make EU policy on human rights more effective in non-EU countries. EU policy includes working to **promote** the rights of women, children, minorities, opposing the death penalty and defending civil rights. All agreements on trade with non-EU countries include a **human rights clause**. The EU has imposed **sanctions** (penalties) for human rights breaches.

The EU is also concerned with justice. It wants a **common legal and judicial culture** across all states. The growth of the single market and online sales has led to greater numbers of **cross-border disputes**. The EU decides which country has jurisdiction to try particular cases. It also ensures judgements in one country are recognised and **enforced** in other EU countries. People can challenge national laws through local courts. If that fails, they can appeal to the **Court of Justice of the European Union**.

Revision Questions

Scan the QR code for more revision questions.

28 Technology and Historical Change

exam focus

If you are asked to explore the **contribution of technological developments and innovation to historical change**, you can write about **any one or more** of the technological developments outlined here.

aims

After studying this chapter, you should be able to:
- Explore the contribution of the printing press to historical change
- Explore the contribution of ships and navigation to historical change
- Explore the contribution of the steam engine to historical change
- Explore the contribution of nuclear energy to historical change.

key point

Historical change is how differences or changes occur in history through **causes** and **consequences** (effects).
Technology refers to the machines and tools that are used to solve practical problems.
Innovation means the development of something new.

Key Words
historical change
technology
innovation
standardisation
vernacular
arms race
inter-continental ballistic missiles (ICBMs)

The Printing Press and Historical Change

The printing press was invented by Johannes Gutenberg. It sped up the printing of books and spread literacy and knowledge.

TECHNOLOGY AND HISTORICAL CHANGE

Before: Before the invention of the printing press, books were **copied by hand** (manuscripts). This was a very slow process, so very few books were produced.

After: Johannes **Gutenberg** invented **moveable metal type** (letters) and the **printing press** around 1450.
- The individual metal letters could be used to set up a **page** in a frame. The letters were then inked and paper was pressed down on them to create a **printed page**. This process was repeated to create **books, posters or prints**.
- Fifty years later, around 1500, there were **236 printers** in cities in Europe.

How did the printing press contribute to historical change?

1. The changes brought about by the **Renaissance** were sped up by the printing press (see Ch. 6).
    - The printing press spread the **learning of Ancient Greece and Rome**.
    - It spread the **new learning and ideas** of the Renaissance, in science, medicine, history and geography, e.g. Vesalius's *On the Fabric of the Human Body* (see page 193) and Copernicus's *On the Revolution of the Heavenly Spheres* (see page 34).
2. The writings of **Shakespeare** (and other writers) were **read widely**. Shakespeare contributed to the standardisation of the English language, making the spelling and writing of it the same all over the country (see page 35).
    - These writers spread the use of the vernacular (the language of the people) rather than the use of Latin, which was the language of educated people in the Middle Ages.
3. The printing press influenced the **Age of Exploration** (see Ch. 7).
    - The learning of Ancient Greece included **Ptolemy's** *Geography*, which interested explorers.
    - Explorers, such as **Amerigo Vespucci**, published **books** about their explorations, which created widespread interest.
4. The printing press influenced the spread of the **Reformation** (see Ch. 8).
    - **Martin Luther's *95 Theses*** were printed and quickly spread over Germany, and other countries.
    - Luther translated the **New Testament into German** and 5,000 copies were sold in two weeks.
    - Luther and his followers used **propaganda** (books, cartoons, drawings) to spread their message.
5. For the **next 500 years**, the printing press was the **main form of news and opinion-making** until the invention of the **radio** and its spread in the early 20th century.

If you are asked to explore the **contribution of technological developments and innovation to historical change**, you should show clearly how **history was changed** by one or more **technological developments**.

Ships and Navigation and Historical Change

In the 15th and 16th centuries, **Portuguese** and **Spanish explorers** began to explore other parts of the world, in what is called the **Age of Exploration (see Ch. 7)**.

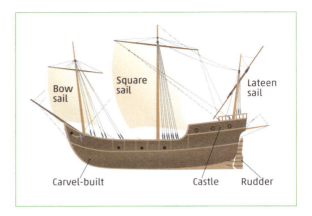

Before: In medieval times, ships had to sail close to the coast. They also found it difficult to sail against the wind. They could not undertake long sea voyages.

After: In the Age of Exploration, **new ships** and **new navigation equipment** contributed to the reasons why the Age of Exploration began (**causes**). Without improvements in ships and methods of navigation, explorers could not have gone on long voyages, far from coasts.

What were the improvements in ships and navigation?

Ships

New ships called **caravels** and **carracks** were **carvel-built** (boards on the hull were fitted edge-to-edge). These sailing ships became longer and could carry more masts.
- Apart from square sails, ships also now had **lateen sails**, which could be used to sail against the wind.
- The caravels and carracks had **rudders** for more accurate steering.

Navigation
- **Compass** – could tell the direction the ships were sailing.
- **Latitude** – the astrolabe, quadrant and cross-staff were used to work out latitude (north and south of the equator).
- **Maps** – became more accurate.

What contribution did improvements in ships and navigation make to historical change?

The Age of Exploration
With the help of new ships and methods of navigation:
- The **Portuguese** explored the coast of Africa, and **Vasco da Gama** found a sea route to India.
- The **Spanish**, led by Columbus, explored the continent of North and South America.
- Both countries **conquered** large territories and created powerful **empires**. They used the ships and navigation methods to develop **great trade routes** between Europe, America, Africa and Asia.
- They were followed by the **English, French and the Dutch**, who also developed large empires.
- In their empires, they spread their own **language**, **culture** and the **Christian religion**, whether Catholic or Protestant.

The slave trade
- About **12.5 million slaves** were shipped from Africa to different parts of the Americas between the 16th and 19th centuries.
- These slaves worked on the **plantations** of the European settlers, harvesting cotton and sugar, mining for gold and silver or working as domestic servants.

War
Ships were **armed with cannons.** These led to **larger and bloodier battles**.
- The **Spanish Armada** planned to invade England but was defeated by the English navy in the English Channel. This saved England from invasion.
- The **French Navy** contributed to the defeat of the British in the **Battle of Yorktown**, which led to American victory in the **American Revolution** and to the independence of the country from Britain (see Ch. 10A).

Decline of the Mediterranean
- The exploration of North and South America and Africa made the **Atlantic Ocean** more important that the **Mediterranean Sea**. Now, much of **world trade** was carried out in the Atlantic.
- Many **new foods** were introduced to Europe, e.g. turkey, potatoes.
- As a result, **cities** along the Atlantic coast – e.g. London and Amsterdam – became larger and more important than the Italian cities of Venice and Genoa.

The Steam Engine and Historical Change

In the 18th century, one of the key factors in the growth of the **Industrial Revolution** was the invention of the **steam engine**.

Before: Before the invention of the steam engine in the 18th century, most power was produced **manually** (by hand) or by **water** (water wheels).

After: The invention of the steam engine provided **much greater power** for mining, manufacturing and transport.

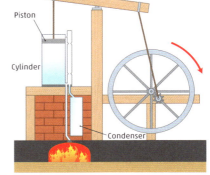

Watt's steam engine

How did the invention of the steam engine contribute to historical change?

Mining

The early steam engines built by **Thomas Newcomen** were used to pump water out of mines. This meant mines could be **dug deeper and greater quantities of coal and tin** could be mined. The coal was used to power steam engines, trains and factories.

Manufacturing

James Watt improved on Newcomen's engine. Watt's steam engine used less fuel, and it had a **flywheel**, which meant it could be used to **power other machines**. As a result, the steam engine could power **large machines** in factories, particularly the cotton mills in England.

- As more and more factories were built, the **cities of Britain** grew rapidly, for example, London, Manchester and Birmingham.
- The **working conditions** in the factories and the **living conditions** in the cities were often **very harsh** for the workers, men, women and children.
- The **government** was forced to intervene to improve the working and living conditions.

Transport

Steam engines were used to create a **transport revolution**. Carts, coaches and canals were replaced by **trains**, which were faster and cheaper.

- The first passenger line was built between **Manchester** and **Liverpool** in 1830.
- Trains also contributed to the **growth of cities**. Better-off people could build houses away from the city centre, creating new **suburbs**, and travel to work by train.
- Trains helped to develop a **growing new industry – tourism** – by enabling people to go on daytrips to seaside resorts, and to travel around Europe.

War

Wars became **bloodier** and **more destructive**.
- **Trains** were used to transport huge numbers of soldiers to the battlefronts. **Armies grew** from thousands to millions by the time of World War I. More soldiers were killed and wounded with each war.
- They were also used to **supply** ammunition, food and clothes to the soldiers.
- The **factories** powered by steam engines produced the weapons, ammunition, clothes and food for the new larger armies.

Nuclear Energy and Historical Change

Before: Various scientists from the end of the 19th century and into the 20th century helped to develop ideas about **nuclear energy**. In 1938, two German scientists named Hahn and Strassmann showed how **nuclear fission** could **split atoms** and release **nuclear energy**.

After: During World War II, the USA used its wealth and technology to become the first country to develop the **atomic bomb**. In the **Manhattan Project**, the USA exploded the first atomic bomb (A-bomb) in the desert in New Mexico. After World War II, nuclear power or energy was also used in other different ways.

How did nuclear energy contribute to historical change?

World War II

In August 1945, the USA dropped atomic bombs on **Hiroshima** (6 August) and **Nagasaki** (9 August) in Japan (see page 125).
- The dropping of these bombs resulted in the **deaths** of up to 120,000 people and injuries to almost 100,000 more.
- The bombing of Hiroshima and Nagasaki helped to bring about the **end of World War II**.
- The bombings **saved** an unknown number of US and Allied soldiers' lives (as well as Japanese lives). If the Allied armies had been forced to invade Japan, many soldiers would have died.

The Cold War

The Cold War between the **superpowers** USA and USSR (Soviet Union) dominated foreign affairs from 1945 to 1990 (see Ch. 22).
- One aspect of the Cold War was the arms race – the race to stay ahead of the opposing side with superior nuclear and other weapons.
- The **USSR** (Soviet Union) soon developed an atomic bomb to match the USA.

- Soon both countries had **hydrogen bombs** (H-bombs), which were much more **destructive**.
- Then both sides built **ICBMs (inter-continental ballistic missiles)** to carry **nuclear warheads** to hit targets in the opposing country.

The danger of nuclear war between the two sides created **great fear around the world**. This was shown during the **Cuban Missile Crisis** in 1962 (see page 152) when the world was brought to the brink of a nuclear war.

- During the 1950s and 1960s in the USA, **bomb shelters** were built in basements or gardens to protect people in the event of a nuclear explosion.

Peaceful use of nuclear power – Electricity

The first **nuclear powered stations** to generate **electricity** were built in the 1950s. The first one was built in the USSR (Soviet Union) in 1954, and this was followed by others in the USA, Britain and France.

- The increased **production of electricity** in these countries contributed to the fast **economic growth** of the 1950s and 1960s.
- However, **accidents** in Three Mile Island, USA (1979), Chernobyl in the USSR (1986) and Fukushima in Japan (2011) slowed down the building of nuclear powered electricity stations. There were fears of more deaths and destruction.
- Worldwide, nuclear energy is responsible for about **10% of electricity generation**, but in some countries, it is much higher. **France**, for example, produces **70% of its electricity** using nuclear power, largely because of a shortage of fossil fuels, such as coal and oil.

The impact of **climate change** created a new interest in building nuclear powered stations since **they do not produce greenhouse gases** and do not contribute to global warming.

Social improvements – Medicine

Radioactive material is used in many cases in medicine, which improves the lives of people.

- **X-rays** and **CT scans** are used in diagnosing illnesses by producing images of parts of the body. This has allowed doctors to see what was happening in the body without having to cut it open.
- **Radiation therapy** (treatment) is used in cancer treatment as high doses of radiation are directed at cancer cells to shrink cancer tumours.

Radioactive material is also used **in other areas of life** – in smoke detectors, in carbon-14 dating of artefacts in archaeology, in insect control and on long space voyages such as the Voyager missions to outer space.

TECHNOLOGY AND HISTORICAL CHANGE

Sample Question

Throughout history, new inventions or discoveries have had a big impact on people's lives. Describe a technological change or innovation from any time period in the history of Europe and the wider world that you have studied.

The printing press was invented in Mainz in Germany by Johannes Gutenberg around 1450. Before the printing press was invented, books were copied by hand (manuscripts). This was a very slow process, so very few books were produced. Gutenberg invented moveable metal type so that individual metal letters could be used to set up a page in a frame. The letters were then inked and paper was pressed down on them to create a printed page. This process was repeated to create a book. Now books could be printed more quickly and they became cheaper to produce.

Give **three examples** how the technological change or innovation you have named had an impact on how people lived or behaved, using evidence to support your answer.

During the Renaissance, new printing presses were set up in many cities in Europe. These printing presses spread the learning of Ancient Greece and Rome as books from that time, such as Ptolemy's 'Geography', were printed and made available to more people.

The printing press also spread the new learning and ideas of the Renaissance, in science, medicine, history and geography. For example, Copernicus said the sun, and not the earth, was the centre of the universe in 'On the Revolution of the Heavenly Spheres'. During the Reformation, Martin Luther's '95 Theses' were printed and quickly spread over Germany, and other countries. These increased support for Luther. Luther also translated the New Testament into German and 5,000 copies were sold in two weeks. This encouraged more people to learn to read and it spread the use of the vernacular language.

For the next 500 years, the printing press, through books, pamphlets and newspapers, was the main form of news and opinion-making until the invention of the radio and its spread in the early 20th century.

Sample 5, NCCA JC History Assessment Items

Revision Questions

Scan the QR code for more revision questions.

29A Patterns of Change – Health and Medicine

After studying this chapter, you should be able to:
- Illustrate changes that have taken place in health and medicine across different time periods
- Identify key personalities in the field of health and medicine.

exam focus

If you are asked to write about **patterns of change over different time periods**, you should write about either **health and medicine OR crime and punishment** (Chapter 29B).

Patterns of change – studying a topic or theme, like health and medicine or crime and punishment, across different time periods.

Key Words
patterns of change
four humours
bloodletting
dissection
barber surgeons
cholera
typhus
antiseptic
dissections
vaccine
pasteurisation

Health and Medicine in Ancient Rome

1. The Romans learnt about health and medicine from the **Greeks**.
2. **Galen** was the most famous doctor in Ancient Rome.
3. He followed Greek ideas about the **four humours**; yellow bile, black bile, blood and phlegm. Galen thought if any of these were **unbalanced**, it would cause sickness.
4. Galen also believed in the **theory of opposites** to cure sickness, e.g. he used hot pepper to cure a cold.
5. Others believed in getting rid of **excess fluid** to restore balance and cure sickness, e.g. **bloodletting**.
6. The Romans also used **herbal remedies**, e.g. broccoli was used to treat skin infections, tarragon was used to treat fatigue (tiredness, lack of energy).
7. People with serious diseases **prayed to the gods** to cure them.
8. The Romans believed that sickness could be caused by dirty water, so **aqueducts** were built to supply towns and cities with clean water.
9. Many houses had toilets, and by 315 AD, Rome had **144 public toilets**. The Romans also built a **sewer system** to remove waste.
10. They also drained swamps to get rid of malaria-carrying mosquitos, e.g. **Julius Caesar** drained the **Codetan Swamp** and planted a forest.
11. Personal hygiene was also important in Ancient Rome, and people used **public baths** every day.

How Did Health and Medicine Change in Medieval Times?

1. Many of the medieval ideas about medicine were based on the writings of **Galen** in Ancient Rome.
2. The dissection of bodies was still banned, this time by the Catholic Church.
3. Like in Ancient Rome, medieval doctors believed that when the **four humours** were unbalanced, this caused disease. Some believed that sickness was the will of God or caused by bad smells or by the patterns in the stars.
4. Most people were treated by 'wise men and women' or barber surgeons.
5. The first medical school was set up in Salerno, Italy.
6. Herbal remedies were often used to cure patients. **Bloodletting** and **leeches** were used to cure a blood imbalance in the four humours. Some people went on **pilgrimages** to holy places to get cured.
7. Unlike Roman towns and cities, medieval towns were unhealthy, so cholera and typhus outbreaks were common. The average life expectancy was about **35 years**.
8. The **Black Death** was the most serious cause of death in medieval times. The plague started in Asia and most historians believed it was spread by fleas on rats. Somewhere between **30–60%** of the population of Europe died.
9. There were some positive developments. Some doctors used wine as an antiseptic to stop the spread of disease. **Opium** was used as a painkiller. St Bartholomew's hospital in London was built in 1123.
10. In 1388, the English parliament passed a law that required streets and rivers to be kept clean.

What Happened to Health and Medicine during the Renaissance?

Several important developments occurred in medicine during the Renaissance:
1. The human body began to be studied in detail.
   - **Vesalius** wrote *On the Fabric of the Human Body*, which reported observations made during dissections of the body. He believed that medicine should be based on **observation,** and he corrected many of the old medical ideas handed down from the Greeks and Romans.
2. A French army surgeon, **Ambroise Paré**, made many developments in **surgery**.
   - He showed how gunshot wounds could be treated with ointment.
   - He developed new surgical instruments.
   - He created artificial limbs and eyes.

3. An Englishman, **William Harvey**, discovered that **blood** circulated around the body. He published his findings in *On the Motion of the Heart and Blood in Animals*.
4. However, there were **little or no improvements in public health**, as streets were still dirty and water was polluted.

What Developments Took Place in Health and Medicine in the 19th Century?

1796	**Edward Jenner** developed a vaccine for smallpox.	1860s	**Louis Pasteur** discovered that **germs caused disease**.
			As a result of this, he discovered **pasteurisation**.
1816	The **stethoscope** was used to listen to a patient's chest.		
1826	Improved **microscopes** were used to see tiny organisms.	1874	**Sophia Jex-Blake** founded the London School of Medicine for Women.
1842	**Edwin Chadwick's** report on the *Sanitary Conditions of the Labouring Population* highlighted the link between bad living conditions, ill health and life expectancy.	1878	**Robert Koch** learned to grow bacteria.
			He was able to figure out which bacteria caused diseases like TB and cholera.
1847	**James Simpson** used **chloroform** as an antiseptic.	1884	**Charles Chamberland** discovered **viruses**.
1860	**Florence Nightingale** wrote *Notes on Nursing* about how nurses could be better trained.	1885	Pasteur developed a vaccine for rabies.
		1895	**Wilhelm Roentgen** discovered the use of X-rays to study broken bones.

What Developments Took Place in Health and Medicine during Modern Times?

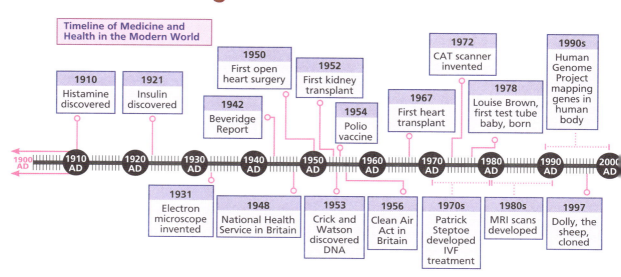

PATTERNS OF CHANGE – HEALTH AND MEDICINE

Overview of Patterns of Change in Health and Medicine

Key developments

Ancient Rome
- Four humours, taken from the Greeks
- Theory of opposites
- Bloodletting
- Herbal remedies
- Prayer
- Aqueducts
- Sewers
- Public toilets

Medieval times
- Dissection still banned
- Four humours
- Bloodletting
- Barber surgeons
- Pilgrimages
- The Black Death
- Wine used as antiseptic
- Opium used as painkillers
- St Bartholomew's hospital in London was built

The Renaissance
- Dissections allowed, which corrected many errors made by the Romans
- New surgical developments
- Artificial limbs created
- Blood circulation discovered

19th-century industrial society
- Smallpox vaccine
- Pasteurisation
- London School of Medicine for Women founded
- Rabies vaccine
- Use of X-rays

Modern times
- Histamine discovered
- Insulin discovered
- NHS established
- First open heart surgery
- First kidney transplant
- Polio vaccine
- First heart transplant
- CAT scanner invented
- MRI scans developed

Key personalities

Ancient Rome
- Galen

Medieval times
- Galen

The Renaissance
- Vesalius
- Ambroise Paré
- William Harvey

19th-century industrial society
- Edward Jenner
- Edwin Chadwick
- James Simpson
- Florence Nightingale
- Louis Pasteur
- Sophia Jex-Blake
- Robert Koch
- Charles Chamberland
- Wilhelm Roentgen

Modern times
- Alexander Fleming
- Crick and Watson
- Christiaan Barnard
- Patrick Steptoe

Revision Questions

Scan the QR code for more revision questions.

29B Patterns of Change – Crime and Punishment

If you are asked to write about **patterns of change** over different time periods, you should write about either **crime and punishment OR health and medicine** (Chapter 29A).

After studying this chapter, you should be able to:
- Illustrate patterns of change in crime and punishment across different time periods.

Key Words
magistrates
decimation
hue and cry
trial by ordeal
trial by combat
court
treason
urbanisation
deterrence
terrorism

Crime and Punishment in Ancient Rome

Who made the laws?
The Romans had a written code of law called the **Twelve Tables**. The laws were made by the senate, the emperor and by **magistrates** (judges). The laws applied to **Roman citizens** only.

Who enforced the laws?
There were **no police** in Ancient Rome.
- **Soldiers** were brought in to keep order when that was needed.
- At nighttime, **vigiles** patrolled the streets to watch for fires and prevent crimes.

Because there were no police, **victims of crime** had to bring criminals to court, to face magistrates.

What were the crimes?
There were **divisions between rich and poor** in Ancient Rome. As a result, robbery and burglary were common crimes. Trade fraud was also common as those making or selling goods **cheated** on those that bought them with **bad or faulty products**.
- Arson and murder were regarded as serious crimes, but they were not that common.
- In a **slave society**, such as Ancient Rome, runaway slaves were also seen as criminals.

What were the punishments?

Romans believed that punishments should be severe enough to **deter crime**. However, punishments also depended on whether you were rich or poor, and whether you were a Roman citizen or non-citizen. If you were a wealthy citizen, you would receive less punishment for the same crimes compared to a slave.

- **Ordinary citizens** were whipped or fined for small crimes. Hanging or beheading was used for more serious crimes. Nobles were executed or exiled for serious crimes.
- **Slaves** were punished harshly – they could be crucified or had to fight in combat.

There were also harsh punishments in the army to impose discipline. Any hint of rebellion was punished by decimation – every tenth man was selected for execution.

Crime and Punishment in Medieval Times

Who made the laws?

The laws in medieval times were made by the kings, parliament, the local lords and the decisions of judges in court.

Who enforced the laws?

The laws were enforced by the **local community**, which was different to Ancient Rome. In medieval times, hue and cry involved asking local people to help capture someone suspected of committing a crime. When a crime was committed, local people would shout after the criminal to alert everybody.

Accused persons had to go through **trial by ordeal** and **trial by combat**.

In trial by ordeal, accused persons had to hold on to a hot bar or be thrown into water. If the hand began to heal quickly, or if you sank, you were innocent.

In trial by combat, the accused faced his accuser in a fight. If he won the combat, he was innocent.

Gradually, trial by ordeal and trial by combat were eliminated. Instead, people were brought before **judges** in courts to be found innocent or guilty.

What were the crimes?

Crimes in medieval times were similar to those in Ancient Rome. These crimes were committed against **people, property and government**. Most of the crime was petty theft and poaching, with little violent crime such as murder. One of the most serious crimes was treason.

Key point

Treason is the crime of betraying one's country either by trying to overthrow the government by force or helping its enemies.

What were the punishments?

There were **no long-term prisons**, so people were only held for a short time until a trial. The most serious punishment was **hanging or beheading**, mostly for **treason**. These were often held in public as an **example to everyone**. There were many **other forms of punishment**.

- One way was to pay **compensation** to victims.
- Another was to **humiliate the person** who broke the law – this could be done by putting people in a pillory or in stocks.
  - In a **pillory**, the guilty person stood with hands and head held in boards with holes.
  - In **stocks**, the guilty person sat with ankles and wrists trapped in boards with holes.
- A shorter and more severe punishment was **flogging**, often done in public with a rod or a leather whip.

When you are illustrating **patterns of change** in **crime and punishment**, it is important to know about crime and punishment in at least **two different time periods**, and **the changes between them**.

Crime and Punishment in Industrial Society

In the 18th and 19th centuries, society changed as the **Industrial Revolution** spread throughout Britain. The population grew rapidly, more people lived in cities and towns, and there were harsh living and working conditions.

Who made the laws?

In the 18th and 19th centuries, the laws were made by **parliaments and/or by kings and queens**. In Britain, for example, parliament had power to make the laws, which the king or queen signed.

Some laws were also made by **local councils**.

Who enforced the laws?

In 1829, **Robert Peel** established the **Metropolitan Police Force** in London. This was the **first professional police force** in Britain, and they became known as **Peelers**. They wore a special uniform and carried a wooden baton.

- It took some decades before similar police forces were set up all over England and Wales.
- The police patrolled the streets to prevent crime.

Robert Peel's early policemen were nicknamed 'Peelers' or 'Bobbies'

Later, a **detective division** was added to the police force. The detective's job was to **investigate** crimes and gather evidence.
- The role of policing also changed as **crime prevention** became as important as catching the criminals.

What were the crimes?

During the 19th century, there was a **rise in crime**. This was largely due to the growing population, increasing urbanisation (more people living in cities) and poverty.
- Crimes were still mostly **petty theft and robbery**, but now **smuggling** became more common.
- Violent crimes, such as assault and murder, represented a small proportion of the overall crimes.

What were the punishments?

Punishments changed during the 19th century. The **Bloody Code** (over 200 offences which carried the death penalty) came to an end, so there were less hangings.
- Later, public hangings ended in 1868, but were still carried on in prisons.
- Another form of punishment ended also in mid-century – **transportation** to Australia.

Demands for **reforms of the prison system** were made by **John Howard** and **Elizabeth Fry.** Their demands led to the **Gaols Act 1823**.
- Male and female prisoners were separated, and gaolers were now paid by the government.
- Later, inspectors were appointed to check that the prisons were well run.

Prison became a **more common form of punishment** as corporal punishment was phased out. Now punishments were meant to match the crime. More prisons were built, e.g. Pentonville in London. Here they used the **separate** and **silent system** – prisoners were kept in **separate cells**, and when prisoners were allowed exercise, they had to do so in **silence**.

There was also a **debate** about whether prisons should be used as a **deterrence** (prevention) or prisoners should be **reformed for life outside prison**.

Deterrence is trying to prevent or discourage crime through fear of punishment.

Crime and Punishment in Modern Times

Who made the laws?

In modern society, laws were made by **parliament**. Laws changed as society changed, so there were **new laws** on cars, driving, drugs and race relations. In other cases, **some laws were scrapped** as society's views changed. An example was the decriminalising of homosexuality.

Who enforced the laws?

There were changes in **policing** to match changes in 20th-century society.
- Police were **motorised** to patrol streets and to catch criminals.
- Police had both **armed and unarmed units**. Most police in Britain were unarmed, except for batons, pepper sprays or tasers, but there were specialist armed units to enforce the law.
- **Specialist police units** were set up to deal with specific crimes, Drug Units, Fraud Squad and Traffic Police.
- **New technology** was adapted by the police all through the 20th century, including:
  - Fingerprinting (1901)
  - Radios
  - Computers
  - CCTV
  - DNA testing.

What were the crimes?

There were **new types of crime** along with the traditional petty theft and robbery. Now **race and drug crimes** featured. So also did **cybercrime**, though these were often new versions of old crimes such as cheating and frauding.

Terrorism became a new crime, as paramilitary groups and Islamist extremists sought to use shootings and bombings to achieve their aims.

The old crime, **smuggling**, became more large scale as huge profits were made from selling drugs and designer clothes.

What were the punishments?

There were changes in the **purpose of prisons** – it was now hoped that prison would make prisoners better people.

The **harsh conditions** of the 19th century were changed. Prisoners could now mix more, they were given better food, and prisons were better heated. Prisoners now had access to education courses.

However, as the 20th century progressed, as the population grew larger, there was more crime and therefore more people in prisons. Prisons got bigger and were sometimes overcrowded.

There were **other changes** in the system of punishment.

- **Community work** and **electronic tagging** were two alternatives to prison.
- Some people got **probation** – they would not go to jail for minor offences if they committed to good behaviour.
- **Young offenders** were sent to **Borstal**, but later in the 20th century, that system was abolished because of the high rate of re-offending.
- Capital punishment (hanging) or the death penalty was abolished except in the case of treason because some innocent people were hanged.

Sample Question

Choose an aspect of life and society that you have studied where you looked at patterns of change over different time periods, such as one of the following: Food and drink; Work and leisure; Fashion and appearance; Health and medicine; Crime and punishment.
Your chosen aspect of life and society does not have to be one of the above.
(a) Name the aspect of life and society that you have studied.
Crime and punishment
(b) Give an account of **three changes** that you have learned about in your chosen aspect of life and society.
The way the laws were made has changed over different times. In Ancient Rome, there was a written code of law called the Twelve Tables. The laws were made by the senate, the emperor and by magistrates (judges). The laws applied to Roman citizens only. In the 18th and 19th centuries, the laws were made by parliaments and/or by kings and queens. In Britain, for example, parliament had power to make the laws, which the king or queen signed. Some laws were also made by local councils. These laws applied to everybody.
There were also changes in who enforced the law. There were no police in Ancient Rome. So, soldiers were brought in to keep order when that was needed. At night, vigiles patrolled the streets to watch for fires and prevent crimes. Because there were no police, victims of crime had to bring criminals to court, to face magistrates.

> The 19th century was very different to Ancient Rome. In 1829, Robert Peel established the Metropolitan Police Force in London. This was the first professional police force in Britain, and they became known as Peelers. They wore a special uniform and carried a wooden baton. The police patrolled the streets to prevent crime. Later, a detective division was added to the police force. The detective's job was to investigate crimes and gather evidence.
>
> Punishments also changed over different time periods. In the Middle Ages, there were no long-term prisons, so people were only held for a short time until a trial. In the 19th century, prisons were the main form of punishment for crime. More prisons were built, e.g. Pentonville in London.
>
> In medieval times, the most serious punishment was hanging or beheading, mostly for treason. These were often held in public as an example to everyone. In the 19th century, the Bloody Code (in which over 200 offences carried the death penalty) came to an end, so there were fewer hangings. Later, public hangings ended in 1868, but were still carried on in prisons.
>
> Sample 18, NCCA JC History Assessment Items

Revision Questions

Scan the QR code for more revision questions.

Assessment Overview

Assessment	Format	Student preparation	Completed	Grade
CBA1: The Past in My Place	• Display • Group, pair or individual • Graded by the class teacher	Maximum of three weeks with support/ guidance from teacher	Towards the end of Year 2	• Exceptional • Above expectations • In line with expectations • Yet to meet expectations Grade will be recorded on the Junior Cycle Profile of Achievement
CBA2: A Life in Time	• Written record • Individual • Graded by the class teacher	Maximum of three weeks with support/ guidance from teacher	Term 2 of Year 3	• Exceptional • Above expectations • In line with expectations • Yet to meet expectations Grade will be recorded on the Junior Cycle Profile of Achievement
The Assessment Task	• Students complete a specified written task which is sent to the SEC for marking	The Assessment Task will link to CBA2: *A Life in Time*	Following completion of CBA2 in Year 3, completed during class time	10% of final grade
Terminal Exam	• Two-hour written exam set and marked by the SEC		June of Year 3	90% of final grade • Distinction • Higher Merit • Merit • Achieved • Partially Achieved • Not Graded

Classroom-Based Assessment Guidelines

Classroom-Based Assessments (CBAs) are projects that you will carry out during your Junior Cycle History course. You will complete **two** History CBAs.

After CBA2, you will complete an **Assessment Task** that will count towards 10% of your final Junior Cycle History grade.

CBA1 – The Past in My Place

What is it? This is a local or family history project.

Where to begin: Firstly, decide if you are going to complete a local or family history project.

If you are completing your CBA on someone from your family, that person does **not** have to be from your locality.

If you are completing a local history project, your locality could be your town, city, county, parish, somewhere that you lived previously, where you were born.

Family history suggestions	Local history suggestions
• A family history or tree • A family member that is historically significant • The experience of a family member during a particular conflict, growing up, or who experienced or witnessed an important event • The role of a family member in a sporting movement or cultural group • The connection between your family and a particular group, company, event or battle • A family member involved in politics.	• A local person that is historically significant • A local building that is historically significant • The history of local place names • A battle or event that took place in your locality • The impact of an event or issue on your locality • The role of your locality in a battle or movement • A survey of how life has changed in your locality • An important local historical incident that caused changed • A historically significant local artefact or archaeological discovery.

Where to find sources

1. Start with a **general search on Google**. Be clear in your online searches. Try to use more than one word to describe what you are searching for. For example, search for 'Michael Collins War of Independence' rather than just 'Michael Collins'.
2. **Avoid Wikipedia** – anyone can edit it, and it isn't reliable. Try Encyclopaedia Britannica, Biography.com or History.com instead.
3. Go to your **school or local library** and ask the librarian for help. If they don't have any books on your topic, they can often order them in from other libraries.
4. Use Google books to search for books: *books.google.ie*. You can often read part, or sometimes all, of a book here.

5. Try **websites** like:
    - RTÉ archives *www.rte.ie/archives*
    - Biography *www.biography.com*
    - BBC History *www.bbc.co.uk/history*
    - History (American history) *www.history.com/topics*
6. If your chosen topic has an official website, look at that, e.g. *www.liverpoolfc.com/history*
7. Use the *Irish Times* **archive** (every school is entitled to a free subscription to this which you can access in school). *www.irishtimes.com/archive*
8. Contact your **local historical society or heritage centre** for help on research into local history, e.g. *www.skibbheritage.com*. If you don't know if your area has a historical society, search for it on Google.
9. For **family or Irish history** in 1901 and 1911, search the census records. Start searching with a surname and county if you are unsure what to look for. *www.census.nationalarchives.ie/search*
10. Look for **news clips or documentaries** on the RTÉ Player, RTÉ Archives or YouTube.
11. Look for relevant **podcast episodes** on Spotify or Apple Music.

How many sources do you need? You should use at least **two** different sources while researching your topic.

Time frame: This will be completed during a three-week window in 2nd Year.

Format: This must be presented as a display, e.g. a poster, PowerPoint presentation, video, booklet, website, model or timeline. This project can be done individually, in a pair or in a group. If you work in a pair or a group, you must clearly identify what you have done during the project as each student will be graded individually.

How it's marked: Your teacher will grade your project and award it one of the following descriptors:
- Exceptional
- Above expectations
- In line with expectations
- Yet to meet expectations.

Checklist for your display	✓
Title	
I have clearly stated the title of this project.	
Creativity and design	
I have demonstrated creativity and put thought and effort into the display I selected.	
I have included relevant images/drawings/maps/graphs with a caption.	
(If creating a poster display) I have made my display eye-catching.	
(If creating a video) I have included suitable music or audio.	
(If creating a model) My model is structurally secure and looks historically accurate.	
Content: I have answered the following questions *(You could use these to structure your display and write a paragraph on each)*	
Why did you do your project on this particular topic?	
For a local history project: What is the connection between your project and your locality?	
What is the historical significance of your topic (why does this topic/subject matter)?	
Provide some background information on your project.	
How does this topic fit into 'the big picture' of national or international history? For example, a local battle could have been part of wider events of the 1798 Rebellion.	
Has the information that you've discovered changed your opinion on anything?	
Have you offered your thoughts and opinions on your subject rather than just repeat what you've found out?	
If your subject is controversial, have you looked at it from more than one perspective?	
Have you presented the information that you have discovered in a clear and logical way?	
Spelling and grammar	
My spelling and grammar are accurate.	
Credits	
I have credited (said where I got) all my maps/images/graphs/information from.	
I have included the name of the source.	
I have included the author or creator.	
I have included the date it was made or published.	
I have included the date I used it (if it's a website).	
I have included the full URL (if it's a website).	
Group work *(If working in a group)*	
I have clearly marked (symbol/initials) what I did.	
Reflection: I have included a reflection section in my display that answers these questions	
What were the most positive things in my experience of working on this CBA?	
What were the main challenges I faced?	
What aspects of my learning about my subject did I find most significant?	
What did I learn about the role of the historian in conducting and presenting research?	

CBA2 – A Life in Time

What is it? This project is about any person from the past that interests you. It does not have to be someone from the Junior Cycle History course. If you select someone from the course, then your project could be on a more in-depth aspect of that person's life.

If you completed your CBA1 on Irish History, then you must complete your CBA2 on a figure from outside of Ireland. If you completed your CBA1 on a topic from outside of Ireland, then you must complete your CBA2 on a figure from Ireland.

Where to begin: Firstly, decide who you are going to complete CBA2 on. Is there anyone historically significant from the world of sport, or politics, or entertainment, or science, or technology, that you would like to learn more about? Have you come across anyone historically significant in class or online or on TV that you could complete this project on?

Your written report must be specific. You should look at one aspect of your chosen person's life. Some suggestions have been included below:

Possible aspects that you could focus on
• How this person contributed to historical change
• This person's early life
• An aspect of this person's career
• What might have influenced or had an impact on this person
• An important relationship in this person's life or career.

Where to find sources: See the guidelines on pages 204–5.

How many sources do you need? You should use at least **two** different sources while researching your topic.

Time frame: This will be completed during a three-week window in 3rd Year.

Format: This must be presented as a written record, such as an essay, a letter, an article, a speech or an obituary. This project must be completed individually.

How it's marked: Your teacher will grade your project and award it one of the following descriptors:

- Exceptional
- Above expectations
- In line with expectations
- Yet to meet expectations.

Checklist for your written record	✓
Title	
I have clearly stated the title of this project.	
Format	
My written record is coherent (logical, makes sense).	
(Where relevant) I have followed chronological order.	
I have used paragraphs.	
I have formatted my written record correctly, e.g. I have included my address and the newspaper's address at the top of my letter.	
Acting like a historian	
My written record is objective.	
Content: I have answered the following questions *(You could use these to structure your written record and write a paragraph on each)*	
Introduction	
What is your written report about?	
Is the focus of your written report specific? Does it focus on one aspect of the life of this person?	
What is the historical significance of your topic (why does this topic/subject matter)?	
Provide some background information on your project.	
Why did you do your project on this particular topic?	
Main body	
Have you presented all of the relevant information that you discovered while researching this topic?	
Have you offered your thoughts and opinions on your subject rather than just repeat what you've found out?	
Have you used different sources to demonstrate your research?	
Have you used evidence (quotes and references) to support your points?	
Conclusion	
Has the information that you've discovered changed your opinion on anything?	
Spelling and grammar	
My spelling and grammar are accurate.	
Credits	
I have listed all of my sources at the end of my record.	
I have included the name of the source.	
I have included the author or creator.	
I have included the date it was made or published.	
I have included the date I used it (if it's a website).	
I have included the full URL (if it's a website).	

Reflection: I have included a reflection section in my display that answers these questions	
What were the most positive things in my experience of working on this CBA?	
What were the main challenges I faced?	
What aspects of my learning about my subject did I find most significant?	
What did I learn about the role of the historian in conducting and presenting research?	

The Assessment Task (AT)

After you have completed your CBA2, you will complete a written Assessment Task. The Assessment Task is directly related to your second Classroom-Based Assessment, *A Life in Time*. The Assessment Task will be submitted to and corrected by the State Examinations Commission. The Assessment Task will count towards 10% of your final Junior Cycle result.

The Assessment Task will have two stages:
1. Engagement with **a short stimulus** in visual, written, audio or audio-visual format to prepare for the written task.
2. **A written task** that tests you in one or more of the following:
    - Your ability to show your understanding of historical concepts by applying your historical thinking to researching the life of a person in history in *A Life in Time*
    - Your ability to evaluate new knowledge or understanding that has emerged through your experience of *A Life in Time*
    - Your capacity to reflect on the process of research, of forming historical judgements based on evidence and other skills demonstrated while working on *A Life in Time*
    - Your reflections on how your experience of *A Life in Time* has influenced your attitudes and values
    - Your general appreciation of the nature of history.

Guidelines for Answering Exam Questions

Questions

2 HOURS | **120 MINUTES** | **8 QUESTIONS**

There are **eight questions** in the **Junior Cycle History examination paper.***
You must **answer all questions**.
Time: The examination is 2 hours.

$$\frac{120 \text{ minutes}}{8 \text{ questions}}$$

= **15 minutes per question.**

*There were eight questions in the final examination in 2022. However, the total number of questions can change from year to year. In an eight-question exam paper, the average time for each question is 15 minutes. In a 10-question exam paper, the average time for each question is 12 minutes.

Marks

TOTAL 360 MARKS | **8 QUESTIONS** | **AVERAGE 45 MARKS PER QUESTION**

In the 2022 examination,

Total marks = $\frac{360}{8}$ = **around 45 marks per question.**

There are **no marks allocated** on the examination paper.
However, some questions have more marks than others.
In the **2022 examination paper**, marks varied from 39 to 51, but half of the questions were marked out of 45 marks.
Even though you could spend more time on some questions than others, **it is best to spend no more time than about 15 minutes on each question.**

Answering questions

1. Read the instructions **carefully**.
2. Read the questions **carefully**.
3. Underline **key words** in each question.
   - **What is being asked in each question?**
   - **Mark the relevant section** of the document where you have found answers.
4. When you are **writing your answer**, keep **within the boxes** provided.
5. If you have extra information, go to the **extra pages** at the end of the booklet.
   - Mark the number and part of the question on any extra work.
6. **Have you answered all of the questions?**

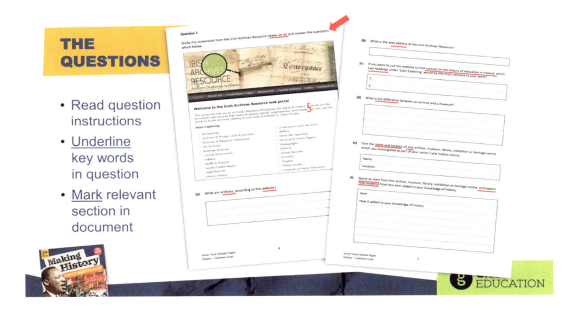

Statement and development

Some answers are **very short**.

> **Example:**
> *Question:* Name a revolution you studied from pre-twentieth-century Europe or the wider world.
> *Answer: The American Revolution*

But many answers **need extra information** to gain full marks.

Writing the answers
- Keep within the boxes.
- Fill out the boxes with information for a very good answer.
- Use back pages for extra information.

The best way to gain those marks is to make a **statement**, and then add more information to **explain** it (**development**). The statement and development together can be called a **key point**. Long answers, especially, are marked out of **the number of key points you have written**.

Statement

Development

Example: Leonardo da Vinci painted the Mona Lisa. This was a painting of a merchant's wife in Florence and it is one of the most famous paintings in the world. Da Vinci used a method of painting called sfumato with fine shading to show a gradual change in colours and to make scenes more realistic. The painting is hanging in the Louvre Museum, Paris, where it is seen by millions of people every year.

What can be learned from Question 1, JC History Examination 2022?

Question 1
An archaeological dig took place at Doon Point in Co. Kerry in May-June, 2021. Use the photograph and report below to answer the questions which follow.

Doon Point is a long, narrow strip of land that extends over 500 metres into the sea. It is one of 95 coastal promontory forts on the Dingle peninsula. All are at risk of coastal erosion.

Sandra Henry, lead archaeologist on the project says, 'The reason we are doing this dig is that we are trying to gather as much information as possible as these places are under increasing risk of erosion, cliff collapse and rising sea levels.'

Local farmer, Dennis Curran, estimates that about half an acre of the promontory fort has fallen into the sea. He has noted rising sea levels and an increase in the number of rock falls.

(a) Where in Ireland is Doon Point located?
    Dingle peninsula   3 marks

(b) When did the dig take place?
    May-June 2021   3 marks

The instructions say, 'Use the photograph and report below to answer the questions which follow.' But answers to Q1 (a) and (b) can be found in the instructions, so you should **read the instructions carefully**.

When the instructions say, 'Use the photograph and report', you should use information from **both** – otherwise you will lose marks.

Stating only '2021' in the answer gained only 1 mark.

GUIDELINES FOR ANSWERING EXAM QUESTIONS 213

(c) What was the role of Sandra Henry at the dig?

> *Lead archaeologist* — 3 marks

You must know **key words** to understand what is **being asked** in questions.

(d) What evidence from the photograph and the report shows the impact of climate change at Doon Point?

> *The photograph shows cliff collapse at the bottom left-hand side.*
> *The report says all promontory forts on Dingle peninsula are at risk of coastal erosion.*
>
> One piece of evidence from both sources = 3 + 3 marks

Note: the question says, 'What evidence from the photograph and the report'. **You will lose marks** if you do not provide evidence from **both**.

(e) The photograph was taken using a drone. Explain why drone technology is a useful tool for archaeologists.

> *Drones allow archaeologists to take photographs of the entire site.*
>
> 1 key point — 3 marks

Sometimes a question will be asked which may be **unexpected**, e.g. drone technology. Always ask yourself 'Can I answer this from something else I know about?' Aerial photography is an example in this case.

(f) Name **two** other tools used by archaeologists and briefly explain how they are used.

Name of tool × 2	2 + 2 marks
e.g. trowel, brush, etc.	
Explain how each tool is used × 2	3 + 3 marks
Use a sliding scale for explanation:	*3m = very good*
	2m = fair/good
	1m = weak
	0m = no attempt

Note this question has **two parts** – 'Name two other tools' **and** 'briefly explain how they are used'. You must answer **both parts**.

(g) Pick a topic from your Junior Cycle History course that you can link to archaeology, e.g.,
- a named ancient or medieval civilisation
- early Christian Ireland
- a pattern of settlement in Ireland
- another named topic of your choice.

How did archaeological evidence help you to learn about **three** different aspects of that topic?

Name of topic: *Ancient Rome.*

How archaeological evidence helped you to learn about the topic:

(1) *Archaeologists found swords when they were excavating in Rome.*

Weak answer (1 mark) = *This helped me to learn about Ancient Rome.*

Better answer (2 marks) = *This helped me learn about the different types of people who lived in Ancient Rome, such as soldiers and gladiators.*

Best answer (3 marks) = *This helped me learn about the different types of people who lived in Ancient Rome, such as soldiers and gladiators. Soldiers wore helmets and they carried shields, swords and bows and arrows. They defended the Roman Empire. Gladiators were slaves who fought other gladiators in the Colosseum, which could hold 50,000 people. They had swords and shields or spears. Sometimes they fought wild animals.*

Annotations:

- There are **two parts** to this question – name a topic **and** link archaeological evidence to life in the named topic.
- What archaeological evidence?
- If you choose an 'ancient or medieval civilisation', you must **name which civilisation** you are writing about, e.g. Ancient Rome or the Normans.
- What did the evidence show you about life in Ancient Rome? – examples of different quality answers and marks
- In relation to the archaeological evidence, you must choose **three different types of archaeological evidence**. Then you must **link each type** to 'different aspects' of life in your named civilisation, e.g. Ancient Rome.
- Develop your answers fully in explaining each of the three different aspects of life.
- One example of archaeological evidence – swords – is laid out above. You must select **two more examples** and **link each** of these **to different aspects** of life in Ancient Rome.

  Other examples of archaeological evidence could be bones, houses or food waste.

GUIDELINES FOR ANSWERING EXAM QUESTIONS

What can be learned from other questions in JC History Examination 2022?

Question 2 (c) – What is being asked in each question?

(c) Describe the main achievements of one Renaissance artist you studied during your Junior Cycle History course.

Artist's name:	2 marks
Achievements:	12 marks

Note key word: 'achievements'.

12 marks = 4 key points @ 3 marks

Key point = statement + development

You must **name the artist**.

You must write about **that artist's achievements**.

e.g. **key point** = name of painting/sculpture/ achievement + development with new information.

Also note you must write about only **one** Renaissance artist. Note also that it is the achievements of an **'artist'**, not a scientist.

Use **'statement and development'** for each achievement. Each achievement will need **at least one key point**.

Question 3 (d) – Writing a key point (using statement and development)

(d) Write an account of **one** of the events/developments mentioned in the timeline. Explain how people in the New World and/or Europe were affected by it.

> 18 marks = at least 6 key points @ 3 marks
> Key point = statement + development

Example of one key point:

The event chosen from the timeline is 1492, Columbus's first voyage to the New World. In 1492, Columbus sailed from Spain with three ships. He sailed westwards across the Atlantic Ocean because he believed the world was round and that he would reach Asia and the Spice Islands this way. He wanted a new trade route to Asia because the trade there was controlled by the Arabs and Italians.

Note: **two aspects** to this question – write an account of **one event/development AND** how the event/development **affected people** in the New World and/or Europe. **You will lose marks if you write about only one event/development.**

Use '**statement and development**' for **each key point** you make.

This key point relates to the account of the event. Other key points should explain how people in the New World/Europe were affected.

GUIDELINES FOR ANSWERING EXAM QUESTIONS

Question 4 (c) – Answering picture questions

Source 1: *United Irishmen upon Duty* by James Gillray, 12 June 1798

When answering questions from **pictures**, **mark or circle** the **relevant** parts of the picture, **then write your answer**.

(c) According to the artist in (Source 1, what is happening in Ireland?) Support your points with evidence from the drawing.

Ireland is in chaos with the United Irishmen on duty. The United Irishman with the red jacket is about to kill the householder with a sword marked 'Liberty' in the middle of the night.

12 marks = at least 4 key points @ 3 marks

Note: when answering the question, 'what is happening in Ireland?', refer to '**evidence** from the drawing'.

Example of **key point** using evidence from the drawing.

Question 5 (c) – Answering written document questions

Question 5

Over one million people emigrated from Ireland in the 1840s/1850s. The following sources relate to a ship containing Irish emigrants which arrived in New York on 30 November 1853. Examine the sources and answer the questions which follow.

Source 1: extract from a newspaper report describing the ship and its passengers.

> The ship, *Marathon*, left Liverpool on the 22nd of September, with 522 passengers, mostly Irish. She arrived at New York after a voyage of 59 days, during which she lost 64 persons to an outbreak of cholera.
>
> The passengers were in a state of the most wretched poverty and filth. They were lodged on two decks, one above the other. The decks were covered with reeking filth.
>
> The passengers' provisions [food supplies] were exhausted three weeks before the ship came into port. Had the ship been delayed for a few days longer, the people would have starved.

When answering questions from **documents**, **mark** or **circle** the **relevant** parts of the document, then write your answer.

(c) In Source 1, what were **three** difficulties faced by passengers on the *Marathon*? Support each point with reference to the source.

Statement of one point → **Example of one point:**

Passengers were sick because of an 'outbreak of cholera' and '64 persons' out of '522 passengers' died. Conditions on board were filthy – 'The decks were covered with reeking filth' – and this would spread the disease.

Development of the statement with supporting information from Source 1, including quotation marks.

Note: you are asked for **three difficulties** faced by **passengers** from **Source 1**.

Note: you must **quote extracts** from the report in **support** of each point.

Note: Some Key Points from the State Examinations Commission on JC History Examination
- Revise all chapters because all questions must be answered.
- Attempt all questions – if there is no answer, there are no marks.
- Read the question carefully. Underline key words.
- Understand the meaning of 'a pattern of settlement', 'the parliamentary tradition', 'the physical force tradition', 'international co-operation', etc.
- Also understand terms such as 'cause and consequence', 'decade', 'impact of', 'significance of', and 'pre-twentieth century'.
- The number of lines in an answer box is a guide to the length of answer required.
- Use the extra space at the end of the answer book if necessary.
- If you want to cross out an answer, only draw a single line through it.

Glossary

Absentee landlords: Landlords who did not live on their estates
Abstentionism: The policy of Sinn Féin in 1918 general election to refuse to sit in parliament in Westminster
Act of Union: Act which closed the Dublin parliament and Ireland was controlled directly from Westminster
AD: Anno Domini; after the birth of Christ
Aerial photography: Photographs taken from drones, helicopters or planes can show crop marks, ditches and walls that might not be visible from the ground
Amphitheatre: An arena such as the Colosseum used for gladiator contests in Ancient Rome
Anatomy: Study of the human body
Ancient civilisation: Developed societies up to the end of Ancient Rome in the fifth century AD
Anglicisation: The process of becoming more English in language and culture
Anglo-Irish relations: Relations between Britain and Ireland
Anschluss: The union of Nazi Germany and Austria; German takeover of Austria
Anti-Semitism: Hatred of the Jews
Antiseptic: A substance used to reduce the risk of infection
Appeasement: The policy of British government in 1930s which held that if governments gave into Hitler's demands, then a world war could be prevented
Apprentice: A person training to become a craftsman
Aqueduct: A bridge for carrying water in Ancient Rome
Archaeology: The study of the past through material remains
Archive: A place where historical documents are kept
Arms race: The competition between USA and Soviet Russia (USSR) to develop more weapons, especially nuclear weapons during the Cold War
Arsenal of democracy: Title given to USA during World War II because it provided supplies to support Britain
Artefact: An object made by people, e.g. sword, axe
Aryan race: The name given to the Nazi genetic ideal of a white race
Astrolabes, quadrants and cross-shafts: Navigation instruments used in the Age of Exploration to find latitude
Astronomy: The study of the stars and the universe
Atrium: The central courtyard in a Roman house
Aural sources: Historical sources obtained through listening
Autarky: The policy of self-sufficiency in goods and food, without imports
Autobiography: The story of a person's life written by themselves
Auxiliaries: Ex-British army officers who were enlisted in the Royal Irish Constabulary during the War of Independence
Aztec Empire: Empire that was based in present-day Mexico
Bailey: Courtyard or open space in a motte and bailey or medieval stone castle
Barber surgeons: Barber who could perform surgical procedures, e.g. pulling teeth and amputations
Bawn: A walled enclosure built for defence in the Plantation of Ulster
BC: Before the birth of Christ
BCE: Before Common Era
Beauty of Labour: A Nazi programme to improve working conditions, e.g. better canteen food
Beveridge Report: The report that led to the creation of the Welfare State in Britain, providing free healthcare
Bias: Deliberately favouring one side over the other; prejudiced
Biography: The story of a person's life written by somebody else
Black and Tans: Ex-soldiers from Britain who were enlisted in the Royal Irish Constabulary during the War of Independence
Black Death: A plague caused by fleas on rats, which spread in the Middle Ages
Black market: An illegal market where goods are bought or bartered for
Blitz: German bombing of British cities after the Battle of Britain during World War II
Blitzkrieg: Lightning war tactics used by Germany in World War II, using planes, tanks and infantry
Blockade: To surround by ships and troops to prevent movement of supplies and people, e.g. Berlin Blockade, Cuban Blockade
Blood sacrifice: Idea of Padraig Pearse that death or self-sacrifice would revive Irish spirit; influenced the 1916 Rising
Bloodletting: A medical treatment in which blood was taken from the patient, used in medieval times and after
Book of Kells: A manuscript copy of the Four Gospels created in Early Christian Ireland

Border (or partition): Line dividing Northern Ireland and the Irish Free State/Republic of Ireland
Bosniak: Bosnian Muslim
Boundary Commission: Group set up to lay out or outline the border between Northern Ireland and the Irish Free State under the Anglo-Irish Treaty
British Commonwealth: An association of states consisting of Britain and former colonies of the British Empire
Brownshirts: Name given to Hitler's Stormtroopers (or SA)
B-Specials: Part-time police in Northern Ireland
c.: 'circa', around, e.g. c. 500 BC
Capitalism: Economic and political system in which industry and agriculture is largely privately owned
Caravel: Ship used by Portuguese and Spanish sailors to explore the coasts of Africa and the Americas in the Age of Exploration
Carbon dating: Technique used to date ancient objects by measuring the amount of carbon-14 in them
Carrack or nao: Large ship used for longer journeys in the Age of Exploration
Carvel-built: Boards on the side of the ship were fitted edge-to-edge
Castle Document: Document which said Dublin Castle planned to arrest leaders of Irish Volunteers in 1916
CAT scanners: Developed 3D images of the inside of the body
Catacombs: Underground tombs used by Christians in Ancient Rome for burials and to hold masses
Cathach: Example of a manuscript in Early Christian Ireland
Catholic Emancipation: Catholic freedom from discrimination, particularly the right to sit in Westminster
Cause: A reason why something happened; explains why events happened
CE: Common Era
Cena: Main meal of the day in Ancient Rome
Censorship: Control of the media
Century: 100 years
Charter: Permission granted by kings or lords to towns to trade
Cholera: Illness caused by dirty water or food
Chronology: The study of time and dates; putting events in order of time (when they happened)
Church abuses: Practices such as nepotism, simony, pluralism and absenteeism, which were common in the Catholic Church before the Reformation
Circus Maximus: Arena in Ancient Rome for chariot racing

Civil rights: The rights of people in a society or country, including freedom of speech, meeting, press and religion
Cloister: Covered walking area in a medieval monastery for monks praying
Coalition government: Government formed by a number of political parties, usually applied to Fine Gael-Labour Party government of the 1970s
Coffin ships: Name given to badly maintained ships used to transport emigrants to America during the Great Famine
Cold War: Period of hostility between the USA and its allies and the Soviet Union and its allies which lasted from after World War II to the collapse of communism in the early 1990s
Collaborator: Person who works with the enemy in control of their country
Collective farms: Private farms joined together to form large farms under government ownership and control in Soviet Russia (USSR)
Collective security: Policy of the League of Nations that each member state was responsible for the security and safety of all other members
Collectivisation: The process of taking farms off of farmers (peasants) and forming collective farms in Soviet Russia (USSR)
Colonisation: Settling among and establishing control over native people
Colony: An area of land controlled by a foreign power, e.g. New York and Virginia were English colonies
Colosseum: Arena in Ancient Rome used for gladiator fighting and other entertainment
Commemoration: A service, monument or celebration as an act of remembrance of a historically significant event or person
Common Agricultural Policy (CAP): Policy of EEC/EU dealing with agriculture/farming and food
Common market: A free trade area with relatively free movement of goods and services, e.g. the EEC/EU
Common Sense: Bestselling book written by Tom Paine that advocated for American Independence
Commons: Public area near the village in medieval times which peasants used to graze animals
Communism: Political belief associated with Soviet Russia and holding that the state (or government) should control industry and agriculture
Community and comprehensive schools: Schools that combined academic subjects of secondary schools with practical subjects of vocational schools
Compass: Tool used to tell direction

GLOSSARY

Concentration camps: Detention centres used by Nazi Germany to imprison opponents without trial, e.g. Bergen-Belsen, Dachau

Confessing Church: Protestant church that opposed the Nazis

Conquest: Forcibly take over

Conquistadors: Spanish conquerors who defeated native empires in Central and South America, e.g. Cortés and Pizarro

Conscription: Forced enlistment in the army

Consequences: Effects; results; impact; showing historical change

Contentious issues: Controversial issues or topics that cause disagreement or conflict

Contentious: Controversial

Continental Army: American army formed by the Second Continental Congress, led by George Washington

Contribution: The part played by a person or organisation in historical events

Controversial issues: Contentious, divisive topics

Convent: A building in which nuns live

Convoys: A group of merchant ships protected by warships, for example, crossing the Atlantic Ocean during World War II

Corbelling: A method of building a roof where flat stones were put on top of one another

Cottier: Farmer renting a small plot of land in pre-Famine Ireland

Counter-Reformation: Efforts by the Catholic Church to reform itself and stop the spread of Protestantism

Course: The progress or development of historical events

Craftsman: Skilled person trained as an apprentice during the Middle Ages, e.g. a carpenter

Crematorium: A place where a dead person's body was cremated or burnt

Crop rotation: Growing different crops in a piece of land each year to make sure the land stays fertile

Cult of personality: Promoting the glorification (worship) of a leader, e.g. Hitler and Stalin were glorified with posters, special festivals and other forms of propaganda

Cultural inheritance: Heritage from the past (history, customs, buildings) which we value and preserve

Cultural nationalism: Where the nation is defined by a common culture, as in cultural revival

Cultural revival: Movement at the end of the 19th century that aimed to promote all things Irish and reduce English influence in Irish life

Cumann na mBan: Irish republican women's paramilitary organisation

Curfew: Rule where everybody had to stay indoors after a certain time

Curtain wall: A stone wall that surrounds a castle

Death marches: People in concentration and extermination camps were forced to march towards Germany, away from the advancing Red Army

Decade: 10 years

Declaration of Independence: A formal statement by the American colonies wanting to choose their own government

Decolonisation: The process of colonies gaining their independence from imperial powers

Decommissioned arms: Putting arms out of use, as in Northern Ireland after the Good Friday Agreement

Demesne: Land that knights kept for their own use

Democracy: A political system that holds that political power comes from the people who vote for leaders in a general election

Dendrochronology (tree-ring dating): Finding out the age of timber by studying the pattern of rings

Dictatorship: A system of government where one man or party has all the power

Dig (excavation): Digging up the earth in order to look for historical objects (artefacts)

Digital archive: Historical sources or documents held online

Direct rule: Where Northern Ireland was ruled directly from London

Discrimination: Treating someone differently because of their religion, race, gender, age, etc.

Dissection: Cutting up dead bodies for medical purposes

Documents: Written, printed or electronic matter that contains historical information

Dole: Free grain given to people in Ancient Rome

Domestic servant: Someone who works in their employer's house, doing jobs such as cooking, cleaning and laundry

Domestic system: The making of goods (such as thread and cloth) in people's houses before the Industrial Revolution

Dominion status: Membership of the British Commonwealth agreed by Ireland in the Anglo-Irish Treaty, similar to Canada and Australia

Domus: Private house of rich Romans (patricians)

Dowry: Money or gifts given by the bride's father to her new family when she got married

Drawbridge: The bridge over a moat in a medieval castle

Ecumenism: Promoting unity among the world's Christian churches

Edelweiss Pirates: A group of German youths who opposed Nazi rule

Einsatzgruppen: SS killing squads during World War II

Emergency: The period of World War II in the south of Ireland, Éire
Emigration: Moving from one country to live in another one
Enabling Act: A law passed by Hitler which gave him power to rule by decree
Encomienda system: Spanish system used in South America in which landowners were given the right to use free native labour on their haciendas (plantations)
Epidemic: When a disease affects a large number of people within a community, population or region
Equality: The right of different groups to receive the same treatment, e.g. in education, job opportunities
European unity: European countries working together to secure lasting peace
Evacuation: Moving people from the city to the countryside, especially in Britain during World War II
Eviction: Forcing somebody or expelling somebody from a property
Evidence: The information which proves or disproves the story of the past. Historians get their evidence from sources.
Excavation: An archaeological dig
Excommunication: Excluding someone from participating in the sacraments of the Christian churches
Extermination camp: A camp designed primarily or exclusively for mass murder, e.g. Treblinka
Fact: Something that happened; a 'true' statement
Fascism: A political ideology, which is anti-democratic and anti-communist, and uses violence to maintain power
Federal government: The division of power between a central national government and local state governments
Feudalism or Feudal system: The system of land ownership and government during the Middle Ages
Fief: An element in feudalism in which land was handed over from the king to the baron/lord
Filigree: Gold wiring on metalwork in Early Christian Ireland
Final Solution: The policy of Hitler and the Nazis of killing all Jews during World War II
First Programme for Economic Expansion: The economic plan developed by T. K. Whitaker that encouraged exports and gave tax concessions to attract foreign industry to Ireland
Five-Year Plans: Economic planning in Soviet Russia (USSR) to boost production in agriculture and industry
Flight of the Earls: Ulster chiefs fled Ireland for the continent in 1607

Flying columns: Small units of the IRA that ambushed British forces during the War of Independence
Forum: A marketplace in the city centre in Ancient Rome
Fosterage: The lord and lady of the castle took the children of other lords and trained them to become knights
Four Freedoms: The free movement of goods, persons, services and capital in EEC/EU
Four humours: A system of medicine in Ancient Roman and medieval medicine; the four humours were believed to be black bile, yellow bile, blood and phlegm
Fraternity: Brotherhood
Freeman: A peasant who was free to move away from the manor in medieval times, if they wanted
Fresco: A painting style in Ancient Rome and in the Renaissance where painting was done on damp plaster
Friar: Member of a religious order who travelled from place to place, preaching and helping the sick and poor
Führer (leader): Title of Hitler after he combined the office of president and chancellor
Gatehouse: Protected the gate of the castle
Genocide: The deliberate extermination of a group of people
Geophysical survey: Used by archaeologists to create a map of features under the surface of the ground
Gerrymander: A system of rigging the boundaries of constituencies to ensure control by a particular party
Gestapo: The secret police in Nazi Germany
Ghetto: A place where Jews were forced to live away from the general population
Gladiator: A slave who was a specially trained fighter in Ancient Rome
Glimmer men: Gas inspectors in Ireland during the Emergency (World War II)
Gothic: A style of architecture in medieval times featuring pointed arches and windows
Great Patriotic War: The name given by Soviet Russia (USSR) to the resistance against the German invasion in World War II
Guild: A trade association for craftsmen and merchants in medieval times
Guillotine: A machine with a heavy blade for beheading people during the French Revolution
Gulags: Slave labour camps used to hold opponents or critics of Stalin's rule in Soviet Russia (USSR)
Haciendas: Large estates in South America bought from or granted by the Spanish king
Hawking: Hunting with hawks in medieval times
Herrenvolk: The Nazi belief that the Germans were the 'Master Race', superior to all other races

GLOSSARY

High cross: A tall stone cross in monasteries in Early Christian Ireland

Histamine: A chemical produced by the body during an allergic reaction

Historical change: How differences occur in history through causes and consequences (effects)

Historical consciousness: Understanding how past, present and future are connected, seeing the world historically with an awareness of time and place

Historical context: Placing events in a wider development to understand how and what happened

Historical empathy: Understanding the motives, actions and beliefs of people in their own time

Historical era/period: A time in history with common features, e.g. Ancient Rome

Historical perspective: Being able to place events, issues and people in their historical context or time

Historically significant: Events or people who had an important impact or effect on history

History: The story of the past based on evidence

Hitler Youth: A Nazi youth group for boys aged 14–18

Holocaust: The killing of 6 million Jews by Nazi Germany during World War II

Home Rule: Irish nationalist policy that wanted self-government in Ireland with a parliament in Dublin dealing with internal Irish affairs

Hue and cry: A loud call to chase and catch a criminal in medieval times

Hunger strike: The refusal to eat for a long time as a political protest

Hutu: An ethnic group primarily in Rwanda and Burundi

Identity: Characteristics that make us who we are

Impact: Having an effect or influence on historical events

Inca Empire: An empire that was based in present-day Peru

Indoctrinated: Brainwashed, persuaded to accept ideas by continually repeating them

Indulgences: Actions that reduced the amount of punishment for sin

Industrial Revolution: The rapid industrial growth that began in England in the 18th century

Industrialisation: The development or growth of factories

Innovation: The development of something new

Inquisition: The Catholic Church court in Italy and Spain used to try Protestants and Jews

Insula: An apartment block in Ancient Rome

Insulin: Breaks down sugar in the body

Inter-continental ballistic missiles (ICBMs): Used to fire nuclear warheads

International relations: Relations between different countries

Internment: The arrest and imprisonment without trial of people suspected of being involved in violence in Northern Ireland during the Troubles

Interpretation: A version of events written by historians, explaining what happened

Intolerable Acts: Acts of the British parliament that closed Boston Port until the tea lost during the Boston Tea Party had been paid for

Intolerance: An unwillingness to respect or tolerate the views of others, usually religious or political

Irish Diaspora: Irish people or people of Irish descent living in other countries

Irish National League: An organisation which wanted to help poor tenant farmers

Irish Women's Franchise League: An organisation that campaigned for women to get the right to vote

Irish Women's Liberation Movement (IWLM): A feminist organisation concerned with gaining equal rights and opportunities for women

Iron Curtain: The border dividing democratic West from communist East during the Cold War

Irregulars: Anti-Treaty forces in Ireland during the Civil War

Jesuits: A religious order founded by Ignatius Loyola to spread the teachings of the Catholic Church

Journeyman: A skilled worker after seven years as an apprentice who could travel around looking for work

Jousting: A sport played by knights during medieval times

Justification by faith: Luther's belief that only faith in God would allow a person to go to heaven

Keep: The tower in a medieval castle where the lord or king lived

Khmer Rouge: A group that ruled Cambodia 1975–79

Kilmainham Treaty: A political agreement between Gladstone and Parnell on improving the Land Act and stopping violence in the countryside

Kinder, Küche, Kirche **(Children, Kitchen, Church):** The Nazi ideal for women

Knight: A specially trained warrior in medieval times

Kulaks: Middle-class farmers in Soviet Russia (USSR)

Laissez-faire: The belief or policy that governments should not be involved in running the economy

Land Act: Provided fair rents for the tenants and a land court to decide the rents

Land War: Increased agrarian outrages (incidents, crimes) in the countryside between landlords and tenants

Lateen sails: Triangular sails
Lay participation: The participation of non-members of the clergy in church ceremonies and activities
League of German Maidens: A Nazi youth group for girls aged 14–18
League of Nations: An association of countries set up after World War I to achieve peace and promote international co-operation
Lebensborn: An organisation with the aim of increasing the birth rate of Aryan children
Lebensraum (living space): The Nazi policy to use Eastern Europe and Russia to provide raw materials and workers for the Nazis
Legion: A division of the army in Ancient Rome, usually 5,000 soldiers
Legionary: A soldier in a legion in Ancient Rome
Liberty: Freedom
Library: A building for storing books
Limitations of sources: Weaknesses of historical sources which make them less valuable or useful
Log and line: Used in ships of the Age of Exploration to work out the speed of the ship
Logbook: Used in ships of the Age of Exploration to record events during the voyage
Loyalists: Extreme unionists in Northern Ireland, strongly opposed to a united Ireland
Luftwaffe: The German air force during World War II
Maginot Line: The defensive line constructed by France along the German border
Manor: A village and the land around it in medieval times
Manuscript: A handwritten book
Matins: Morning prayers in a monastery
Medieval society: Life and how it was lived in medieval times
Medieval times: Also called the Middle Ages, this was the time between the fall of Ancient Rome and the start of the Renaissance
Merchant: Someone who buys and sells goods
Military Council: Committee of the Irish Republican Brotherhood (IRB) that organised the 1916 Rising
Minstrels: Musicians, jugglers and entertainers in a medieval feast
Missionary: A person sent abroad to convert locals to Christianity
Moat: A trench filled with water around a medieval castle
Modernised: Brought up to date
Monastery: A building or series of buildings where monks live, work and pray
Monster rallies: Huge rallies, organised by Daniel O'Connell, as part of the campaign to repeal the Act of Union
Mosaics: Tiled patterns on floors, often in Ancient Rome
Mother's Cross of Honour: A medal awarded to mothers with large families in Nazi Germany
Mothers' Schools: Schools to educate women in household work in Nazi Germany
Motte and bailey: A castle built of timber in the Middle Ages, with a mound and a courtyard
Motte: A mound of earth with a timber tower or keep
MRI scanners: Machines that look at the workings of the brain
Murals: Paintings done on walls
Museum: Collects and stores objects (artefacts) for study and display
Nationalised: Putting industry and agriculture under government ownership
Nationalism: The political idea or belief that identifies with one's own nation and supports its interests
Nationalist: In the context of Ireland, someone who wants Irish unity under Irish rule
Navigation Acts: Acts of British parliament that said some American products, like sugar, could only be sold through England
Nazi Soviet Pact: A 10-year pact of non-aggression signed by Germany and Russia, also agreed to split Poland between them
Neutral: Not taking sides
Neutrality: Policy of Irish government during World War II not to take part in the war
Night of the Broken Glass (*Kristallnacht*): The night Hitler's SA attacked Jews, their shops and synagogues after a Polish Jew killed a German diplomat in Paris
Night of the Long Knives: The night Hitler commanded his SS to arrest and kill leaders of the SA, including Ernst Röhm, because they threatened his leadership
Nine Years' War: The war between Gaelic chiefs in Ulster and the English government over the spread of English culture and customs in Ireland
No taxation without representation: The belief that American colonists should not be taxed when they are not represented in parliament in London
North Atlantic Treaty Organisation (NATO): A defensive association of countries including the USA and countries in Western Europe
Northern Ireland Civil Rights Association (NICRA): An association established to end discrimination against Catholics
Novice: Someone training to become a monk or nun
Nuclear war: A war fought with nuclear weapons
Nuremberg Laws: Nazi laws against the Jews, which deprived them of German citizenship, banned marriages with non-Jews and forced them to wear the Star of David

GLOSSARY

Nuremberg Rallies: A large festival/series of parades held to celebrate and glorify the Nazis
Oath of Allegiance: The oath taken by deputies of Dáil Éireann
Objective: Not influenced by personal feelings or opinions in judging the facts
One man, one vote: An aim of NICRA that meant that each person, regardless of whether they owned property or not, should be able to vote
Operation Barbarossa: The German battle plan for the invasion of Soviet Russia during World War II
Operation Dynamo: The evacuation of soldiers from Dunkirk in World War II
Operation Overlord: The code name for Allied plan to invade France during World War II
Operation Sea Lion: The Nazi plan to invade Britain in World War II
Operation Vittles: The code name for airlift of food and supplies to West Berlin during the Berlin Blockade
Opinion: A view or belief about something that happened or is about to happen
Oral sources: Historical sources that are spoken, such as interviews and recordings
Oratory: A small church
Page: The first stage in the training of a knight in medieval times
Pandemic: An epidemic that is spread over many countries or continents
Panzer: A German tank during World War II
Paramilitary: An armed organisation, not part of the official armed forces, an unofficial army
Parchment: Paper made out of sheepskin
Parliamentary tradition: Using peaceful methods and politics to get greater independence for Ireland
Partition: The division of Ireland and creation of Northern Ireland
Passive resistance: Resisting or opposing government laws without the use of violence, peacefully
Pasteurisation: Sterilising something, usually by heating it, to destroy bacteria
Patricians: Rich people in Ancient Rome
Patron: A supporter of artists during the Renaissance
Peasants: Farmers who rented land from lords under the feudal system
Penal Laws: Laws passed in 17th- and 18-century Ireland to control and discriminate against Catholics and Presbyterians
People's Radio: A cheap radio that was used to listen to Hitler's speeches
Personalities: Famous or influential people
Perspective: A technique used by artists in the Renaissance to create the illusion of depth (3D effect)
Phoenix Park murders: Two high-ranking officials in the British government were murdered by a Fenian group in 1882
Physical force tradition: Using an armed rebellion or uprising to get an independent Ireland
Pilgrimage: A symbolic journey to a holy place
Pillory: A wooden frame with holes to put your head and hands through, used as punishment in medieval times
Plantation: The policy of the English government to bring in English and Scottish planters to Ireland
Plantations: Large farms that grew crops like cotton, tobacco and sugar in the Americas
Plebeians: Poorer people in Ancient Rome
Pogrom: A violent massacre aimed at a particular group of people, e.g. Jews
Policy of containment: The policy of USA during the Cold War to stop the spread of communism
Polish Corridor: A piece of land that connected Germany and East Prussia
Political prisoner: Prisoners jailed for political reasons; this status was often given to those who did not want to be treated the same way as criminals
Pollen: A substance produced by plants; analysis of pollen found in ancient sites helps archaeologists to find out what plants were growing at the time, when forests were cleared and when farming
Portcullis: An iron-and-timber gate at the entrance to a castle that could be raised and lowered for defence
Portolan charts: The earliest maps used during the Age of Exploration that showed places along the coast joined by straight lines
Pottage: A thick stew
Prehistory: The history of people before writing was invented, based on archaeological evidence
Primary source: A source that came directly from the time that is being studied. It is a first-hand account of what happened.
Propaganda: The use of information to influence people's opinions or to convince people that a particular belief is true
Protectionism: Taxing imports to protect industry at home
Protestant Ascendancy: Members of the Church of Ireland who controlled the Irish parliament
Protestant: A member of Christian churches that separated from the Catholic Church in the Reformation
Purge: Removing people from an organisation because they do not agree with you e.g. purging of Communist Party in Stalin's Russia
Quadrant: A navigation instrument used in the Age of Exploration to find latitude
RAF: Royal Air Force (United Kingdom)

Rationing: Use of coupons and ration books to control the amount of food, clothes, footwear and petrol given to each person during the Emergency (World War II) in Ireland (also in Britain and Germany)
Rearmament: Increasing the size of the army, creating arms and weapons
Refectory: The dining room in a monastery in Early Christian Ireland or in a medieval monastery
Reformation: A movement that protested against abuses in the Catholic Church and led to the establishment of the Protestant churches
Reformer: Someone who wants to make changes for the better
Refugee: A person who has been forced to leave home and cannot safely return home
Regulars: Pro-Treaty forces in Ireland during the Civil War
Reign of Terror: A time of bloodshed and repression during the French Revolution
Reliable source: A source that you can trust; the information in it is accurate and true
Renaissance: The time of revival of interest in learning of Ancient Greece and Rome, begun in Italy
Reparations: Compensation
Repository of historical evidence: A museum, archive, library or similar institution
Republic: A form of government where people vote for their leaders and the country is led by an elected representative like a president
Republicanism: The political belief in Ireland that advocated complete independence from Britain and the establishment of a republic (a government without a monarch) by physical force (rebellion)
Resistance movement: Opposition to German army in World War II
Revolution: The forcible overthrow of a government; also huge change in society and economy
Romanesque: A type of architecture in medieval times that followed the style of Ancient Rome
Round tower: A tall tower built in monasteries in Early Christian Ireland for safety
Royal charter: Gave towns permission to form a town government, hold fairs and markets and hold their own courts
Royal Ulster Constabulary (RUC): The police force in Northern Ireland
Rudder: Used for steering the ship
Rule by decree: A situation in which rulers such as Hitler make laws without having to pass them in parliament
Rule of St Benedict: A set of rules that monks and nuns must follow
SA: A Nazi paramilitary organisation led by Ernst Röhm, also known as the Brownshirts
Sans-culotte: The working class in Paris during the French Revolution
Scorched-earth policy: A war tactic used by the Soviet soldiers during World War II of burning crops and destroying bridges and towns as they retreated before the Germans
Scriptorium: The manuscript room in a monastery in Early Christian Ireland or in a medieval monastery
Secondary source: A source that comes from after the time being studied. Secondary sources are based on primary sources and other secondary sources.
Sectarian riots: Riots between people from different religious groups, e.g. violence between Catholics and Protestants
Sectarian violence: Violence between people from different religious groups
Sectarianism: Prejudice or hatred between people from different religions or racial groups
Separatist tradition: The belief that full revival of Gaelic culture could not be achieved without a fully independent country
Serf: A peasant who worked the land for a lord in the Middle Ages
Servitors: English soldiers and officials who were granted land in the Plantation of Ulster
Seven Years' War: British and American conflict against the French in Canada
Sfumato: A painting technique associated with Leonardo da Vinci which used blended colours
Shortages: When there is not enough food or other goods for people
Show trials: Public trials in Soviet Russia used to influence the people of the country
Socialism: The political belief that favours state (government) control of industry and agriculture
Solar: The private rooms of the lord's family in a castle
Sons of Liberty: A group of revolutionary American colonists who fought against British taxation
Source: A historical source provides the evidence for writing history
Soviet partisans: Soldiers who resisted the German army with guerrilla warfare tactics during World War II
Space Race: The competition between the USA and the Soviet Union to get the first people on the Moon
Spices: Ingredients used to give flavour to food, brought from the Spice Islands (Maluku Islands)
Squad: The group of IRA volunteers formed by Michael Collins to kill British spies and others during the War of Independence
SS: A paramilitary group originally formed to serve as Hitler's bodyguards, also known as the Blackshirts

GLOSSARY

Stakhanovite Movement: Propaganda campaign in Soviet Russia to encourage people to work harder for the country

Stamp Act: Newspapers and legal documents stamped and taxed by a government official in colonial America

Stocks: A wooden frame with holes for your feet or head and hands, used as a punishment in the Middle Ages

Stola: A long dress worn by women in Ancient Rome

Stratigraphy: A method of dating objects where the oldest layers are at the bottom and the youngest layers are at the top

Strength Through Joy: An organisation set up to create leisure activities for workers in Nazi Germany

Strigil: An instrument to scrape oil and dirt off the body in Ancient Roman baths

Subdivision: When larger farms were split into smaller farms

Subjective: Historical views influenced by a person's opinions or feelings; opposite to objective

Superpowers: The USA and the Soviet Union (USSR) during the Cold War

Swastika: A Nazi symbol in the form of a crooked cross

Swinging Sixties: The nickname given to the 1960s because of the many changes that took place in music, fashion and culture

Tactile sources: Sources that can be touched, such as artefacts and buildings

Technology: The machines and tools that are used to solve practical problems

The Troubles: The 30-year-long period of violence in Northern Ireland

Timeline: A line or graph which shows the dates when events happened; puts events in chronological order

Tithe: A tax paid to the church

Toga: A long robe worn by men in Ancient Rome

Toll: Tax

Tories: Gaelic Irish who lived in the mountains and woods

Treaty ports: Three ports in Ireland that the British could use for bases after the Anglo-Irish Treaty

Trial by combat: Where a person, usually a nobleman, faced his accuser, and if he won the combat or fight, he was innocent

Trial by ordeal: Where accused persons had to hold on to a hot bar or be thrown into water and survive to prove their innocence

Tunic: A short garment worn by men and women in Ancient Rome

Tutsi: An ethnic minority primarily found in Rwanda and Burundi

Typhus: An illness caused by fleas

U-boat: A German submarine

Ulster Solemn League and Covenant: The declaration of Ulster unionists to resist Home Rule by all means, signed by over 200,000 people

Undertakers: English planters who received land during the Plantation of Munster, or English and Scottish planters who received land during the Plantation of Ulster

Unionism: The political belief that Ireland's union with Britain must be retained, and that parliament in Westminster should continue to make laws for Ireland

Unionist: An Irish or Northern Irish person who wants to maintain the link with Britain

United Irishmen: Group founded in Belfast to unite all religions and to reduce English power in Ireland

Usefulness (of a source): A source is useful when it provides information about the topic you are researching

Vaccine: A substance that stimulates the immune system to produce antibodies and develop immunity to a disease

Vassal: A person who has been granted land by a lord in the Middle Ages

Vatican II: A major church council in the 1960s that introduced reforms in the Catholic Church

Vellum: Paper made from calfskin

Vernacular: The language of the people

Vespers: Evening prayers in a monastery

Vichy France: The part of France ruled by French leaders under Nazi German control during World War II

Viewpoint: The point of view (or perspective) from which historians view events. Viewpoint can be influenced by gender, beliefs, values and interests.

Villa: A country house or estate in Ancient Rome

Visual source: Historical sources that can be seen, such as photographs, paintings and cartoons

Wannsee Conference: A meeting of senior Nazi officials that formulated the Final Solution to exterminate all Jews

Wattle and daub: Interwoven sticks covered with mud and used to make walls

With Burning Anxiety: A 1937 statement in which Pope Pius XI criticised the Nazis

Wolfpacks: Groups of German U-boats which attacked Allied shipping in the North Atlantic during World War II

Women's Liberation Movement: A wide group of women who demanded equal rights for women, beginning in the 1960s in the USA

Workhouse: A place where poor people can live if they have no recourses; used in 19th-century Ireland and UK

Written sources: Historical sources which are written, typed or printed

Youth culture: The lifestyle of young people, particularly in the 1960s and later

Zyklon B: A poisonous gas used to kill Jews in Nazi extermination camps